Safety-Critical Systems:
Problems, Process and Practice

T0143024

Related titles:

Towards System Safety
Proceedings of the Seventh Safety-critical Systems Symposium, Huntingdon, UK, 1999
Redmill and Anderson (Eds)
1-85233-064-3

Lessons in System Safety
Proceedings of the Eighth Safety-critical Systems Symposium, Southampton, UK, 2000
Redmill and Anderson (Eds)
1-85233-249-2

Aspects of Safety Management
Proceedings of the Ninth Safety-critical Systems Symposium, Bristol, UK, 2001
Redmill and Anderson (Eds)
1-85233-411-8

Components of System Safety
Proceedings of the Tenth Safety-critical Systems Symposium, Southampton, UK, 2002
Redmill and Anderson (Eds)
1-85233-561-0

Current Issues in Safety-critical Systems
Proceedings of the Eleventh Safety-critical Systems Symposium, Bristol, UK, 2003
Redmill and Anderson (Eds)
1-85233-696-X

Practical Elements of Safety
Proceedings of the Twelfth Safety-critical Systems Symposium, Birmingham, UK, 2004
Redmill and Anderson (Eds)
1-85233-800-8

Constituents of Modern System-safety Thinking
Proceedings of the Thirteenth Safety-critical Systems Symposium, Southampton, UK, 2005
Redmill and Anderson (Eds)
1-85233-952-7

Developments in Risk-based Approaches to Safety
Proceedings of the Fourteenth Safety-critical Systems Symposium, Bristol, UK, 2006
Redmill and Anderson (Eds)
1-84628-333-7

The Safety of Systems
Proceedings of the Fifteenth Safety-critical Systems Symposium, Bristol, UK, 2007
Redmill and Anderson (Eds)
978-1-84628-805-0

Improvements in System Safety
Proceedings of the Sixteenth Safety-critical Systems Symposium, Bristol, UK, 2008
Redmill and Anderson (Eds)
978-1-84800-099-5

Chris Dale • Tom Anderson
Editors

Safety-Critical Systems: Problems, Process and Practice

Proceedings of the Seventeenth Safety-Critical Systems Symposium, Brighton, UK, 3–5 February 2009

Safety-Critical Systems Club

The publication of these proceedings is sponsored by BAE Systems plc

BAE SYSTEMS

 Springer

Editors
Chris Dale
Dale Research Ltd
33 North Street
Martock, TA12 6DH
UK

Tom Anderson
Centre for Software Reliability
University of Newcastle
Newcastle upon Tyne, NE1 7RU
UK

ISBN 978-1-84882-348-8   e-ISBN 978-1-84882-349-5
DOI 10.1007/978-1-84882-349-5

British Library Cataloguing in Publication Data
A catalogue record for this book is available from the British Library

Library of Congress Control Number: 2009920216

Printed on acid-free paper

Springer Science+Business Media
springer.com

Preface

The Safety-critical Systems Symposium (SSS), held each February for seventeen consecutive years, offers a full-day tutorial followed by two days of presentations of papers. This book of Proceedings contains all the papers presented at SSS'09.

The first paper accompanies the tutorial, which addresses one of the most important and fundamental disciplines in the safety field, that of hazard analysis, and advocates a new approach for dealing with the increasing complexity of the systems being built today.

The Symposium is for engineers, managers, and academics in the field of safety, across all industry sectors, so its papers always cover a range of topics. Given that system safety engineering involves spending money in order to reduce the chances and consequences of accidents, moral and economic questions inevitably arise concerning the amount of money that is, or should be, spent on safety. This year, three papers address these questions.

Case studies of the application of safety techniques to real systems are always popular with audiences at the Symposium, and this year's event featured a number of such papers, including two in a section on transport safety, looking at examples on the roads and railways.

Recent changes in the law have been made in response to major accidents occurring in the past few years, but controversy still rages about the use of criminal law as a tool for improving safety. These matters are raised in a section on safety in society, as are issues relating to professionalism in system safety engineering.

Every year sees new challenges, in the safety field as in others, and two of this year's papers focus on very different types of challenge: one highly technological, and the other concerned with the introduction of well established safety approaches into a new domain.

The final two sections address safety assessment and safety standards, both areas of perennial interest and of continuing active development. Some of these papers bring new insights to established areas of practice, some report practical experience, some reflect major developments in the regulatory arena; all have something important to say to those working in the field of system safety engineering.

Overall, the papers in this volume address many of the topics that are of current concern to the safety-critical systems community, and we are grateful to the authors for their contributions. We also thank our sponsors for their valuable support, and the exhibitors at the Symposium's tools and services fair for their participation. And we thank Joan Atkinson and her team for laying the event's foundation through their planning and organisation.

CD & TA
October 2008

THE SAFETY-CRITICAL SYSTEMS CLUB

organiser of the

Safety-critical Systems Symposium

What is the Safety-Critical Systems Club?

This 'Community' Club exists to support developers and operators of systems that may have an impact on safety, across all industry sectors. It is an independent, non-profit organisation that co-operates with all bodies involved with safety-critical systems.

Objectives

The Club's two principal objectives are to raise awareness of safety issues in the field of safety-critical systems and to facilitate the transfer of safety technology from wherever it exists.

History

The Club was inaugurated in 1991 under the sponsorship of the UK's Department of Trade and Industry (DTI) and the Engineering and Physical Sciences Research Council (EPSRC). Its secretariat is in the Centre for Software Reliability (CSR) at Newcastle University, and its Meetings Coordinator is Chris Dale of Dale Research Ltd. Felix Redmill of Redmill Consultancy is the Newsletter Editor.

Since 1994 the Club has been self-sufficient, but it retains the active support of the EPSRC, as well as that of the Health and Safety Executive, the Institution of Engineering and Technology, and the British Computer Society. All of these bodies are represented on the Club's Steering Group.

The Club's activities

The Club achieves its goals of awareness-raising and technology transfer by focusing on current and emerging practices in safety engineering, software engineering, and standards that relate to safety in processes and products. Its activities include:

- Running the annual Safety-critical Systems Symposium each February (the first was in 1993), with Proceedings published by Springer-Verlag;

- Organising a number of 1- and 2-day seminars each year;
- Providing tutorials on relevant subjects;
- Publishing a newsletter, *Safety Systems*, three times annually (since 1991), in January, May and September; and
- A web-site http://www.scsc.org.uk providing member services, including a safety tools directory.

Education and communication

The Club brings together technical and managerial personnel within all sectors of the safety-critical-systems community. Its events provide education and training in principles and techniques, and it facilitates the dissemination of lessons within and between industry sectors. It promotes an inter-disciplinary approach to the engineering and management of safety, and it provides a forum for experienced practitioners to meet each other and for the exposure of newcomers to the safety-critical systems industry.

Influence on research

The Club facilitates communication among researchers, the transfer of technology from researchers to users, feedback from users, and the communication of experience between users. It provides a meeting point for industry and academia, a forum for the presentation of the results of relevant projects, and a means of learning and keeping up-to-date in the field.

The Club thus helps to achieve more effective research, a more rapid and effective transfer and use of technology, the identification of best practice, the definition of requirements for education and training, and the dissemination of information. Importantly, it does this within a 'club' atmosphere rather than a commercial environment.

Membership

Members pay a reduced fee (well below the commercial level) for events and receive the newsletter and other mailed information. Not being sponsored, the Club depends on members' subscriptions: these can be paid at the first meeting attended, and are almost always paid by the individual's employer.

To join, please contact Mrs Joan Atkinson at: The Centre for Software Reliability, Newcastle University, Newcastle upon Tyne, NE1 7RU; Telephone: 0191 221 2222; Fax: 0191 222 7995; Email: csr@newcastle.ac.uk

Contents

Tutorial Paper

The Economics of Safety

Transport Safety

Safety in Society

New Challenges

Safety Assessment

Safety Standards

Tutorial Paper

The Need for New Paradigms in Safety Engineering

Nancy G. Leveson

Massachusetts Institute of Technology

Cambridge, MA, USA

Abstract The world and technology are changing, but these changes are not reflected in our safety engineering approaches. Many of the underlying assumptions of the traditional techniques no longer hold for the complex, high-tech systems being built today. We need new models of accident causality and engineering techniques built on them that handle these new systems and problems. An example of a new model, based on systems theory rather than reliability theory, is described and some uses of such a model are discussed.

1 Introduction

Most of the safety engineering techniques and tools we use today were originally created for first mechanical and later electro-mechanical systems. They rest on models of accident causation that were appropriate for those types of systems, but not the majority of the systems we are building today. After computers and other new technology became important in most new systems, the primary approach to handling safety was to try to extend the traditional techniques and tools to include software. We have now attempted that for at least three decades with little real success. I believe that it is time to conclude that this approach may not lead to great success and that something else is needed (Leveson 2008, Leveson et al. 2009).

Software allows us to increase the complexity of the systems we build (in particular, *interactive* complexity and coupling) such that new types of accidents are occurring that do not fit the traditional accident causation model. These new accidents arise not from the failure of individual system components, but from dysfunctional interactions among components, none of which may have failed, i.e., they operated as specified in their requirements. The loss of the Mars Polar Lander was attributed to noise (spurious signals) generated when the landing legs were deployed during descent (JPL Special Review Board 2000). This noise was normal and expected and did not represent a failure in the landing leg system. The onboard software interpreted these signals as an indication that landing occurred (which the software engineers were told they would indicate) and shut the engines

C. Dale, T. Anderson (eds.), *Safety-Critical Systems: Problems, Process and Practice*,
DOI 10.1007/978-1-84882-349-5_1, © Springer-Verlag London Limited 2009

down prematurely, causing the spacecraft to crash into the Mars surface. The landing legs and the software performed correctly with respect to their specified requirements but the accident occurred because the system designers did not account for all interactions between the leg deployment and the descent-engine control software.

A model of accident causation and the engineering techniques built on it that consider only component failures will miss system accidents, which are the most common software-related accidents. In addition, the role of human operators is changing from direct control to supervisory positions involving sophisticated decision-making. Once again, the types of mistakes humans are making are different and are not readily explained or handled by the traditional chain-of-failure-events models. Finally, there is more widespread recognition of the importance of management, organizational, and cultural factors in accidents and safety: the traditional models, which were never derived to handle these factors, do so poorly if at all.

I believe that to make significant progress in safety engineering, we need to rethink the old models and create new accident causality models and engineering techniques and tools based on them that include not only the old accident causes but also the new types of accidents and accident causality factors. In this paper, I suggest one such model and some tools based on it, but it is not the only such model possible and other tools and techniques might be built on it or on other models. Our new model is based on system theory (rather than the reliability theory of the traditional models) and our experience with it has shown that it allows much more powerful accident analysis and root cause analysis, hazard analysis, design-for-safety techniques, and general approaches to risk management in complex, socio-technical systems.

2 STAMP: An Accident Causality Model Based on System Theory

Traditional accident causation models explain accidents in terms of a chain of events that leads up to the accident. The relationships assumed between events in the chain are direct and relatively simple. Using this model of causation, the most appropriate approaches to preventing accidents is to somehow 'break the chain' by either preventing an event or by adding additional 'and' gates in the chain to make the occurrence of the events in the chain less likely. Because the events usually included almost always involve component failures or human errors, the primary mechanism for increasing safety is to make the individual components more reliable or failure free. Such models are limited in their ability to handle accidents in complex systems, organizational and managerial (social and cultural) factors in accidents, human error, and the systemic causes of the events.

For the past seven years, I have been developing a new, more comprehensive model of accident causation, called STAMP (System-Theoretic Accident Model and Processes), that includes the old models but expands them to better handle the levels of complexity and technical innovation in today's systems (Leveson 2004, Leveson 2008). STAMP extends the types of accidents and causes that can be considered by including non-linear, indirect, and feedback relationships among events. Accidents or unacceptable losses can result not only from system component failures but also from interactions among system components – both physical and social – that violate system safety constraints.

In systems theory, emergent properties associated with a set of components are related to *constraints* upon the degree of freedom of those components' behaviour. *Safety constraints* specify the relationships among system variables or components that constitute the non-hazardous or safe system states – for example, the power must never be on when the access door to the high-power source is open; pilots in a combat zone must be able to identify targets as hostile or friendly; and the public health system must prevent the exposure of the public to contaminated water. Accidents result from interactions among system components that violate these constraints – in other words, from a lack of appropriate constraints on component and system behaviour.

Major accidents rarely have a single root cause but result from an adaptive feedback function that fails to maintain safety as performance changes over time to meet a complex and changing set of goals and values. The accident or loss itself results not simply from component failure or human error (which are symptoms rather than root causes) but from the inadequate control (i.e., enforcement) of safety-related constraints on the development, design, construction, and operation of the entire socio-technical system.

System safety, then, can be reformulated as a system *control* problem rather than a component failure or reliability problem: accidents or losses occur when component failures, external disturbances, and/or dysfunctional interactions among system components are not handled adequately or controlled – where controls may be managerial, organizational, physical, operational, or manufacturing – such that required safety constraints on behaviour are violated.

Note that the use of the term 'control' does not imply a strict military command and control structure. Behaviour is controlled not only by engineered systems and direct management intervention, but also indirectly by policies, procedures, shared values, and other aspects of the organizational culture. All behaviour is influenced and at least partially 'controlled' by the social and organizational context in which the behaviour occurs. Engineering this context can be an effective way of creating and changing a safety culture, i.e., the subset of organizational culture that reflects the general attitude about and approaches to safety and risk management.

Three important concepts in STAMP are hierarchical safety control structures, process models, and migration toward states of high risk.

2.1 Hierarchical Safety Control Structures

Hierarchies are a basic concept in systems theory. At any given level of a hierarchical model of complex systems, it is often possible to describe and understand mathematically the behaviour of individual components when the behaviour is completely independent of other components at the same or other levels. But emergent properties like safety do not satisfy this assumption and require a description of the acceptable interactions among components at a level higher than the components; these interactions are controlled through the imposition of constraints upon the component interactions at the level below.

Figure 1 shows an example of a hierarchical safety control structure for a typical U.S. regulated industry, such as aircraft. Each industry and company will, of course, have its own unique control structure. There are two basic hierarchical control structures in Figure 1 – one for system development (on the left) and one for system operation (on the right) – with interactions between them. An aircraft manufacturer, for example, might only have system development under its immediate control, but safety involves both development and operational use of the aircraft and neither can be accomplished successfully in isolation: safety must be designed into the aircraft and safety during operation depends partly on the original design and partly on effective control over operations. Manufacturers must communicate to their customers the assumptions about the operational environment in which the original safety analysis was based, e.g., maintenance quality and procedures, as well as information about safe aircraft operating procedures. The operational environment, in turn, provides feedback to the manufacturer about the performance of the system during operations. Each component in the hierarchical safety control structure has responsibilities for enforcing safety constraints appropriate for that component; together these responsibilities should result in enforcement of the overall system safety constraint.

Hierarchies, in system theory, are characterized by control and communication processes operating at the interfaces between levels. The downward communication channel between levels in the hierarchy provides information necessary to impose behavioural constraints on the level below and an upward feedback channel provides information about how effectively the constraints were enforced. For example, in Figure 1, company management in the development safety control structure may provide a safety policy, standards and resources to project management and in return, receive status reports, risk assessment, and incident reports as feedback about the status of the project with respect to the safety constraints.

To completely understand the cause of accidents and to prevent future ones, the system's hierarchical safety control structure must be examined to determine why the controls at each level were inadequate to maintain the constraints on safe behaviour at the level below and why the events occurred – for example, why the designers arrived at an unsafe design (in the case of the space shuttle Challenger loss, there were political and other non-technical influences) and why management decisions were made to launch despite warnings that it might not be safe to do so (again, there were political and economic reasons).

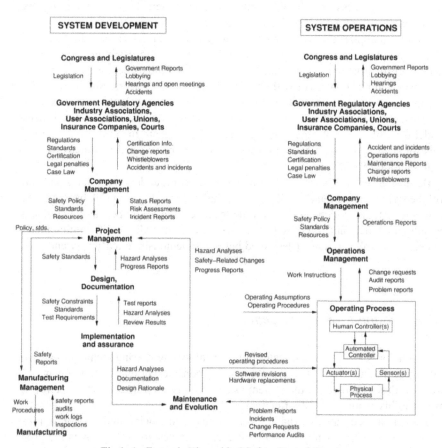

Fig.1. An Example Hierarchical Safety Control Structure

When designing a new system or analyzing an existing system using STAMP as the foundation, required safety constraints are identified at the system level first and then a top-down iterative process is used to identify required safety constraints that must be imposed at each of the lower levels. The entire safety control structure must be carefully designed and evaluated to ensure that the controls are adequate to maintain the constraints on behaviour necessary to control risk.

2.2 Process Models

Another important part of STAMP is the concept of process models. In basic system (and control) theory, the controller must contain a model of the system it is controlling. For human controllers, this model is usually called the *mental model.* Accidents in complex systems often result from inconsistencies between the model of the process used by the controller and the actual process state. For example, the autopilot software thinks the aircraft is climbing when it really is descending and applies the wrong control law or the pilot thinks a friendly aircraft is hostile and shoots a missile at it. Part of the challenge in designing an effective safety control structure is providing the feedback and inputs necessary to keep the controller's model consistent with the actual state of the process. Similarly, an important component in understanding accidents and losses involves determining how and why the controller was ineffective; often this is because the process model used by the controller was incorrect or inadequate in some way. The reasons for such an inconsistency are used in the new hazard and risk analysis techniques built on STAMP.

Because STAMP is based on a firm mathematical foundation (systems and control theory), computational modelling and analysis of safety and risk becomes feasible: the process models, along with the feedback control loops, can be computationally modelled and analyzed. We have experimentally built computational models of complex systems (described below) to demonstrate feasibility and practicality.

2.3 Migration toward Accidents

Traditional models of accident causation and safety engineering techniques are not only limited in the types of causal factors they consider, primarily component failures, but they usually treat the system as static. This simplification, however, limits our ability to manage risk effectively.

Systems are continually changing under physical, social, and economic pressures. In STAMP, systems are not treated as static designs, but as dynamic processes that are continually adapting to achieve their ends and to react to changes in themselves and their environment. For safety, the original system design must not only enforce appropriate constraints on behaviour to ensure safe operation (the enforcement of the safety constraints), but the system must continue to operate safely (safety constraints must continue to be enforced) as changes and adaptations occur over time, for example, operators change how they use the system once they become familiar with it, managers demand different performance such as increased throughput, or doctors spend less time talking with patients.

Accidents in complex systems often involve a migration of the system and changes in the safety control structure toward a state where a small deviation (in the physical system or in human operator behaviour) can lead to a catastrophe. The foundation for an accident is often laid years before. One event may trigger the loss, but if that event had not happened, another one would have led to a loss. Union Carbide and the Indian government blamed the Bhopal MIC (methyl isocyanate) release, one of the worst industrial accidents in history in terms of human death and injury, on the improper cleaning of a pipe at the chemical plant. The maintenance worker, however, was in fact only a minor and somewhat irrelevant player in the loss (Leveson et al. 2003). Instead, degradation in the safety control structure occurred over time and without any particular single decision to do so but rather as a series of independent decisions that moved the plant toward a situation where any slight error would lead to a major accident:

> 'The stage for an accidental course of events very likely is prepared through time by the normal efforts of many actors in their respective daily work context, responding to the standing request to be more productive and less costly. Ultimately, a quite normal variation in someone's behavior can then release an accident. Had this "root cause" been avoided by some additional safety measure, the accident would very likely be released by another cause at another point in time. In other words, an explanation of the accident in terms of events, acts, and errors is not very useful for design of improved systems.'
> (Rasmussen 1997)

Degradation of the safety-control structure over time may be related to *asynchronous evolution* (Leplat 1987), where one part of a system changes without the related necessary changes in other parts. Changes to subsystems may be carefully designed, but consideration of their effects on other parts of the system, including the safety control aspects, may be neglected or inadequate. Asynchronous evolution may also occur when one part of a properly designed system deteriorates. In both these cases, the erroneous expectations of users or system components about the behaviour of the changed or degraded subsystem may lead to accidents. One factor in the E. coli contamination of the water supply of a small town in Ontario, Canada, was the privatization of the government water testing laboratory without establishing feedback loops from the private labs to the government overseers of the water system to detect when conditions were degrading (Leveson 2008). A factor in the loss of contact with the SOHO (Solar Heliospheric Observatory) spacecraft in 1998 was the failure to communicate to the operators that a functional change had been made in a procedure to perform gyro spin-down (NASA/ESA Investigation Board 1998). A factor in the friendly fire shoot down of a U.S. Army Blackhawk helicopter by a U.S. Air Force fighter over northern Iraq in 1996 was that the Air Force had upgraded their radio technology while the Army had not, thus violating the safety constraint that U.S. forces would be able to communicate over their radios (Leveson 2008).

3 Applying STAMP to System Safety Problems

Using this basic model of accident causation as the foundation, powerful new approaches to system safety can be developed, just as techniques such as Fault Tree Analysis and Failure Modes and Effects Analysis were constructed atop the basic chain of events model. Because the foundations of STAMP are mathematical, computation models and tools can be used to support these new techniques.

Basic structural control models, such as shown in Figure 1, will be used in most new tools. To augment the static structural models, formal models can be used of changes over time and the physical and social influences that can lead to these changes. One such modelling technique we have found useful is system dynamics (Sterman 2000). The field of system dynamics, created at MIT in the 1950s by computer pioneer Jay Forrester, is designed to help decision-makers learn about the structure and dynamics of complex systems, to design high leverage policies for sustained improvement, and to catalyze successful implementation and change. System dynamics provides a framework for dealing with dynamic complexity, where cause and effect are not obviously related. It is grounded in the theory of non-linear dynamics and feedback control, but also draws on cognitive and social psychology, organization theory, economics, and other social sciences (Sterman 2000):

> 'All too often, well-intentioned efforts to solve pressing problems create unanticipated "side effects". Our decisions provoke reactions we did not foresee. Today's solutions become tomorrow's problems. The result is policy resistance, the tendency for interventions to be defeated by the response of the system to the intervention itself. From California's failed electricity reforms, to road building programmes that create suburban sprawl and actually increase traffic congestion, to pathogens that evolve resistance to antibiotics, our best efforts to solve problems often make them worse. At the root of this phenomenon lies the narrow, event-oriented, reductionist worldview most people live by. We have been trained to see the world as a series of events, to view our situation as the result of forces outside ourselves, forces largely unpredictable and uncontrollable…System dynamics helps us expand the boundaries of our mental models so that we become aware of and take responsibility for the feedbacks created by our decisions.' (Sterman 2002)

System behaviour is modelled in system dynamics by using feedback (causal) loops, stocks and flows (levels and rates), and the non-linearities created by inter-actions among system components. In this view of the world, behaviour over time (the dynamics of the system) can be explained by the interaction of positive and negative feedback loops (Senge 1990). The combined STAMP and system dynamics models can be used to devise and validate fixes for technical and organizational safety problems and to design systems with lower risk.

4 Uses for STAMP

A major advantage of this new approach to system safety engineering is that it can handle very complex systems and both the technical and social (organizational and cultural) aspects of accident understanding and prevention. STAMP can be applied to accident and incident investigation; hazard analysis (i.e., investigating an accident before it occurs); enhanced preliminary hazard analysis that allows safety to be considered during early system architecture selection; design for safety (at the technical and social level); risk analysis of organizational safety policies and designs and identification of leading indicators of migration toward increasing organizational risk; and programmatic risk analysis of the tradeoffs between safety, performance, schedule, and budget.

4.1 Accident and Incident Investigation and Analysis

All current accident models and accident analysis techniques suffer from the limitation of considering only the events underlying an accident and not the entire accident *process*. The events preceding the loss event, however, reflect only the *results* of dysfunctional interactions and inadequate enforcement of safety constraints. The inadequate control itself is only indirectly reflected by the events.

A focus on proximal events often makes it appear that accidents are the result of an unfortunate coincidence of factors that come together at one particular point in time and lead to the loss. This belief arises from too narrow a view of the causal time line. As argued above, systems are not static. Rather than accidents being a chance occurrence of multiple independent events, they tend to involve a migration to a state of increasing risk over time. A point is reached where an accident is inevitable (unless the high risk is detected and reduced) and the particular events involved are somewhat irrelevant: if those events had not occurred, something else would have led to the loss. This concept is reflected in the common observation that a loss was 'an accident waiting to happen'. The proximate cause of the Columbia Space Shuttle was the foam coming loose from the external tank and damaging the re-entry heat control structure. But many potential problems that could have caused the loss of the Shuttle had preceded this event and an accident was avoided by luck or unusual circumstances. The economic and political pressures had led the Shuttle program to drift to a state where any slight deviation could have led to a loss (Leveson 2007).

Understanding and preventing or detecting system migration to states of higher risk requires that our accident models consider the *processes* involved in accidents and not simply the events and conditions: processes control a sequence of events and describe system and human behaviour as it changes and adapts over time (perhaps as a result of feedback or a changing environment) rather than considering individual events and human actions. Accident causation is a complex process involving the entire socio-technical system including legislators, government agencies, industry associations and insurance companies, company management, technical and engineering personnel, operators, etc. To understand why an accident has occurred, the entire process needs to be examined, not just the proximal events in the event chain. Otherwise, only symptoms will be identified and fixed, and accidents will continue to recur.

Instead of decomposing behaviour into events over time, systems theory (and STAMP) focuses on systems taken as a whole. It assumes that some system properties can only be treated adequately in their entirety, taking into account all facets relating the social to the technical aspects (Ramo 1973). These system properties derive from the relationships among the parts of the system: how the parts interact and fit together (Ackoff 1971). Thus, the system approach concentrates on the analysis and design of the whole as distinct from the components or the parts and provides a means for studying emergent system properties, such as safety (Leveson 2008). Using this approach as a foundation, new types of accident analysis (both retroactive and proactive) can be devised that go beyond simply looking at events and can identify the processes and systemic factors behind the losses and also the factors (reasons) for migration toward states of increasing risk. This information can be used to design controls that prevent hazardous states by changing the design to prevent or control the hazards and migration and, in operational systems, detect the increasing risk before a loss occurs.

To completely understand the cause of accidents and to prevent future ones, the system's hierarchical safety control structure must be examined to determine why the controls at each level were inadequate to maintain the constraints on safe behaviour at the level below and why the events occurred. The goal is not to assign blame – blame is the enemy of safety[1] – but to determine why well-meaning people acted in ways that contributed to the loss. If the hierarchical safety control structure has not already been documented, then that should be done and then used to identify and understand the safety control inadequacies in the engineered system (the physical system), the aspects of the design and the environment that affected the loss, and the systemic factors that contributed to the loss.

The first step in the accident analysis is to understand the physical factors involved in the loss, including:

- The limitations of the physical system design. For the sinking of the Herald of Free Enterprise (Sheen 1987), for example, the ferry's loading ramp was too low to reach the upper car deck at high tide,
- The failures and dysfunctional interactions among the physical system components, e.g., the Assistant Bosun did not close the doors to the Herald's car deck, and
- The environmental factors, e.g., the high spring tides in Zeebrugge where the sinking occurred, that interacted with the physical system design.

Most accident analyses include this information, although they may omit dysfunctional interactions and look only for component failures.

Understanding the physical factors leading to the loss is only the first step, however, in understanding why the accident occurred. The next step is understanding how the engineering design practices contributed to the accident and how they could be changed to prevent such an accident in the future. Why was the hazard (capsizing as a result of flooding) not adequately controlled in the design? Some controls were installed to prevent this hazard (for example, the doors themselves, and the assignment to close them to the Assistant Bosun), but some controls were inadequate or missing (a lack of watertight compartments). What parts

---

[1] In the Herald of Free Enterprise loss, for example, many of the individuals at Townsend Thoresen (the owner of the ferry) were prosecuted for manslaughter, as was the operating company. Such reactions do not increase safety. See recent work on *Just Culture*, e.g., (Dekker 2007).

of the design and analysis process allowed this flawed design to be accepted? What changes in that process, e.g., better hazard analysis, design, or review processes, could be used to ensure that designs have adequate hazard controls in the future?

Many of the reasons underlying poor design and operational practices stem from management and oversight inadequacies due to conflicting requirements and pressures. Identifying the factors lying behind the physical design starts with identifying the safety-related responsibilities (requirements) assigned to each component in the hierarchical safety control structure along with their safety constraints. As an example, a responsibility of the First Officer on the Herald of Free Enterprise is to ensure that the doors are closed before the ferry leaves the dock, management has the responsibility to ensure their ferries have a safe design and are operated safely, the responsibility of the International Maritime Organization is to provide regulations and oversight to ensure that unsafe ships are not used for passenger transportation, etc. Using these safety-related responsibilities, the inadequate control actions for each of the components in the control structure can be identified. In most major accidents, inadequate control is exhibited throughout the structure, assuming an adequate control structure was designed to begin with. But simply finding out how each person or group contributed to the loss is only the start of the process necessary to learn what needs to be changed to prevent future accidents. We must first understand why the 'controllers' provided inadequate control. The analysis process must identify the systemic factors in the accident causation, not just the symptoms.

To understand why people behave the way they do, we must examine their mental models and the environmental factors affecting their decision making. All human decision-making is based on the person's mental model of the state and operation of the system being controlled. For example, the Herald's First Officer assumed that the Assistant Bosun had closed the doors, the Assistant Bosun may have thought that someone else would notice that the doors were open and close them, and the Captain thought the doors had been closed. Preventing inadequate control actions in the future requires not only identifying the flaws in the controllers' mental models (including those of the management and government components of the hierarchical safety control structure) but also why these flaws existed. For example, the Captain's inadequate mental model (thinking the doors were closed) resulted from lack of feedback about the state of the doors. All of them thought that leaving the doors open would not cause a loss of the ferry because a year earlier one of the Herald's sister ships sailed from Dover to Zeebrugge with bow doors open without incident, i.e., they had inadequate knowledge about the potential ferry hazards.

The impact of the operating environment (including environmental conditions, cultural values, etc.) must also be identified. For example, the problematic ferry design features were influenced by the competitive ferry environment in which the ferry was to operate.

The accident report blamed a 'disease of sloppiness and negligence at every level of the corporation's hierarchy' (Sheen 1987). But this superficial level of analysis (management sloppiness and negligence) is not useful in preventing future accidents – it simply provides someone to blame and to prosecute. It does not eliminate the underlying pressures that led to the poor decision making nor the inadequate design of the hierarchical safety control structure. Without changes that respond to those factors, similarly flawed and risky decision-making is likely again in the future, although the actual accident details may be very different. We have used system dynamic models to understand the complex environmental, social, and economic factors contributing to poor decision making in order to provide policy and other changes to improve risk-related decision making in the future (Dulac et al. 2007, Leveson et al. 2009).

A complete accident/incident analysis based on STAMP usually finds dozens of causal factors contributing to the accident process and points to many changes that could prevent future losses. Leveson provides several examples of such analyses of major accidents (Leveson 2008).

4.2 STPA: A New Hazard Analysis Technique

To create new approaches to both technical system hazard analysis and organizational risk analysis based on STAMP, we have identified a set of factors that can lead to violation of safety constraints, such as inadequate feedback to maintain accurate mental (process) models. These factors are derived from basic control theory. We used these factors in creating a new, more powerful hazard analysis technique called STPA (STamP Analysis) (Dulac and Leveson 2004, Leveson 2008), which we have applied to both technical system hazard analysis and organizational risk analysis.

The goals of STPA are the same as any hazard analysis: (1) to identify the system hazards and the safety-related constraints necessary to ensure acceptable risk; and (2) to accumulate information about how the safety constraints may be violated and use this information to eliminate, reduce, and control hazards in the system design and operation. STPA supports a System Safety approach to building safer systems as specified in the U.S. MIL-STD-882. The process starts with identifying the system safety requirements and design constraints. The technique then assists in top-down refinement into requirements and safety constraints on individual system components. At both the system and component levels, STPA helps to identify scenarios in which the safety constraints can be violated. Information about the scenarios can be used to eliminate or control them in the system and component design.

STPA is a top-down system hazard analysis technique as opposed to bottom-up techniques like FMEA or FMECA. It considers more than just component failure events although these are included. STPA is perhaps closest to HAZOP (in terms of current techniques). Both are applied to a model of the system—a structural model in the case of HAZOP and a functional model in STPA. Both also provide guidance in performing the analysis, with guidewords being used in HAZOP and basic control theory concepts in STPA. In comparisons with fault trees, STPA found all the scenarios identified by the fault trees but also others that could not be identified in a fault tree because of their nature.

4.3 Early System Architectural Trades

Ideally, safety should be a part of the early decision making used in conceptual system design. However, effectively evaluating safety-related risk early enough to inform the early trade studies is not possible with current technology. We have created a new approach to preliminary hazard analysis (PHA) that can be performed prior to system architecture selection and thus can influence key decisions that will be difficult and costly or impossible to change later in the system lifecycle (Dulac and Leveson 2005). After an architecture is selected, the information generated in these early analyses can be used to design hazards out of the system during the detailed design process as the original analyses are revised and refined.

Risk in a PHA is usually evaluated using a matrix with various categories representing severity along one dimension and likelihood along the other. While severity (the consequences of the worst possible loss related to the hazard being considered) is easily determined, there is no way to determine likelihood before any system design or even architecture has been selected, especially in systems where new technology or new functions are included. Our new analysis technique uses the hazard mitigation of potential candidate architectures to estimate hazard likelihood. Hazards that are more easily mitigated in the design and operations are less likely to lead to accidents, and similarly, hazards that have been eliminated during system design cannot lead to an accident. The goal of the new analysis process is to assist in selecting an architecture with few serious hazards and inherently high mitigation potential for those hazards that cannot be eliminated, perhaps because eliminating them would reduce the potential for achieving other important system goals.

We chose mitigation potential as a surrogate for likelihood for two reasons:

1. the potential for eliminating or controlling the hazard in the design has a direct and important bearing on the likelihood of the hazard occurring (whether traditional or new designs and technology are used); and
2. mitigatability of the hazard can be determined before an architecture or design is selected – indeed, it helps in the design selection process.

The new process has been demonstrated in a MIT/Draper Labs project to perform an early concept evaluation and refinement for the new NASA space exploration mission (return humans to the Moon and then go on to Mars). The goal was to develop a space exploration architecture that fulfils the needs of the many stakeholders involved in manned space exploration. Because safety is an important property to many of the stakeholders, using it to influence early architectural decisions was critical as most of the architectural decisions would be very costly or impossible to change later in the development process.

The hazard-based safety risk analysis developed is a three-step process:

1. Identify the system-level hazards and associated severities.
2. Identify mitigation strategies and associated impact.
3. Calculate safety/risk metrics for a given transportation architecture.

The first two steps are performed only once, at the beginning of the process. They may have to be repeated if the architectural design space changes or if additional hazards are identified. The third step is repeated in order to evaluate as many candidate architectures and variations as necessary.

Hazard mitigation metrics are defined and used to evaluate and rank potential architectures. By systematically selecting and de-selecting options in the architecture description, it is possible to perform a first-order assessment of the relative importance of each architectural option in determining an Overall Residual Safety-Risk Metric.

Hundreds of architectures were evaluated for their inherent hazard mitigation potential. An automated tool was created to perform multiple evaluations based on the needs of the team responsible for designing the manned space architecture. The analysis started at the very beginning of the conceptual design phase and the methodology proved flexible and extensible enough to carry the team from Day 1 of conceptual design up to the beginning of the detailed design phase, at which point, a more detailed hazard analysis methodology such as STPA (Dulac and Leveson 2004, Leveson 2008) will be necessary and safety-driven design of the system and its components can be started (see below).

Details are beyond the scope of this paper. The interested reader is referred to Dulac and Leveson 2005.

4.4 Safety-Driven Design

Ideally, hazard analysis should precede or at least accompany system design in order to avoid the problems associated with changing design decisions after they have been made. The problem is that most of the existing hazard analysis techniques require a detailed design before they can be applied, because they rely on identifying potential component failures and their impact on system hazards. STPA is based on control rather than failure analysis and can be applied to hazards before a design is developed. The development of the design and the hazard analysis can go hand-in-hand, starting with the requirements for control of the high-level hazards and then refinement of the analysis as design decisions are made.

To demonstrate this safety-driven design process on a real system, we designed a spacecraft for outer planets exploration for NASA JPL (Jet Propulsion Laboratory) using safety-driven design procedures (Owens et al. 2008).

4.5 Safety Assessment of Complex Systems

Most current safety assessment techniques are impractical on very complex 'systems of systems' but STAMP-based methods will work. We have applied the new approach to assessing the vulnerability of the U.S. Missile Defense System to inadvertent launch. The latter is a vast system of systems, including radars, launch platforms, early warning systems, interceptors, etc., some of which have been used for decades and others of which are new. While some of these components had been analyzed using traditional safety analysis techniques, an analysis of the hazards at the integrated system level was needed. STAMP-based methods were tried after nobody could figure out how to apply any existing techniques to such a complex system. The assessment was successfully completed on the integrated system and, in fact, the analysis found so many paths to inadvertent launch that deployment and testing was delayed six months while these vulnerabilities were fixed. STAMP and STPA have now been adopted by the government for all future missile defence system analysis.

4.6 Organizational Risk Analysis

STAMP can go beyond physical system design. New approaches to organizational risk analysis based on STAMP involve creating a model of the social and organizational control structure and identifying the safety constraints each component is responsible for maintaining, a model of the social dynamics and pressures that can lead to degradation of this structure over time, process models representing the view of the process by those controlling it, and a model of the cultural and political context in which decision-making occurs. To model the social dynamics and pressures, we use system dynamics as described earlier.

We have completed a demonstration of applying STAMP to organizational and cultural risk analysis in the U.S. manned space program, specifically the current Space Shuttle operations program (Leveson et al. 2005). Our models start with Congress and the White House and continue down through the NASA management structure to the engineering project offices and the actual operations (in the case of the Space Shuttle). In this analysis, we identified system-level requirements to reduce poor engineering and management decision-making leading to an accident, identified gaps and omissions in the operational program design and changes made after the Columbia accident, and performed a rigorous risk analysis to evaluate proposed policy and structure changes and to identify leading indicators and metrics of migration toward states of unacceptable risk over time.

4.7 Programmatic Risk Analysis

STAMP-based modelling and analysis can be used to create sophisticated pro-grammatic risk management tools. While looking at safety alone is important, practical risk management requires understanding the tradeoffs among safety, per-formance, schedule, and budget risks. In another demonstration project for NASA, we showed how STAMP-based methods could be used for programmatic risk analysis in the new NASA space exploration mission (to return humans to the Moon and go on to Mars) (Dulac et al. 2007). Again, the models included the en-tire socio-technical system from Congress and the Executive Branch down to en-gineering processes and management. A major difference between this demonstra-tion and the one for the current Space Shuttle program described above is that this project involves development as well as future operations. A second difference is that we modelled and analyzed performance, budget, and schedule risks along with safety and showed how the results could be used for management decision making. For example, we found that attempting to speed up development resulted in surprisingly little improvement in schedule (less than two percent) primarily because of resulting increases in rework, but the attempted schedule reduction had a very high negative impact on the safety of the resulting design. At the same time, early emphasis on safety led to improvements in both schedule and budget due, again, to less required changes and rework when problems are discovered late. Although this result is probably not surprising to safety engineers, it was to managers and provided, in addition, a mathematical analysis of the differences and rationale. Another example result, in the area of workforce planning, was that the development of the Space Shuttle replacement (called Orion) would not be possi-ble within the time frame anticipated unless Congress relaxed hiring constraints on NASA.

5 Conclusions

STAMP is not the only possible expanded model of accident causation that could be devised. The purpose of this paper is not to sell STAMP, but to encourage those working in this field to expand beyond the techniques and models created for simple electro-mechanical systems whose underlying assumptions no longer match the majority of the systems we are building today.

By creating new models, we will be able to provide much more powerful safety engineering techniques and tools. This hypothesis is supported by our experience with STAMP as described above. To make significant progress, we need to get beyond the limiting assumptions about accidents and accident causality of the past and build on new foundations that better reflect the types of systems and engineer-ing prevalent today.

We are currently exploring the limits of STAMP and applying it so a large variety of risk management problems including safety in pharmaceutical testing, hospitals, the process industry, and the air transportation system as well as non-safety problems such as corporate fraud and security of national infrastructure systems.

References

Ackoff RL (1971) Towards a system of systems concepts. Management Science 17:661–671

Dekker S (2007) Just Culture: Balancing Safety and Accountability. Ashgate, Aldershot

Dulac N, Leveson N (2004) An Approach to Design for Safety in Complex Systems. International Conference on System Engineering (INCOSE), Toulouse, France

Dulac N, Leveson, N (2005) Incorporating Safety into Early System Architecture Trade Studies. Int. Conference of the System Safety Society

Dulac N, Owens B, Leveson N et al (2007) Demonstration of a New Dynamic Approach to Risk Analysis for NASA's Constellation Program. CSRL Final Project Report. http://sunnyday.mit.edu/ESMD-Final-Report.pdf. Accessed 27 August 2008

JPL Special Review Board (2000) Report on the Loss of the Mars Polar Lander and Deep Space 2 Missions. NASA Jet Propulsion Laboratory, 22 March 2000

Leplat, J (1987) Occupational accident research and systems approach. In: Rasmussen J, Duncan K, Leplat J (eds) New Technology and Human Error. Wiley, New York

Leveson N (2004) A New Accident Model for Engineering Safer Systems. Safety Science 42: 237–270

Leveson N (2007) Technical and Managerial Factors in the NASA Challenger and Columbia Losses: Looking Forward to the Future. In: Kleinman DL, Cloud-Hansen KA, Matta C, Handelsman J (eds) Controversies in Science and Technology, Vol. 2: From Chromosomes to the Cosmos, Mary Ann Liebert, New Rochelle, NY

Leveson N (2008) System Safety Engineering: Back to the Future. Unfinished manuscript. http://sunnyday.mit.edu/book2.html. Accessed 27 August 2008

Leveson N, Daouk M, Dulac N, Marais K (2003) Applying STAMP in Accident Analysis. Second Workshop on the Investigation and Reporting of Accidents, Williamsburg, September 2003

Leveson N, Dulac N, Barrett B et al (2005) Risk Analysis of NASA Independent Technical Authority. CSRL Final Report. http://sunnyday.mit.edu/ITA-Risk-Analysis.doc. Accessed 27 August 2008

Leveson N, Marais K, Dulac N, Carroll J (2009) Beyond Normal Accidents and High Reliability Organizations: The Need for an Alternative Approach to Safety in Complex Systems. To appear in Organizational Studies

NASA/ESA Investigation Board (1998) SOHO Mission Interruption. NASA, 31 August 1998

Owens B, Herring M, Leveson N et al (2008) Application of a Safety-Driven Design Methodology to an Outer Planet Exploration Mission. In: IEEE Aerospace Conference, Big Sky, Montana

Ramo S (1973) The systems approach. In: Miles RF (ed) Systems Concepts: Lectures on Contemporary Approaches to Systems. Wiley, New York

Rasmussen, J (1997) Risk Management in a Dynamic Society: A Modelling Problem. Safety Science 27: 183–213

Senge, PM (1990) The Fifth Discipline: The Art and Practice of the Learning Organization. Doubleday, New York

Sheen B (1987) Herald of Free Enterprise Report. Marine Accident Investigation Branch, Department of Transport (originally Report of Court No 8074 Formal Investigation, HMSO, London)

Sterman, J (2000) Business Dynamics: Systems Thinking and Modeling for a Complex World. McGraw Hill, New York

Sterman, J (2002) All models are wrong: reflections on becoming a systems scientist. System Dynamics Review 18:501-531

The Economics of Safety

Risk Management: the Economics and Morality of Safety Revisited

John Adams

University College London

London, UK

Abstract   The introduction to the proceedings of the Royal Academy of Engineering 2006 seminar on *The Economics and Morality of Safety* (RAEng 2006) concluded with a list of issues that were 'worthy of further exploration'. I have reduced them to the following questions:

- Why do moral arguments about 'rights' persist unresolved?
- Why can risk managers not agree on a common value for preventing a fatality?
- Why do governments and the media react differently to different causes of death?
- Why do some institutions profess to be pursuing zero risk, knowing that achieving it is impossible?
- Why do some institutions pretend that their risk management problems can be reduced to a calculation in which *all* significant variables can be represented by a common metric?
- Why are societal attitudes and risk communication still seen as problematic after many years of investigation?
- Why are certain accident investigations, criminal or civil, seen as 'over zealous' by some and justifiable by others?

These questions are addressed with the help of a set of risk framing devices. For some my conclusion will be discouraging: all of these issues are likely to remain unresolved. Risk is a word that refers to the future. It has no objective existence. The future exists only in the imagination, and a societal consensus about what the future holds does not exist.

1 Background

In April 2006 the Royal Academy of Engineering published the proceedings of a seminar on *The Economics and Morality of Safety* (RAEng 2006, henceforth referred to as TEAMOS). The proceedings were published with an introduction by John Turnbull. Unusually for such an introduction he focused not on the achievements of the conference, but on the problems that it had failed to resolve. He con-

C. Dale, T. Anderson (eds.), *Safety-Critical Systems: Problems, Process and Practice*,
DOI 10.1007/978-1-84882-349-5_2, © Springer-Verlag London Limited 2009

cluded his introduction with six bullet points. They provide a useful summary of key issues of concern in current debates about risk management. Although not framed interrogatively they all contained implicit questions.

His points, and the implicit questions (*in italics*) that I will seek to answer, are:

1. Moral arguments surrounding the differing 'rights' of individuals, enterprises and the state to cause potential harm to third parties.
   Why do moral arguments about 'rights' persist unresolved?
2. The case for a common Value for Preventing a Fatality or varying it according to the economic status of the potential victims and factors such as life expectancy and health.
   Why can risk managers not agree on a common value for preventing a fatality?
3. The wide variations in approach to safety in the transport sector between road, rail, marine and air.
   Why do governments and the media react differently to different causes of death?
4. The potential conflicts between a 'Zero Tolerance' approach to accidents and Cost Benefit Analysis.
   Two questions:
   Why do some institutions profess to be pursuing zero risk, knowing that achieving it is impossible?
   *Why do some institutions pretend that their risk management problems can be reduced to a calculation in which **all** significant variables can be represented by a common metric?*
5. Societal attitudes and the influences on them. Strategies for communication and dialogue.
   Why are societal attitudes and risk communication still seen as problematic after many years of investigation?
6. The threats posed to technical investigation and prevention of accidents by over zealous criminal investigations.
   Why are certain accident investigations, criminal or civil, seen as 'over zealous' by some and justifiable by others?

Turnbull observes (TEAMOS p3) that 'there would still be risk even if we applied all our resources to safety'. All his points and my questions listed above relate to the underlying problem of managing risk in a world in which absolute safety is not attainable. I will explore them with the help of a number of risk framing devices that I have found applicable to a wide range of risk management problems.

2 What are we trying to manage?

There are many ways in which one can categorize problems of risk management. Typing the single word 'risk' into Google produces hundreds of millions of hits. One need sample only a small fraction in order to discover unnecessary and often acrimonious arguments caused by people using the same word to refer to different things and shouting past each other. Figure 1, Types of Risk, I proffer as a fundamental typology in the hope that it might help to dispose of some unnecessary arguments and civilize others.

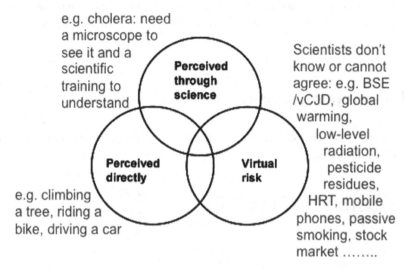

Fig. 1. Types of risk

We all routinely manage *directly perceptible* risks in everyday life. We do so using *judgement* – some combination of instinct, intuition and experience. We do not undertake formal, probabilistic risk assessments before we cross the road.

The circle labelled *perceived through science* contains most of the published risk literature. Here we find books, reports and articles with verifiable numbers, cause-and-effect reasoning, probability and inference. This is the domain of, amongst many others, biologists with microscopes, astronomers with telescopes, evidence based medicine, highway engineers and vehicle designers, bridge builders, epidemiologists, statisticians and insurance company actuaries.

The circle labelled *virtual risk* contains contested hypotheses, ignorance, uncertainty and unknown unknowns. During the seminar (TEAMOS p35) John McDermid observed that 'we have been talking all along as though we know how to quantify risk'. But if an issue cannot be settled by science and numbers we rely, as with directly perceptible risks, on *judgement*. Some find this enormously liberating; all interested parties feel free to argue from their beliefs, prejudices or superstitions. It is in this circle that we find the longest-running and most acrimonious arguments. Virtual risks may or may not be real, but beliefs about them have real consequences.

Moral arguments can get particularly heated in the zones of overlap in Figure 1. While we all might cross the road exercising our judgement others, institutional risk managers armed with statistics and different safety standards, often conclude that our behaviour ought to be managed to make us safer than we apparently choose to be.

Laws that criminalize self-risk, such as seat belt laws, and laws compelling the wearing of motorcycle helmets, and in some jurisdictions bicycle helmets, provoke fierce debate between civil libertarians and those who argue that sometimes even adults need to be compelled, in their own interest, to be careful (Adams 2006).

3 How do we manage it?

Figure 2, the Risk Thermostat, presents the essence of a phenomenon that Wilde called 'risk compensation' (Wilde 2001).

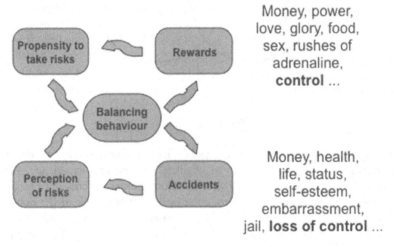

Money, power, love, glory, food, sex, rushes of adrenaline, **control** ...

Money, health, life, status, self-esteem, embarrassment, jail, **loss of control** ...

Fig. 2. The Risk Thermostat

Risk management involves balancing the rewards of actions whose outcomes are uncertain against potential losses. Figure 2 is a model of this balancing act. The model postulates that

- everyone has a propensity to take risks
- this propensity varies from one individual to another
- this propensity is influenced by the potential rewards of risk taking
- perceptions of risk are influenced by experience of accident losses – one's own and others'
- individual risk taking decisions represent a balancing act in which perceptions of risk are weighed against propensity to take risk

- accident losses are, *by definition*, a consequence of taking risks; the more risks an individual takes, the greater, on average, will be both the rewards and losses he or she incurs.

The model might be called cost-benefit analysis without the £ or $ signs. It is a conceptual model, not one into which you can plug numbers and from which you can extract decisions; the Rewards and Accidents boxes contain too many incommensurable variables; our reasons for taking risks are many and diverse, and vary from culture to culture and person to person.

3.1 Institutional risk management and bottom loop bias

Frequently after an accident people chorus that risk was not managed properly. Not necessarily so. Culpable negligence must contend with bad luck as the explanation. If people take risks there will be accidents.

Figure 2 can help to explain the clash, referred to above, between individual risk managers and institutional risk managers. When I am managing my own risks while crossing the street or riding my bike I am performing the balancing exercise described by the Risk Thermostat. If I am late for dinner and I see my bus approaching on the other side of the road, I will risk shorter gaps in the traffic to get across the road to catch it.

But institutional risk managers frequently suffer from *bottom loop bias*. Their job descriptions commonly enjoin them not to have their judgement about what is safe or dangerous compromised by contemplation of the rewards of risk. Their job is to reduce accidents. Their role in commercial institutions frequently brings them into conflict with other departments, such as product development, sales and marketing who are more focused on the rewards of risk taking.

In the most affluent countries of the world there is a trend toward increasing institutional risk aversion. We all in our daily lives routinely manage risks by balancing perceived rewards against the perceived risk of accidents. But some of us (not me) are promoted to the ranks of the institutional risk managers. Their job is to reduce accidents, and then get them lower still. For them, one accident is one too many.

In many cases, in Britain the domain of education provides a good example, there is no effective top-loop counterweight. The unopposed demands for ever more safety result in significant opportunity costs. Interesting experiments in chemistry classes, field trips, games and sports are lost, not to mention the uncounted hours of productive teaching and research time devoted to the filling in of fatuous risk assessments.

In Britain at the time of writing one-sided institutional risk aversion and lack of trust are promoting defensive medicine, the practice of medicine in which doctors' fears of liability compromise the welfare of the patient. Medicine in Britain is now burdened with minutely detailed audit trails, risk assessments and expensive, unnecessary and sometimes risky tests. More widely, fear of liability, ever more stringent health and safety regulations, and the rising cost of insurance are leading to the abandonment of traditional fairs, fetes and street parties, the chopping down of many mature trees, the removal of hanging flower baskets and the banning of conkers played without goggles. Perhaps the single most worrying manifestation of risk paranoia in Britain is the Safeguarding Vulnerable Groups Bill that will require up to one third of the adult working population to be subject to continuous criminal-records vetting (Appleton et al. 2006).

3.2 Top-loop bias and weapons of financial mass destruction

At the time of writing (August 2008) the world is in a state of financial turmoil that might be attributed to *top-loop bias*. The 'subprime crisis' and the 'credit crunch' can be viewed as the consequences of financial risk taking in a context in which the rewards for playing successfully with other people's money are enormous. In a good year the Christmas bonus of a foreign exchange dealer or hedge fund manager can be enough to retire on for life. And if he has a financial 'accident' and loses his clients or shareholders a lot of money, the worst that is likely to happen is that he will need to find another job – while still retaining his earlier bonuses. On a more modest, but far more widespread scale, this distortion of incentives has led commission-hungry providers of mortgages to persuade large numbers of people to assume debts that they had no hope of repaying, especially in a climate of collapsing property prices.

The problem has been compounded by the hubris that confuses luck with financial genius, a condition nicely described by Nassim Nicholas Taleb in *Fooled by Randomness* (Taleb 2005). The financial instruments devised by the so-called financial 'rocket scientists' – famously labeled *weapons of financial mass destruction* by Warren Buffett – have become complex beyond the comprehension of most people trading them, and often beyond the comprehension of their devisers. Their apparent mathematical sophistication has led many who dealt in them to believe that they were safely within the scientific circle of Figure 1.

In reality they were in the Virtual Risk circle where the available numbers provided spurious support for judgments based on speculation, superstition and prejudice – and greed and vanity. A famous example has been compellingly documented by Roger Lowenstein in *When Genius Failed* (Lowenstein 2002). It is the story of the spectacular fall, in September 1998, of Long Term Capital Management, a fall that came close to bringing down the global financial markets. The principal 'geniuses' in this story were Robert Merton and Myron Scholes who shared a Nobel Prize for Economics in 1997 for their discovery of 'a new method to determine the value of derivatives'. So long as the assumptions embodied in their model held, so long as the phenomena they were modeling could be confined within the scientific circle of Figure 1, their genius trumped all competitors, and produced astonishing profits. But their vanity, arrogance and early success deceived them into believing that they had a formula for managing uncertainty.

3.3 What kills you matters

Figure 3 illustrates another way of classifying risks that can also help clear out of the way some unnecessary arguments.

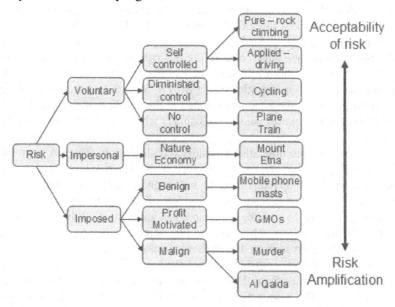

Fig. 3. Risk acceptability and risk amplification: what kills you matters

Acceptance of a given actuarial level of risk varies widely with the perceived level of control an individual can exercise over it and, in the case of imposed risks, with the perceived motives of the imposer.

With 'pure' voluntary risks, the risk itself, with its associated challenge and rush of adrenaline, is the reward. Most climbers on Mount Everest and K2 know that it is dangerous and willingly take the risk (the fatality rate on K2 – fatalities/those reaching the summit – is reported to be 1 in 4).

With a voluntary, self-controlled, applied risk, such as driving, the reward is getting expeditiously from A to B. But the sense of control that drivers have over their fates appears to encourage a high level of tolerance of the risks involved.

Cycling from A to B (I write as a London cyclist) is done with a diminished sense of control over one's fate. This sense is supported by statistics that show that per kilometre travelled a cyclist is much more likely to die than someone in a car. This is a good example of the importance of distinguishing between relative and absolute risk. Although much greater, the absolute risk of cycling is still small – 1 fatality in 25 million kilometres cycled; not even Lance Armstrong can begin to cover that distance in a lifetime of cycling. And numerous studies have demonstrated that the extra relative risk is more than offset by the health benefits of regular cycling; regular cyclists live longer.

While people may voluntarily board planes, buses and trains, the popular reaction to crashes in which passengers are passive victims, suggests that the public demand a higher standard of safety in circumstances in which people voluntarily hand over control of their safety to pilots, or bus, or train drivers.

Risks imposed by nature – such as those endured by people living on the San Andreas Fault or the slopes of Mount Etna – or by impersonal economic forces – such as the vicissitudes of the global economy – are placed in the middle of the scale. Reactions vary widely. Such risks are usually seen as motiveless and are responded to fatalistically – unless or until the risk can be connected to base human motives. The damage caused by Hurricane Katrina to New Orleans is now attributed more to willful bureaucratic neglect than to nature. And the search for the causes of the economic devastation attributed to the 'credit crunch' is now focusing on the enormous bonuses paid to the bankers who profited from the subprime debacle.

Imposed risks are less tolerated. Consider mobile phones. The risk associated with the handsets is either non-existent or very small. The risk associated with the base stations, measured by radiation dose, unless one is up the mast with an ear to the transmitter, is orders of magnitude less. Yet all around the world billions of people are queuing up to take the voluntary risk, and almost all the opposition is focused on the base stations, which are seen by objectors as impositions. Because the radiation dose received from the handset increases with distance from the base station, to the extent that campaigns against the base stations are successful, they will increase the distance from the base station to the average handset, and thus the radiation dose. The base station risk, if it exists, might be labeled a benignly imposed risk; no one supposes that the phone company wishes to murder all those in the neighbourhood.

Even less tolerated are risks whose imposers are perceived to be motivated by profit or greed. In Europe, big biotech companies such as Monsanto are routinely denounced by environmentalist opponents for being more concerned with profit than the welfare of the environment or the consumers of its products.

Less tolerated still are malignly imposed risks – crimes ranging from mugging to rape and murder. In most countries in the world the number of deaths on the road far exceeds the numbers of murders, but far more people are sent to jail for murder than for causing death by dangerous driving. In the United States in 2002 16,000 people were murdered – a statistic that evoked far more popular concern than the 42,000 killed on the road – but far less concern than that inspired by the zero killed by terrorists.

Which brings us to terrorism and Al Qaida. How do we account for the massive scale, world-wide, of the outpourings of grief and anger attaching to its victims, whose numbers are dwarfed by victims of other causes of violent death? In London 52 people were killed by terrorist bombs on 7 July 2005, about six days worth of death on the road. But thousands of people do not gather in Trafalgar Square every Sunday to mark, with a three minute silence, their grief for the previous week's road accident victims.

At the time of writing the British Government is proposing legislation that would permit the detention of terrorist suspects without charge for 42 days. The malign intent of the terrorist is amplified by governments who see it as a threat to their ability to govern. To justify forms of surveillance and restrictions on liberty previously associated with tyrannies 'democratic' governments now characterize terrorism as a threat to Our Way of Life.

4 Who is 'we'?

How 'we' manage risk depends on who 'we' are. Figure 4 presents in cartoon form a typology of cultural biases commonly encountered in debates about risk.

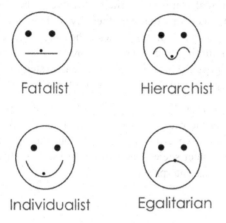

Fig. 4. A typology of cultural biases

These are caricatures, but nevertheless recognizable types that one encounters in debates about threats to safety and the environment. With a little imagination you can begin to see them as personalities. In a report for Britain's Health and Safety Executive (Adams and Thompson 2002) they are described as follows:

- *Individualists* are enterprising 'self-made' people, relatively free from control by others, and who strive to exert control over their environment and the people in it. Their success is often measured by their wealth and the number of followers they command. They are enthusiasts for equality of opportunity and, should they feel the need for moral justification of their activities, they appeal to Adam Smith's Invisible Hand that ensures that selfish behaviour in a free market operates to the benefit of all. The self-made Victorian mill owner or present-day venture capitalist would make good representatives of this category. They oppose regulation and favour free markets. Nature, according to this perspective, is to be *commanded* for human benefit.

- *Egalitarians* have strong group loyalties but little respect for externally imposed rules, other than those imposed by nature. Human nature is – or should be – cooperative, caring and sharing. Trust and fairness are guiding precepts and equality of outcome is an important objective. Group decisions are arrived at by direct participation of all members, and leaders rule by the force of their arguments. The solution to the world's environmental problems is to be found in voluntary simplicity. Members of religious sects, communards, and environmental pressure groups all belong to this category. Nature is to be *obeyed*.
- *Hierarchists* inhabit a world with strong group boundaries and binding prescriptions. Social relationships in this world are hierarchical with everyone knowing his or her place. Members of caste-bound Hindu society, soldiers of all ranks and civil servants are exemplars of this category. The hierarchy certifies and employs the scientists whose intellectual authority is used to justify its actions. Nature is to be *managed*.
- *Fatalists* have minimal control over their own lives. They belong to no groups responsible for the decisions that rule their lives. They are non-unionised employees, outcasts, refugees, untouchables. They are resigned to their fate and see no point in attempting to change it. Nature is to be *endured* and, when it's your lucky day, *enjoyed*. Their risk management strategy is to buy lottery tickets and duck if they see something about to hit them.

It was explained to the HSE that in the terms of this typology they were statuary Hierarchists who make the rules and enforce the rules. For the foreseeable future we predicted they could expect to be attacked from the Egalitarian quadrant for not doing enough to protect society, and from the Individualist quadrant for over regulating and suffocating enterprise.

5 Conclusion

Returning to Turnbull's list of unresolved issues and the questions that they contain, what, with the help of the risk framing devices set out above, might we conclude?

1. Moral arguments surrounding the differing 'rights'of individuals, enterprises and the state to cause potential harm to third parties.

   Why do moral arguments about 'rights' persist unresolved? Individuals, enterprises and the state have different perceptions of the rewards and potential costs of risk. *Enterprises* are led by entrepreneurs, 'individualists' (top loopers) in the lower left quadrant of Figure 4 who tend to focus more on the 'rewards' of risk in Figure 2 than on the risk of 'accidents. The *state* is represented by 'hierarchists' in the upper right quadrant of Figure 4 who seek to manage risk by balancing its costs and benefits. 'Egalitarians' (bottom loopers) will complain about the callous profit-seeking activities of the individualists and the failure of the government 'the Hierarchy' to protect society. The rest of us can be found in all four quadrants but most are either 'egalitarians' protesting at the unfair distribution of the costs and benefits of risk, or 'fatalists' who are resigned to being unlucky but nevertheless continue to buy lottery tickets. The moral arguments remain unresolved because *there are many moralities, and they are unlikely ever to agree.*

2. The case for a common Value for Preventing a Fatality or varying it according to the economic status of the potential victims and factors such as life expectancy and health.

Why can risk managers not agree on a common value for preventing a fatality? This question reflects a frustration common to most cost benefit analysts. The frustration is rooted in their assumption that there ought to be a common cash value for a life. Discovering it is proving difficult, they will admit, but find it they must. Otherwise their method is useless. So, despite decades of failure, they persist with their surveys and revealed preference studies in hopes of uncovering it.

Above I describe the various 'rewards' and 'accidents' in Figure 2 as 'incommensurable'. They are so for a number of reasons:

a) Most people are simply incapable of reducing the pleasures of 'money, power, love, glory, food, sex, rushes of adrenaline...' to a common denominator.

b) There is great uncertainty about what prevents fatalities – or other losses. In the realm of road safety, the effect of most accident prevention measures is greatly reduced, if not completely nullified, by risk compensation – the balancing act described by Figure 2; after the use of seat belts became mandatory more pedestrians and cyclists were killed by motorists enjoying an enhanced sense of safety (Adams 2006).

c) Any 'value' that people attach to a risk is hugely influenced by whether it is perceived as voluntary or imposed. In the jargon of conventional cost benefit the analysts ask 'what would you be willing to pay' (WTP) to reduce your risk of death and 'what would you be willing to accept as compensation' (WTA) for an imposed increase in your risk of death. Figure 3 suggests that these answers will differ greatly – so greatly that cost benefit analysts usually do not ask the WTA question. The person being questioned is entitled to say 'no amount of money will compensate me for a particular imposed risk' and it takes only one infinity to blow up a cost benefit analysis.

d) Within any given society there is no common value system. Individuals differ greatly in the value that they attach to any given risk or reward. *Assuming* that they could express these values in monetary terms, the average to which cost benefit analysis would reduce them would irritate almost everyone because the average would not represent their values.

Cost benefit analysis settles no arguments – except amongst economists prepared to accept the unrealistic assumptions upon which it depends.[1]

3. The wide variations in approach to safety in the transport sector between road, rail, marine and air.

Why do governments and the media react differently to different causes of death? The reactions of both governments and the media reflect the range of risk acceptance and risk amplification described by Figure 3.
  What kills you matters.

4. The potential conflicts between a 'Zero Tolerance' approach to accidents and Cost Benefit Analysis.

a) Why do some institutions profess to be pursuing zero risk, knowing that achieving it is impossible? The professed pursuit of zero risk is a defense mechanism. It is a paranoid response to the fear of the no-win-no-fee lawyer in an increasingly litigious society. It is unlikely to be much help. Accidents will happen. When they do the zero risk management plan will be closely examined, and assist the no-win-no-fee lawyer in identifying precisely where the human failure occurred.

b) Why do some institutions pretend that their risk management problems can be reduced to a calculation in which all significant variables can be represented by a common metric? Cost benefit analysis is an ineffectual comfort blanket. The senior management, the hierarchy, find numbers reassuring. They are precise (or have precise error bands) and can be produced as evidence that the management is in control of affairs. But in court they have turned out to be an 'aggravating offence'. Many years ago Ford did a cost benefit analysis of a proposal to make the fuel tank of a Ford Pinto safer. They calculated the cost of the safety improvement and the benefit of the lives and limbs that might be saved – using the then current values for lives and limbs. The cost benefit analysis concluded that the proposed safety benefit did not justify the cost. But a jury, after an accident, found this calculation so callous that they awarded unprecedented punitive damages.
  Both the 'zero tolerance' approach and cost benefit analysis offer hostages to the no-win-no-fee lawyers.

---

[1] In TEAMOS p 40 Michael Jones-Lee observes that 'when one does an empirical willingness-to-pay exercise, one is asking people to wear a "self interested" hat, whereas when considering societal concerns, you are asking them to behave as citizens. I will say no more than that.' This is a remarkable concession from someone who for many years has been a leading defender of cost benefit analysis. The procedure is commonly called 'social cost benefit analysis' because it purports to capture non-market costs and benefits, sometimes called 'externalities'. Jones-Lee appears to be conceding that social cost benefit analysts cannot capture the social aspect of issues that they are called upon to resolve.

5. Societal attitudes and the influences on them. Strategies for communication and dialogue.

Why are societal attitudes and risk communication still seen as problematic after many years of investigation? They will remain eternally problematic. The 'risk communicators' are mostly to be found in the hierarchist quadrant of Figure 4. These are the risk experts who know, quantitatively, what the risks are, or pretend they know when the risks fall into the 'virtual' circle of Figure 1 – as most of them do. They are the legislators and regulators, and regulation enforcers. They despair of the 'irrationality' that they see implicit in the diverse responses to risk illustrated by Figure 3. They are frustrated by the phenomenon of risk compensation illustrated by Figure 2; extending sight lines should make roads safer – but motorists respond by driving faster. And they are bemused by the attacks from the different cultural biases illustrated by Figure 4; the egalitarians complain that the hierarchy is not doing enough to protect them, while the individualists complain that they are over regulating and suffocating enterprise.

There is no such thing as society.

6. The threats posed to technical investigation and prevention of accidents by over zealous criminal investigations.

Why are certain accident investigations, criminal or civil, seen as 'over zealous' by some and justifiable by others? Over zealousness is in the eye of the beholder. Those pursuing criminal investigations, commonly found in the Hierarchist quadrant of Figure 4, would rarely, if ever, concede that they were being over zealous; their job is to prosecute wrongdoers and thereby make the world safer. The different reactions to their works have been briefly described above.

An impressionistic view of media coverage of risk stories at the time of writing (September 2008) is that there is a consensus that the Hierarchy has been over-zealous in the pursuit of the risks posed by hanging flower baskets and the playing of conkers without goggles, and under-zealous in the regulation of hedge funds and providers of subprime mortgages. But it is a fragile consensus; *'over zealous' is a value judgment not universally shared.*

6 And finally

The drunk notoriously searches for his keys not in the dark where he dropped them, but under the lamppost where he can see. This is an apt metaphor for much of what is written on the subject of risk management.

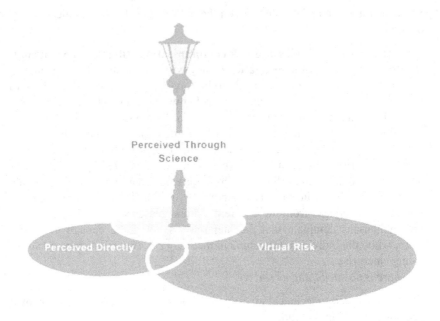

Fig. 5. Risk management: Where are the keys?

Lord Kelvin famously said, 'When you cannot measure your knowledge is meagre and unsatisfactory'[1].

This dictum sits challengingly alongside that of another famous scientist, Peter Medewar who observed, 'If politics is the art of the possible, research is the art of the soluble. Both are immensely practical minded affairs. Good scientists study the most important *problems they think they can solve* [my emphasis]. It is, after all, their professional business to solve problems, not merely to grapple with them.' (Medawar 1967)

Risk is a word that refers to the future. It has no objective existence. The future exists only in the imagination. There are some risks for which science can provide useful guidance to the imagination. The risk that the sun will not rise tomorrow can be assigned a very low probability by science. And actuarial science can estimate with a high degree of confidence that the number of people killed in road accidents in Britain next year will be 3,000, plus or minus a hundred or so. But these are predictions, not facts. Such predictions rest on assumptions; that tomorrow will be like yesterday; that next year will be like last year; that future events can be foretold by reading the runes of the past. Sadly, the history of prediction contains many failures – from those of stock market tipsters to those of vulcanologists seeking to predict eruptions, earthquakes and tsunamis.

---

[1] Words carved in stone over the entrance to the Social Science building of the University of Chicago.

In the area lit by the lamp of science one finds risk management problems that are potentially soluble by science. Such problems are capable of clear definition relating cause to effect and characterized by identifiable statistical regularities. On the margins of this circle one finds problems framed as hypotheses, and methods of reasoning, such as Bayesian statistics, which guide the collection and analysis of further evidence. As the light grows dimmer the ratio of speculation to evidence increases. In the outer darkness lurk unknown unknowns. Here lie problems with which, to use Medawar's word, we are destined to 'grapple'.

There is a distinction, frequently insisted upon in the literature on risk management, between 'hazard' and 'risk'. A hazard is defined as something that could lead to harm, and a risk as the product of the probability of that harm and its magnitude; risk in this literature is hazard with numbers attached. So, relating this terminology to Figure 5, it can be seen that risk can be placed in the circle illuminated by science while the other two circles contain different types of hazard.

Typing 'hazard management' into Google at the time of writing yielded 120,000 hits; 'risk management', 36.6 million – 300 times more. But the number of potential harms in life to which useful numbers can be attached is tiny compared to the number through which we must navigate using unquantified judgement. The Kelvinist, approach to risk, with its conviction that everything in the outer darkness must be quantifiable, can only lead to self-deception. And following Medawar's dictum that we should confine our efforts to the quantitatively soluble, threatens to divert attention from larger, more complicated, more urgent problems with which we ought to be grappling.

References

Adams J (2006) The Failure of Seat Belt Legislation. In: Verweij M, Thompson M (eds) Clumsy Solutions for a Complex World. Palgrave Macmillan, Basingstoke. See also http://john-adams.co.uk/wp-content/uploads/2006/failure%20of_%20seatbelt%20legislation.pdf and http://john-adams.co.uk/wp-content/uploads/2008/08/seat-belts-for-significance-2.pdf. Accessed 10 September 2008

Adams J, Thompson M (2002) Taking account of societal concerns about risk. Health and Safety Executive Research Report 035. http://www.hse.gov.uk/research/rrpdf/rr035.pdf. Accessed 11 September 2008

Appleton J, Ball J, Weldon F et al (2006) Children's cost in safety bill. Letter to the Times, 16 October. http://www.timesonline.co.uk/tol/comment/letters/article601499.ece. Accessed 11 September 2008

Lowenstein R (2002) When Genius Failed: the rise and fall of Long Term Capital Management. Fourth Estate, London

Medawar PB (1967) *The Art of the Soluble.* Methuen, London

RAEng (2006) The Economics and Morality of Safety. The Royal Academy of Engineering, London. http://www.raeng.org.uk/news/publications/list/reports/Safety Seminar.pdf. Accessed 10 September 2008

Taleb NN (2005) Fooled by Randomness. Random House, New York

Wilde GJS (2001) Target Risk 2: A New Psychology of Safety and Health. PDE Publications, Toronto

The Morality and Economics of Safety in Defence Procurement

Tim Clement

Adelard

London, UK

Abstract Ministry of Defence policy is to conform as closely as possible to UK health and safety legislation in all its operations. We consider the implications of the law and the guidance provided by the Health and Safety Executive for the arguments we need to make for the safety of defence procurements, and extract four general principles to help in answering the questions that arise when considering the safety of systems with complex behaviour. One of these principles is analysed further to identify how case law and the guidance interpret the requirement for risks to be reduced so far as is reasonably practicable. We then apply the principles to answer some questions that have arisen in our work as Independent Safety Auditors, including the limits to the tolerability of risk to armed forces personnel and civilians in wartime, and the acceptability of the transfer of risk from one group to another when controls on risk are introduced.

1 Introduction

Perhaps because of the clear level of risk involved, the safety of personnel and their equipment has long been a concern in defence procurement and operations. The Ordnance Board, the forerunner of the Defence Ordnance Safety Board, has had formal responsibility for munitions safety since the Second Boer War, and its origins go back to Tudor times. The Accidents Investigation Branch of the Royal Flying Corps was established in 1915. These bodies implemented a classic approach to improvement in safety through the investigation of accidents and incidents, and the embodiment of lessons learned in policy, guidance and good practice.

More recently, the UK defence community has, like other areas of high risk and public concern, adopted a rigorous approach to safety management in procurement and operation, based around the construction of a safety case. There has been a parallel move to give up some legal exemptions from health and safety legislation and adopt legal requirements as policy where the exemptions remain. As a result,

C. Dale, T. Anderson (eds.), *Safety-Critical Systems: Problems, Process and Practice*,
DOI 10.1007/978-1-84882-349-5_3, © Springer-Verlag London Limited 2009

safety in defence has become more like safety in the regulated civil sectors (oil, rail, nuclear and civil aviation) discussed at the recent Royal Academy of Engineering seminar on the economics and morality of safety (Turnbull 2006). Like them, it has the problems of applying legislation primarily concerned with widespread and well understood hazards to systems with complex behaviour, novel implementation and risk resulting from functional failure as much as from inherent hazards. Unlike them, the armed forces routinely and deliberately place their employees in harm's way and attempt to harm others, while trying to preserve the safety of third parties.

Being practitioners rather than legislators (or philosophers) we try to understand and work within the current framework rather than to alter it. This paper summarises the legal and policy framework for defence safety in Section 2. In Section 3, we try to extract some key principles behind the legislation and the supporting guidance to make it easier to apply consistently to novel questions. We then apply these principles to arrive at answers to questions that have arisen in the course of our work: to the establishment of criteria for the tolerability of risk in war in Section 4; to the acceptability of the transfer of risk between groups in Section 5; and to a selection of common minor questions (with economic rather than moral dimensions) in Section 6.

2   The legal position

The Health and Safety At Work *etc* Act of 1974 (HSWA) imposes on an employer the duty to ensure the health and safety at work of all his employees, and to ensure that persons not in his employment who may be affected by his undertaking are not exposed to risks to their health or safety. In addition, any person who supplies an article for use at work must ensure that the article is designed and constructed to be safe and when properly used. In each case, these duties are to be carried out *so far as is reasonably practicable*, a phrase we shall consider in more detail in the next section.

It is widely believed that Crown Immunity, the ancient legal principle that action cannot be taken against the sovereign (and by extension, her government) in her own courts, means that the Act does not apply to the Ministry of Defence (MoD). This is not quite the case. The provisions of the Act, including the power of the Health and Safety Executive (HSE) to inspect and issue Improvement Notices where breaches are observed, apply to the MoD as to any other employer. The difference is that MoD cannot be prosecuted under it: in circumstances where a prosecution would be brought against a civil employer, HSE can only issue a Crown Censure.

It is the stated policy of the Secretary of State for Defence (MOD 2003) that MoD will comply with the requirements of the HSWA and its subordinate provisions within the United Kingdom. This is essentially an acceptance of the need to comply within its jurisdictional scope. Some specific legislation explicitly states that it does not apply to MoD, and in this case it is policy to introduce arrangements that are at least as good. In addition, UK standards will be applied overseas as well as complying with relevant host nations' standards. In each case, the policy will be applied only where it is reasonably practicable.

Legislation may include powers for the Minister to disapply it when considered necessary for national security. Such provisions appear fairly regularly in the regulations supporting the HSWA, including the Noise at Work Regulations (HSE 2005) where the exemption requires that the health and safety of employees is ensured *as far as possible* (not, in this case, so far as is reasonably practicable). Policy is to do so only when essential to maintain operational capability. For example, exemptions have been given for the firing of noisy weapons if the inherent noise levels cannot be further reduced and the available hearing protection cannot achieve the statutory noise levels. These can apply to training as well as use on operations because this is part of maintaining operational capability.

The recent Corporate Manslaughter Act (HMG 2007) allows organisations to be fined for gross breaches of their duty of care to employees or the public where these stem from systematic failures of management. Crown bodies, including MoD, are explicitly included within its scope. This is in line with recommendations from the HSE and other bodies that government bodies should be subject to the same judicial process as private organisations.

Civil actions by armed forces personnel against MoD for injuries sustained on service have been permitted since the Crown Proceedings (Armed Forces) Act 1987 (HMG 1987). However, current case law (Multiple Claimants 2003) is that the MoD is not under a duty to maintain a safe system of work for service personnel engaged with an enemy in the course of combat, based on the common law principle of 'combat immunity'. This applies not only in the presence of the enemy or the occasions when contact with the enemy has been established but also to active operations against the enemy in which service personnel are exposed to attack or the threat of attack. It also covers the planning of and preparation for these operations. It covers peace enforcement operations as well as war.

3   The moral argument

We recognise that most of the activities we undertake, whether individually or collectively, involve some risk of injury to ourselves, to other people, to property or to the environment. The question is therefore what justification do we have for imposing risk on others, and in particular, what determines the extent to which the state, in carrying out its defence activities, is entitled to subject people to risk.

Parliament, in not granting a general exemption to defence activities from the HSWA, has taken the view that this is a particular instance of an undertaking with a duty of care to its employees and the general public, although as we have seen there are some possibilities for specific exemptions. By choosing to conform with the Act under most circumstances even when not compelled to do so, and while not under threat of civil action, the Secretary of State has taken the view that the moral arguments for this duty of care and how it should be discharged retain their force even outside the scope of jurisdiction of the law. We shall therefore consider the moral basis for the general legislation.

The HSE has set out the reasoning behind its policy on interpreting and enforcing HSWA (HSE 1992, HSE 2001), in the interests of better understanding of how it acts on behalf of the public. We can identify two main principles that are common to the two documents:

- A person's exposure to risk from an undertaking is justified by the benefit that they or society receive from the undertaking.
- A person should not be exposed to unjustified risk.

The first of these provides the moral justification for imposing the risk. In general, employees can be seen as deriving most of their benefit directly from the undertaking as earnings. The armed forces, fire service and police are unusual in that they are expected to expose themselves to high risks in their employment for the general good rather than personal benefit (and with reduced legal recourse in the event of injury)[1].

Risk to the general public is usually justified by the benefit brought to the public in general. In the case of the armed forces, these benefits are the defence of national interests and support to the civil powers in the event of disaster. In some cases, the general public benefit includes a direct benefit to the individual: the person living next to a nuclear power station gains from the stability of their electricity supply. (The French take this one stage further by providing discounted electricity and other amenities to local residents (HSE 1992).) However, the rest of society has the benefit without the risk, and a vegetarian might well consider they get no benefit from a poultry factory.

The argument for this principle is framed by the HSE in utilitarian terms, producing the greatest total amount of good. Kantians could also accept the morality of imposing risk on others on the basis that while they might want an absolute prohibition on others imposing risk on them, this is not a restriction that they would accept for themselves because of the restrictions on liberty and opportunity that it would imply, and so a prohibition cannot be willed as a universal law (Kant and Bennett 2008).

The acceptability of the second principle depends on what is meant by unjustified risk. We have seen that the legal requirement is that the risk shall be reduced so far as is reasonably practicable. (In the guidance, the alternative formulation that the risk is As Low As Reasonably Practicable – ALARP – is more widely used.) The interpretation of this rests on a small body of case law: in particular,

---

[1] The Military Covenant, expressed by (MoD 2008) as 'In putting the needs of the nation, the army and others before their own, they forgo some of the rights enjoyed by those outside the armed forces. So, at the very least, British soldiers should always expect the nation and their commanders to treat them fairly, to value and respect them as individuals, and to sustain and reward them and their families', seeks to strike an appropriate balance.

the Court of Appeal, in its judgment in Edwards v. National Coal Board in 1949 (under the Coal Mines Act of 1911, which also uses the wording), ruled that 'reasonably practicable' is a narrower term than 'physically possible', and that a measure can be considered not reasonably practicable if the cost of implementation is grossly disproportionate to the reduction in risk achieved (Edwards 1949). Gross disproportion is not defined in the judgement but guidance from the HSE (HSE 2008a) suggests that factors between 2 and 10 can be reasonable depending on circumstances. The test is therefore stricter than a simple cost-benefit analysis but shares with it the idea that a value can be placed on avoiding death or injury.

'Putting a value on human life' is always controversial, particularly when talking about particular lives lost in the aftermath of an accident. Prospective risk assessments usually use the more positive phrase 'value of a prevented fatality'[2]. Most people would prefer that risks that apply to them are reduced wherever physically possible, the interpretation rejected by the Edwards judgement mainly on the grounds that 'reasonably practicable' must mean something different from 'practicable'. The European Court appears to agree with them (CEC 2005) in its judgement on the action by the Commission of the European Communities against the UK, for failing to transpose the requirement from the European directive on workplace safety (CEC 1989) that 'the employer shall have a duty to ensure the safety and health of workers in every aspect related to the work'[3].

This can be seen as a debate between utilitarian and Kantian moral positions. The utilitarian argues that the money spent on achieving safety at all costs is better spent on other benefits to society (although they might be uncomfortable if it appears as company profits instead, even though these produce indirect societal benefits through economic activity). The National Institute for Clinical Excellence (NICE) attempts exactly this argument when allocating fixed National Health Service resources between competing treatments. In contrast, Kant takes the view that 'Everything has either a *price* or a *dignity*. Whatever has a price can be replaced by something else as its equivalent; on the other hand, whatever is above all price, and therefore admits of no equivalent, has a dignity' (Kant and Bennett 2008). On this basis we can deny that life can be traded for other benefits and insist that all practical steps should be taken to reduce risk: public reaction to NICE decisions tends to adopt this position, the corollary being that the resources allocated must be increased.

In setting out the basis for their regulatory framework (HSE 2001), HSE do not seek to defend the legal definition of reasonably practicable except in relation to the straw man of absolute safety. Instead, they modify it to bring the concept of

---

[2] There is a large literature on how this value should be assessed, which leads to moral discussions of its own (the Green Book (HM Treasury 2008) provides an introduction), but the resulting figures tend to be in the range from £1M to £10M.

[3] The judgement is in favour of existing UK law on the grounds that civil liability is not limited in the way that the Health and Safety at Work Act limits criminal liability. Employment in the UK is also safer than in most other European countries.

justified risk closer to unavoidable risk, a position that the Kantian would accept as consistent with the dignity of life.

This is done first by setting limits to exposure to particular hazards, such as noise, vibration or particular hazardous chemicals, at levels where no observable harm will be caused if they are experienced continuously. They must be met even if the cost of achieving them is grossly disproportionate to the harm caused by a higher level of exposure. This is precisely the area of regulation where disapplication tends to be permitted for the armed forces, although as we have seen the requirement to reduce the risk as far as possible remains. The principle that the risk is justified because it is unavoidable is therefore maintained.

The second modification is to require that commonly occurring hazards should be controlled by application of good practice, which is essentially a broad consensus on the steps that are reasonable to take to achieve safety, as expressed in standards, codes of practice, or increasingly in the form of European regulations[4]. They define a minimum set of risk controls to be applied in relevant situations, again regardless of the cost compared with the benefit in any particular case although general acceptance normally implies some degree of cost-effectiveness. The residual risk should then be further reduced by special-to-situation measures if their costs are not grossly disproportionate to the benefits.

HSE also further modify the utilitarian position by introducing two further principles. The first is motivated by considerations of equity:

- There is a limit to the level of risk that it is equitable to impose on a person or group, irrespective of the benefit gained.

Essentially, this principle says that there shall be no scapegoats to bear the risk for the rest of us. HSE guidance (HSE 2001) suggests a limit to the risk that a person should experience from all hazards associated with their work, or from their exposure to the activities of a single undertaking.

The second, related principle stems from public concern about large scale accidents, resulting in tens of fatalities or worse (the so-called societal accidents). These are rare, and so the risks that give rise to them are well below the limits set on tolerable risk to an individual in accordance with the previous principle. However, their magnitude and rarity means that they receive a high degree of public attention and hence the perceived risk is high, with a corresponding demand for it to be reduced[5]. They also typically involve risks that are outside the immediate control of the affected individual. This has historically resulted in specific regulation of safety in the affected areas, and so public disquiet takes on a political dimension. This results in the principle that:

---

[4] HSE's policy on codes of practice is that the legal requirements for safety can be discharged by alternative means that are equally effective, whereas legislation must be complied with.

[5] The classic example here is the contrast between the public perception of the risks of road and rail travel. We may also contrast the risk of dying in an act of terrorism with that of death by handgun in the United States.

- There is a limit to the level of risk that it is equitable for an undertaking to incur, irrespective of the benefit it produces.

As a principle, it appears to be pragmatically rather than morally based. It is also difficult to estimate the likely frequencies of accidents killing many people, because of the number of uncertainties involved. As a result, this particular criterion has not been much used, even for undertakings where an accident of this magnitude is credible. However, HSE has recently conducted a consultation (HSE 2007) on whether it should be applied, in addition to the limits on individual risk, when considering housing developments in the neighbourhood of high risk installations such as chemical plants. This was given extra topicality by the Buncefield incident.

4   Setting a limit of tolerability for wartime risk[6]

We have identified a moral principle underlying health and safety legislation that there is a limit to the level of risk that any person should be expected to accept, but this principle does not determine what that risk should be, and it is hard to see how it could be determined purely from philosophical considerations. Instead, the level has to be determined by social consensus.

We would expect general agreement that the risk to a person from their employment or from their exposure to risk from a particular undertaking should represent only a small part of their risk of death from all causes (about 1 in 100 per year averaged over the whole population, somewhat lower for people of working age). In (HSE 1992), the HSE consider the tolerability of risk to workers in nuclear power stations, and set the 'limit of tolerability for any significant group of workers over an extended period' at 1 fatality in 1,000 person-years. This is a fairly small contribution to total risk, and because it is based on the actual fatality levels amongst the highest risk occupations there is an argument that it is tolerable because historically it has been tolerated by society. They then argue that the risk to the general population in the vicinity of a nuclear power station should be an order of magnitude lower on the basis of it being an imposed risk. The resulting limit of 1 fatality in 10,000 person-years is about the same as the risk of dying in a road traffic accident, which again is tolerated as a daily risk, in this case by most of the population. In the nuclear context, where the main contribution to risk comes from radiation-induced cancer, it is also a small contribution to the rate of fatality from cancer of 1 in 300 person-years.

(HSE 2001) uses these figures as suggested limits for broader application. It also makes the point that good practice and regulation ensure that these limits are rarely reached, and so the main issue is whether risks have been reduced so far as is reasonably practicable rather than whether they are tolerable. The limits remain

---

[6] This section is based on work originally undertaken for BATCIS IPT.

useful in risk assessment because they give a basis for distinguishing large risks from small risks on an absolute scale, and thus guide the allocation of effort in risk management.

In peacetime, working for the armed forces is not that different from working for any other undertaking. There is no obvious civilian equivalent of piloting fast jets (one of the riskier military occupations). The routine use of weapons is also unusual, but weapons training is tightly controlled to reduce the risk. As a consequence, occupational death and injury rates for the armed forces in peacetime are comparable with those in manufacturing industry, at around 1 fatality in 100,000 person-years[7], and the civilian limit for tolerability of risk is widely adopted as the appropriate criterion for military risk assessments. Similarly, military activity generates risk to the public from such sources as road traffic, storage and transport of hazardous materials, and air traffic, all of which have civilian counterparts so the criteria for risk to the general public also seem appropriate.

War and peace enforcement activities carry the risk of attack by hostile forces, and there is an expectation that injuries will be sustained as a result. The risks of injury from carrying out operations are also likely to increase, because although the inherent hazards and dangerous failure modes of the equipment remain unchanged, operational circumstances mean that it will be used nearer to its limits where failure is more likely, or where procedural controls on risk such as range safety cannot be applied. In extreme cases, a judgement may need to be made between the safety of a particular action and the wider operational need. This is summarised in JSP 454 (MoD 2006, Part 2, paragraph 4.4) as:

> A system should be intrinsically safe in training, during peacetime and on operations. However, it may not be possible to maintain safety performance in times of hostility, and safety requirements may need to be relaxed if, in the judgement of the appropriate operating authority or Commanding Officer, the operational risks outweigh the safety benefits. It is the project team's responsibility to ensure that safety issues, *i.e.* emergency and contingency arrangements and limitations of use *etc.*, are clearly reflected in the relevant equipment publications to allow the Operating Authority or Commander to make such an informed decision if he/she decides to take this course of action.

The Release To Service procedures applied to aircraft (MoD 2007a) make specific provision for recording areas where the Commanding Officer may exercise judgement by providing Operational Emergency Clearance for actions that are not normally permitted.

Def Stan 00-56 (MoD 2007b) expects a risk assessment to demonstrate that risks are tolerable and ALARP. This means that we need a limit of tolerability for the risk to personnel from own forces' activities during operations. To derive this, we can follow the strategy used by HSE and take as tolerable what has been historically tolerated. Table 1 shows numbers deployed and fatalities for a series of wars in the 20th century. The calculations are necessarily approximate, since not all personnel will have been in service for the whole period of conflict.

---

[7] For land forces, this has been adopted as a safety target (MoD 2006, Part 2, paragraph 4.3.2).

Table 1. Wartime casualty rates

Conflict	Number deployed	Fatalities	Duration (years)	Death rate (per thousand per year)
1st World War	9,000,000 (British Empire)	900,000	4	25
2nd World War	8,720,000 (British Empire)	452,000	6	9
Korea	270,000 (US)	27,000	3	33
Malaya	40,000	1,300	12	3
Vietnam	500,000 (US, 1968)	14,000	1	28
Falklands	28,000 (UK)	236	0.2	42
1st Gulf War	45,000 (UK)	47	1	1

The First Gulf War is generally assumed to have had a very low casualty rate. This is placed in perspective when we observe that it was at the boundary of tolerability for industrial fatalities. The First World War is now seen as an instance of appalling carnage. The fatality rate seems in fact to be comparable with many other conflicts, although the numbers involved are enormous. The Falklands conflict, generally seen as a military success, had a higher fatality rate but was of relatively short duration and involved only professional military personnel rather than conscripts. Each of these was a war where the territorial integrity of the combatants was at stake. The Vietnam War had a similar casualty rate, but largely amongst conscripts, for a less direct cause, and was eventually ended at least in part due to popular dissent. The Korean War caused similar but less extreme protest. Broadly, then, the evidence suggests that the historically tolerated long term fatality rate in wartime is around 30 per thousand per year. These levels begin to generate dissent, particularly when the war aims are abstract, so they can be taken as a reasonable socially determined limit of tolerability for likely future conflicts.

This is the maximum tolerable fatality rate from all causes, but for risk assessment we need a tolerability limit for fatalities resulting from operational failures rather than hostile action. In the First Gulf War, 20% of the fatalities resulted from friendly fire incidents, which represent the extreme and most visible cases of operational error. Allocating one third of the historically just tolerated wartime fatality rate to operational failures gives a conveniently round tolerability limit of 1 fatality per 100 person years that has some justification behind it.

Risk assessment will also need a limit of tolerability of risk to third parties. Accidents to these groups arouse public concern, but the public acceptability of an operation seems to be determined more by injuries to the nation's own forces. We can instead estimate a tolerability limit for third parties in wartime using the existing peacetime limit, our first principle that risk is justified by the benefit that it provides, and the extent to which the risk is imposed rather than accepted voluntarily, which the HSE has identified as a factor in social acceptability.

Third parties in wartime take a number of forms, and derive different degrees of benefit from the operations:

- Native civilians. Where the aim of the military action is to remove an occupying power (as in the First Gulf War), liberation can be taken as a larger and more direct benefit than the guarantee of national security provided to third parties by peacetime training. Where the objective is to achieve a regime change (as in Afghanistan), the civilian population may not see liberation as such a clear-cut benefit, and casualties could strengthen opposition. This group usually has little alternative but to remain exposed to the risk.
- Foreign residents. Their governments will normally advise that they leave the war zone and may help with evacuation. Those that remain are therefore mostly present voluntarily, and so may be deemed to accept a higher degree of risk. One exception to this general principle is that refugees from the hostile power may not want to return. However, they still have the option to seek refuge elsewhere.
- Neighbouring third parties. This category includes civilians of bordering countries, and those in transit through those countries or in international space near the hostilities. We can assume aircraft and ships will normally avoid known areas of conflict, but citizens of neighbouring countries cannot do so. They may gain little benefit from such actions, although the military aims may include improved political stability in an area, including a reduced threat of invasion of these third parties.

We can justify some increase in the level of risk considered tolerable to third parties, on the basis that most have potential benefits from action that are greater than those from armed forces in peacetime and have some ability to move out of the most dangerous areas. Increasing the limit by an order of magnitude would maintain the relative tolerability of risks to armed forces and civilians the same as in peacetime. However, civilians in neighbouring countries need to be paid special attention, perhaps by extra procedures to minimise the associated risk. (There are of course political as well as humanitarian reasons to do so.)

5   The morality of transferring risk

In the simplest cases of risk reduction, a potential cause of an accident is identified and then it is either eliminated or controls are put in place to reduce the likelihood of it becoming the actual cause of an accident. In more complex cases, the controls we adopt result in new risks, which may affect a different population. The question is then whether it is morally justifiable to increase the risk on one group of people in order to reduce it for another. The issue is raised in (HSE 2001, p.34) but no specific guidance is given. We have therefore fallen back on the general principles and their interpretation.

To take a concrete example, military bases in areas where peace enforcement operations are being conducted often come under attack from rockets and mortars fired by hostile forces. Radar can be used to detect these attacks and sound a warning, which achieves a significant reduction in risk but cannot eliminate it entirely because the time between the warning and the arrival of the incoming round is too short to allow everyone to find effective cover.

A further level of risk control can be provided by using radar to determine the trajectory of the munition and direct the fire of a machine gun on to it (Wikipedia.2008). This clearly will not be completely effective as a control. Like most active control systems, it also introduces new risks to the system.

One such risk is the accidental engagement of an aircraft flying in the area of the base. Introducing such a system therefore transfers risk from military personnel on the ground to people in the air. This is potentially a different group, but in practice there is not likely to be civilian air traffic in the base area, and hence the people in the air are military personnel who will eventually be on the ground and protected rather than threatened by the system. They therefore derive benefit in accordance with the first principle. Provided the design and operation of such systems includes controls for this risk that make it tolerable, it is permitted by the third principle. It may be greater than that of other personnel who never fly, but this is not a violation of the principles we have identified, or of any legal requirement. (By setting a limit to the level of risk that is tolerable, we have ensured some level of equity between groups but have not required complete equity.) The second principle requires that the risk to this group should be ALARP, which is addressed by the detailed design of the system and its operating procedures. It also influences the higher level decision of whether to deploy the system or not given the transfer of risk. If the extra risk to people in the air is outweighed by the reduced risk to people on the ground, then deployment is the lower risk choice at the architectural design level and should be adopted if reasonably practicable (HSE 2008b).

There is another risk, which is that most of the rounds fired during an engagement miss their target. The risk can be controlled by providing a self-destruct capability that detonates the explosive charge and reduces the round to small fragments that are not expected to carry damaging levels of kinetic energy when they reach the ground. However, such self-destruct mechanisms have a failure rate that could result in a significant number of rounds falling intact on the ground. The risk of being struck by a round or by fragments after detonation on landing can be controlled by keeping the ballistic endpoint of the rounds in a sparsely populated area (which also mitigates any residual risk from fragments) but there can be a significant quantity of unexploded ordnance that represents a long-term risk to the local population.

It may be possible to show that it would normally be considered tolerable as a risk to the general public, justified on the basis of the benefit of the peace enforcement operation to the local society as in Section 4. In this case, provided the risk to third parties is controlled so far as is reasonably practicable and the overall risk of death and injury to all affected parties is reduced by fielding the interception capability, the ALARP principle applied at the architectural design level again requires that it should be done unless the cost is grossly disproportionate to the net improvement in safety.

The risk to the surrounding population can be controlled by maintaining or improving the self-destruction rate by appropriate manufacturing controls (such as batch lot acceptance tests), maintaining appropriate storage conditions through life, recording where rounds could fall and how many may be involved, providing information on the identification and safe disposal of rounds, educating the local population about the risks, and securing the affected area. The local security situation may make some of these measures impractical for the peace enforcers, although the assistance of humanitarian agencies can be sought. These measures are defined as good practice for controlling risks from unexploded and abandoned ordnance in the Protocol on Explosive Remnants of War (ICRC 1980), which represents a codification of another set of moral principles into international humanitarian law.

6   Some other examples

The HSE has adopted a number of principles from different philosophical backgrounds in determining its approach to managing risk. This raises the question of whether they are internally consistent, and consistent with common sense when applied in particular cases.

There are times when they appear not to be. For example, it is not uncommon to find that at the point where a new piece of equipment is to be deployed, there are further actions that can be taken to reduce the risk that have been identified but have not yet been implemented. These might include safety-related software faults that have been found and not yet corrected, or specific control measures that are not yet in place. (We assume that these controls do not represent good practice or a legislative requirement.) In these cases the risk from the equipment is not ALARP from the perspective of the detailed design.

However, if implementing the controls necessarily causes a delay in deployment we have two alternatives: to delay deployment until the equipment is perfected, or to deploy the imperfect system now. Again, this is an architectural design level choice and the lowest risk option (in this case, deployment) should normally be chosen, although it is acceptable to provide a cost-benefit justification for an alternative.

The apparent paradox is resolved by the temporal aspects of the situation. If it were possible to implement the controls without delay then we would not be justified in not doing so unless the cost grossly outweighed the benefits. Because this is not an option, our best alternative is to deploy the equipment we have (possibly with compensating limitations on use). We are, however, obliged to implement the improvements as soon as is reasonably practicable.

The situation is essentially the same as with a fault reported just after fielding. In that case we must determine the best option from continuing to operate with no changes, imposing an operational limitation, or withdrawing the capability until the fault can be resolved. Similarly, technical developments may allow improvements in risk after deployment but these do not need to be implemented immediately.

The viewpoint that time can be considered as an issue when assessing reasonable practicability is supported by the legal ruling in Edwards v National Coal Board (Edwards 1949) where the judge explicitly states that the defendants would have discharged their duty of care had they had a plan to make the necessary safety improvements but it had not been reasonably practicable to implement it in the time available before the accident occurred.

The interpretation of what is a justified risk in terms of reasonable practicability strikes a balance between the benefits of a measure and its cost of implementation without considering the ability to meet that cost. This accords with a general public unwillingness to sacrifice safety for someone else's profits, but where MoD Integrated Project Teams are allocated budgets at an early stage of a project and contractors operate on fixed price contracts to supply, the possibility of a design change that could save several lives over the lifetime of the project, and hence be reasonably practicable even with a seven figure price tag has caused concern. Most compliance with the HSWA requires that common hazards should be addressed by the application of good practice, and the costs are predictable and in many cases small. This is no longer the case when designing complex and novel systems where the major risks come from functional failure rather than inherent hazards.

The situation in practice is unlikely to be that bad. The airworthiness requirement for a military aircraft (which contractors know in advance and agree to meet) is that it should demonstrate a rate of technical failure leading to the death of any aircrew or passengers of 10^{-6}/flying hour. For most aircraft types, this is comparable with the total flying hours accumulated by the fleet across the service life (for example, Tornado GR1 and GR4 had accumulated about 815,000 flying hours at the end of 2006 (MoD 2007c). Using typical values in a cost-benefit analysis would make the cost of steps to eliminate all the residual risk from a fleet of fast jets meeting the target grossly disproportionate if it exceeded £10M. No single step would be likely to achieve this much risk reduction, and hence be worth so much. Man-portable munitions will typically have tolerable major accident rates of around 10^{-6}/weapon, and a similar calculation places the disproportionate cost of eliminating the risk at around £5 per weapon. In each case the sums involved are small in comparison with the lifetime cost of the system. When safety targets require that no fatalities are expected over the lifetime of the system, the difference between an approach that makes risks as low as reasonably practicable and one that makes them as low as possible is very small.

Showing that the risk from a system is ALARP does raise some interesting contractual issues. The equipment Design Authority is typically responsible for producing an equipment safety case (the Part 2 safety case in the terminology of

(MoD 2006)) and a hazard log. The hazard log can be used to manage the argument that all reasonably practicable controls have been implemented (the detailed design part of the ALARP argument). These controls will include both aspects of the equipment design, which the Design Authority controls and can assess, and procedural controls, which are typically suggested by the Design Authority as desirable but are subject to acceptance as reasonably practicable by the Operating Authority (and will be supported by evidence of implementation in the operational – Part 3 – safety case). The equipment safety case cannot, formally, say that the risk is ALARP, since this depends on the procedural controls being in place. All they can say is that the risk has been reduced so far as is reasonably practicable within the scope of the design. If the Operating Authority rejects a procedural control as not reasonably practicable the ALARP status of the system does not necessarily change. However, it could be that the increased risk makes a design control for the same issue, previously considered only practicable, a reasonably practicable control, thereby invalidating the design safety case. This possibility is rendered less likely by the preference for design controls over procedural controls, but emphasises the need for early discussion and acceptance of proposed procedural controls.

This paper has not so far considered one aspect of the HSE regulatory framework, which is that some risks are considered small enough to be broadly acceptable. This is defined in (HSE 2001) as 'comparable to those that people regard as insignificant or trivial in their daily lives', and has a guideline risk of fatality (from employment or from exposure to an undertaking) of 1 in a million person-years. The motivation for this does not lie in a philosophy of acceptability of risk, since the principle that exposure to risk must be justified continues applies even to broadly acceptable risks. (This is in line with HSE guidance in (HSE 2001) and is applied to defence contractors through the requirement in (MoD 2007b) that 'all identified safety risks are reduced to levels that are ALARP and broadly acceptable or, when this is not possible, tolerable and ALARP'. The requirement to be ALARP as well as broadly acceptable was one of the few changes from interim Issue 3). Instead it represents a pragmatic view that the effort of risk management should be concentrated where it has most effect, and risks above this level deserve more attention.

7 Summary

MoD policy is to conform as closely as possible to UK health and safety legislation in all its operations. We extracted four underlying principles from the guidance that HSE has provided on their regulation of health of health and safety:

- A person's exposure to risk from an undertaking is justified by the benefit that they or society receive from the undertaking.
- A person should not be exposed to unjustified risk.

- There is a limit to the level of risk that it is equitable to impose on a person or group, irrespective of the benefit gained.
- There is a limit to the level of risk that it is equitable for an undertaking to incur, irrespective of the benefit it produces.

The last of these principles, which reflects public concern about large scale accidents, is less frequently applied than the remainder.

We then explored the definition of unjustified risk used in the second principle. This principle reflects the legal duty of care to control risk so far as is reasonably practicable, which is the only general legal requirement, and in case law it has been defined as a risk that could be controlled at a cost that was not grossly disproportionate to the reduction in risk achieved. The guidance modifies this position, both by introducing the third and fourth principles to cap even justified risks, and also by expecting general good practice to be followed everywhere. For common hazards, this good practice may be codified by regulations with legal force, and may be strong enough to control the hazard to the point where there is no observable risk.

The principles provide a basis for answering the novel questions that tend to arise when dealing with systems with complex behaviour, where functional failure contributes most of the risk. We considered how limits could be set for the tolerability of risk to armed forces personnel and civilians in wartime, as required by the third principle. We also considered the justification for transferring risk from one group to another. Finally, we considered the interaction between ALARP arguments at the conceptual design and detailed design levels, and some of the economic implications of justifying risk.

References

CEC (1989) Council Directive 89/391/EEC of 12 June 1989 on the introduction of measures to encourage improvements in the safety and health of workers at work

CEC (2005) Case C-127/05 Commission of the European Communities v United Kingdom of Great Britain and Northern Ireland. http://curia.europa.eu/jurisp/cgi-bin/form.pl?lang=en&Submit=Submit&alldocs=alldocs&numaff=C-127/05, Opinion, paragraphs 138-141. Accessed 27 September 2008

Edwards (1949) Edwards v National Coal Board. All ER 743 CA. Court of Appeal, London

HMG (1987) Crown Proceedings (Armed Forces) Act 1987. HMSO, Norwich

HMG (2007) Corporate Manslaughter and Corporate Homicide Act 2007. HMSO, Norwich

HM Treasury (2008) The Green Book: Appraisal and Evaluation in Central Government, Annex 2: valuing non-market impacts. http://greenbook.treasury.gov.uk/annex02.htm. Accessed 13 September 2008.

HSE (1992) The tolerability of risk from nuclear power stations. HMSO, Norwich

HSE (2001) Reducing risks, protecting people: HSE's decision making process. HMSO, Norwich

HSE (2005) Statutory Instrument 2005 No. 1643: The Control of Noise at Work Regulations 2005. HMSO, Norwich

HSE (2007) CD212 - Proposals for revised policies to address societal risk around onshore non-nuclear major hazard installations. http://www.hse.gov.uk/consult/condocs/cd212.htm. Accessed 13 September 2008

HSE (2008a) HSE principles for Cost Benefit Analysis (CBA) in support of ALARP decisions. http://www.hse.gov.uk/risk/theory/alarpcba.htm. Accessed 13 September 2008

HSE (2008b) Policy and guidance on reducing risks as low as reasonably practicable in Design. http://www.hse.gov.uk/risk/theory/alarp3.htm. Accessed 13 September 2008

ICRC (1980) Protocol on Explosive Remnants of War (Protocol V to the 1980 Convention on Conventional Weapons). ICRC, Geneva

Kant I, Bennett J (ed) (2008) Groundwork for the Metaphysic of Morals. http://www.earlymoderntexts.com/pdf/kantgw.pdf. Accessed 13 September 2008

MoD (2003) Ministry of Defence Health and Safety Handbook. Joint Service Publication (JSP) 375

MoD (2006) MoD System Safety and Environmental Assurance for Land Systems, Issue 4. Joint Service Publication (JSP) 454. Land Systems Safety Office, Bristol

MoD (2007a) Military Airworthiness Regulations, Edition 1, Change 5. Joint Service Publication (JSP) 553

MoD (2007b) Def Stan 00-56: Safety Management Requirements for Defence Systems, Issue 4. UK Defence Standardization, Glasgow

MoD (2007c) UK Defence Statistics Table 4.5: Thousand flying hours by aircraft role and type. http://www.dasa.mod.uk/applications/newWeb/www/apps/publications/pubViewFile.php?content=10.405&date=2007-09-26&type=html. Accessed 13 September 2008

MoD (2008) Core Values and the Military Covenant. http://www.armyjobs.mod.uk/howdoijoin/rolesranks/Pages/CoreValuesandtheMilitaryCovenant.aspx. Accessed 13 September 2008

Multiple Claimants (2003) Multiple Claimants v MoD – The PTSD Group Actions. EWHC/1134 QB. Royal Courts of Justice, London

Turnbull J (2006) Report and proceedings of a seminar on the economics and morality of safety. Royal Academy of Engineering, London

Wikipedia (2008) Phalanx CIWS. http://en.wikipedia.org/wiki/Phalanx_CIWS. Accessed 13 September 2008

Safety Expenditure: where should we draw the Line?

Mike Jones-Lee

Newcastle University

Newcastle upon Tyne, UK

Abstract The argument developed in this paper takes two points as axiomatic. First, it will be assumed that virtually every activity that we engage in carries some risk of death or injury. And second, it will be taken that in most situations safety can be improved, but typically only at a cost. This then raises the question of the extent to which society's scarce resources should be devoted to safety improvement, rather than to other beneficial uses, such as education, environmental protection, crime prevention and so on. In particular, the paper considers the extent to which procedures such as the application of safety standards, social-cost-benefit analysis or decision theory can be relied upon to provide answers to the controversial but vitally important question of how much society should spend on safety.

1 Introduction

The ongoing debate about nuclear power generation and the recent controversy over the public provision of life-extending drugs for cancer patients are just two manifestations of the way in which safety effects have come to feature centrally in many public and private sector allocative and investment decisions.

Essentially, this is the result of two inescapable facts of life. First, it is the case that virtually every activity that we engage in carries some risk of death or injury. And second, while in most situations safety can improved, this will typically be achievable only at cost. This then raises the difficult question of the extent to which society's scarce resources should be devoted to safety improvement, rather than to other desirable uses, such as education, environmental protection, crime prevention and so on.

The purpose of this paper is to consider the various ways in which this contentious but important question might be addressed in a civilised society.

C. Dale, T. Anderson (eds.), *Safety-Critical Systems: Problems, Process and Practice*,
DOI 10.1007/978-1-84882-349-5_4, © Springer-Verlag London Limited 2009

2 The Alternative Approaches to Safety Expenditure Decision-Making

Essentially, there would appear to be five broad avenues of approach open to both public and private sector decision makers when confronted with safety expenditure decisions. Specifically:

- Rely on well-informed, balanced judgement
- Apply safety standards
- Use cost-effectiveness analysis
- Use some form of cost-benefit analysis
- Apply decision theory

While there has been a tendency in the past to view these five approaches as mutually exclusive alternatives, in practice it is becoming increasingly the case that decision-making agencies in both the public and private sectors are, in fact, relying on more than one of these procedures in their appraisal of safety projects and hence treating them as complementary, rather than competing analytical tools. Nonetheless, given the clear differences that exist both in the underlying methodology and practical application of these approaches it would seem most fruitful to give a brief account of the key features of each separately.

3 Well-Informed Judgement

In an area fraught with so many difficult ethical, technical and practical questions there is clearly a strong temptation to avoid any attempt at formal analysis and to rely instead on well-informed, balanced judgement. While there are, undoubtedly, issues over which judgement will inevitably have to be exercised (as in, for example, a criminal trial), exclusive reliance on this approach to the resolution of questions concerning the allocation of scarce resources to safety improvement will almost inevitably lead to inconsistencies both between different decision makers and, indeed – taken over time – on the part of any given decision maker. Thus, for example, examination of decisions for and against the implementation of safety projects taken round about the middle of the last century (i.e. prior to the widespread application of more formal project appraisal procedures) reveals implicit values for the prevention of a fatality ranging from less than £1,000 per life saved to more than £20 million (Card and Mooney 1977).

4 Safety Standards

A second approach which – at least in its implementation – also avoids the need to apply any sort of formal decision making procedure involves the application of safety standards. Thus, for example, in enforcing the Health and Safety at Work Act 1974 (HSWA), the Management of Health and Safety at Work Regulations 1992 (MHSW) and the Railways (Safety Case) Regulation 1994, the UK Health and Safety Executive (HSE) imposes an upper bound on the fatality risk to which members of the public and those in the workplace may be exposed. In particular, in specifying its 'Tolerability of Risk' (TOR) framework the HSE sets an upper bound above which fatality risks are deemed to be unacceptable (or 'intolerable') and, save in exceptional circumstances, must be reduced whatever the cost, even if this means discontinuing the activity giving rise to the risk.

While in its most recent publications the HSE does not give a precise specification of the level at which the upper bound should be set (HSE, 1999), there are indications that, broadly speaking, the HSE continues to endorse its earlier recommendation that for fatality risks the upper bound should be 1 in 10,000 per annum for individual members of the public and 1 in 1,000 per annum for workplace risks (HSE 1992 paras 169-175, HSE 1999 paras 117-121).

But of course the application of safety standards per se leaves open two key questions:

- By what criteria are such standards to be set?
- What, if anything, should decision makers do about risks that do not breach the specified standards?

As far as the first of these two questions is concerned, it seems difficult to escape the conclusion that those bearing the responsibility for setting the standard in any particular context must, to some extent, rely on well-informed, balanced judgement. But at least once the standard is set, then provided that it is effectively enforced, one can be assured of a degree of consistency within the context concerned. What does not follow, however, is the assurance of consistency between different contexts. More specifically, if – as will almost certainly be the case – the cost of meeting the safety standard set in context A differs markedly from the corresponding cost in context B, then there will inevitably exist a serious inconsistency in that the straightforward transference of resources from the high to the low cost context would, on balance, save lives at no additional cost overall. Arguably, this is precisely the situation that now prevails in the UK Transport sector, given the differential that exists between road and rail safety expenditure per fatality prevented (with the former falling well below the latter), particularly following implementation of the recommendations of the Cullen-Uff Inquiry (Cullen and Uff 2001).

Turning to the second question – i.e. what are decision makers to do before the limits set by safety standards are reached? – the answer is again provided by the HSE's TOR framework. Thus, in addition to setting an upper bound on tolerable risk, the so-called 'TOR Triangle' also involves a lower bound below which risks are treated as being 'broadly acceptable' and are generally regarded as insignificant and sufficiently controlled (this is treated as being in the region of one in a million per annum). But this then leads on to what is, from a practical point of view, arguably the most significant feature of the TOR framework, namely the stipulation that, between the upper and lower bounds of the TOR Triangle, risks are viewed as being 'tolerable' provided that they have been reduced to levels that are as low as reasonably practicable (ALARP).

As far as 'ALARP' is concerned the Courts have ruled that this term should be interpreted as requiring that safety improvement must be undertaken provided that the costs of implementing the improvement are not disproportionate to the resultant risk reduction. Thus, in the Court of Appeal in Edwards v National Coal Board (Edwards 1949), Lord Justice Asquith's judgement was to the effect that:

> 'Reasonably practicable' is a narrower term than 'physically possible' and seems to me to imply that a computation must be made by the owner, in which the quantum of risk is placed on one scale and the sacrifice involved in the measures necessary for averting the risk (whether in money, time or trouble) is placed on the other; and that if it be shown that there is a gross disproportion between them – the risk being insignificant in relation to the sacrifice – the Defendants discharge the onus on them.

The issue of reasonable practicability was also considered by the House of Lords in Marshal v Gotham Co Ltd (Marshal 1954), the headnote of which states:

> The test of what is (reasonably practicable) is not simply what is practicable as a matter of engineering, but what depends on the consideration, in the light of the whole circumstances at the time of the accident, whether the time, trouble and expense of the precautions suggested are or are not disproportionate to the risk involved, and also an assessment of the degree of security which the measures suggested may be expected to afford.

While these two rulings clearly indicate that in reaching a decision concerning 'reasonable practicability' it is appropriate to weigh the costs of implementing a risk-reduction against the resultant benefits, the fact that the first judgement refers to 'gross disproportion', while the second stipulates only that costs should not be 'disproportionate' to the risk reduction, has – perhaps not surprisingly – raised serious questions that are essentially unresolved. Thus, in its document *Reducing Risks, Protecting People* (R2P2, HSE 1999 p73), the HSE focuses on the 1949 Edwards v National Coal Board 'gross disproportion' judgement and stipulates that '...when weighing risks against costs...at least, there is a need to err on the side of safety in the computation of safety costs and benefits.

By contrast, several recent reports call into question the appropriateness of the 'gross disproportion' requirement (e.g. RSSB 2005, House of Lords Select Committee on Economic Affairs 2006). Thus, for example, does the gross disproportion condition mean that a safety improvement has to be undertaken provided that its costs do not exceed its benefits by a factor of two, or three, or ten or what?

And even if one were to be specific about the factor, what defence is there for setting it at any level greater than one, given that the ethical principles underpinning standard Social Cost-Benefit Analysis will recommend adoption of a project only if its benefits (appropriately defined) exceed its costs.

Given all of this, it seems fair to say that the current weight of opinion is strongly in favour of basing safety policy on the more specific and less-extreme 'disproportion' (as opposed to 'gross disproportion') interpretation of the ALARP criterion, with this requirement being treated as equivalent to the standard Cost-Benefit criterion. Indeed, in some of its recent publications the HSE itself recommends the application of what would appear to be standard Cost-Benefit Analysis. For example, in its document *The Tolerability of Risk from Nuclear Power Stations*, the HSE states that:

> ...in pursuing any further safety improvements to demonstrate ALARP account can be taken of cost. It is in principle possible to apply formal cost-benefit techniques to assist in making decisions of this kind (HSE, 1992, para. 35),

and in its more recent publication, *Reducing Risks, Protecting People*, that:

> ...cost-benefit analysis (CBA) offers a framework for balancing the benefits of reducing risk against the costs incurred in a particular option for managing risks. (HSE 1999, Annex 3, para. 8).

Furthermore, in *Managing Risks to the Public: Appraisal Guidance*, it is argued that in relation to decisions affecting health and safety:

> Once a range of options has been created, they should be assessed by estimating their costs and benefits, and/or by their cost effectiveness. (H.M. Treasury 2005, para 4.1).

In view of all this, it is therefore not surprising that the techniques of social cost-benefit analysis, cost-effectiveness analysis and, more recently, decision theory, have come to feature centrally in the public and private sector safety decision-making process. To the extent that cost-effectiveness analysis is the most straightforward (but arguably the most limited) of these procedures, this will be considered first.

5 Cost-Effectiveness Analysis

Essentially, cost-effectiveness analysis seeks to maximise the level of achievement of a given well-defined and numerically quantifiable objective within a predetermined budget. Thus, for example, in the case of healthcare this typically involves maximisation of the number of so-called 'Quality Adjusted Life Years' (or 'QALYs') provided to patients within a given safety budget. In principle, this is done by computing a 'cost-effectiveness' ratio for each possible project and then selecting projects, starting with those having the lowest cost per unit of the specified objective and 'working up' until the budget is exhausted. From a conceptual point of view, this is clearly a relatively straightforward procedure, but it has two clear limitations. First, it provides no indication of the appropriate size of the budget in any given context. And second, it cannot resolve the problem of project selection whenever different projects generate more than one kind of beneficial effect, with the proportionate mix of benefits differing between projects. In such circumstances what is needed is a common unit in which to measure and then aggregate the various different types of benefit, and this is precisely what cost-effectiveness analysis fails to do. By contrast, both cost-benefit analysis and decision theory explicitly address the problem of measurement and aggregation.

6 Social Cost-Benefit Analysis

The fundamental prescriptive (or ethical) principle underpinning Social Cost-Benefit Analysis (CBA) is that decisions concerning the allocation of society's scarce resources should, so far as is possible, reflect the preferences – and more particularly the *strength of preference* – of those members of society who will be affected by the decision concerned. Naturally, there is the implicit requirement that these preferences should, so far as is possible, be well-informed and carefully considered.

Given that an individual's maximum willingness to pay for a good or service is a clear indication of what that good or service is worth to the individual concerned relative to other potential objects of expenditure – and given that willingness to pay is ultimately constrained by ability to pay (i.e. income) and hence reflects the overall scarcity of resources – individual willingness to pay constitutes a natural measure of strength of preference and is hence used as the fundamental measure of value or 'benefit' in CBA.

In view of all this, under what had naturally come to be known as the 'willingness-to-pay' (WTP) approach to the valuation of safety, one attempts to determine the maximum amounts that people would individually be willing to pay for (typically small) improvements in their own and (possibly others') safety. These amounts are then simply summed across all affected individuals to arrive at an overall value for the safety improvement concerned. The resultant figure is thus a clear indication of what the safety improvement is 'worth' to the affected group, relative to the alternative ways in which each individual might have spent his or her limited income. Furthermore, defining values of safety in this way effectively 'mirrors' the operation of market forces – in circumstances in which markets do not exist – given that such forces can be seen as vehicles for allowing individual preferences to interact with relative scarcities and production possibilities in determining the allocation of a society's scarce resources.

In order to standardise values of safety that emerge from the WTP approach, the concept of the prevention of a 'statistical' fatality or injury is employed. Thus, suppose that a group of 100,000 people enjoy a safety improvement that reduces the probability of premature death during a forthcoming period by, on average, 1 in 100,000 for each and every individual in the group. While the safety improvement might, in the event, prevent no deaths, or one death (in fact, the most likely outcome) or two deaths (with a lower probability) and so on, the arithmetic mean (or statistical expectation) of the number of deaths prevented is precisely one and the safety improvement is therefore described involving the prevention of one 'statistical' fatality.

Now suppose that individuals within this group are, on average, each willing to pay £x for the 1 in 100,000 reduction in the probability of death afforded by the safety improvement. Aggregate willingness to pay will then be given by £x times 100,000. This figure is naturally referred to as the WTP-based value of preventing one statistical fatality (VPF). An alternative term often used is the 'value of statistical life' (VSL). Thus, if on average, the members of the population were willing to pay £15 per year to reduce their risks of death to this extent, the VPF (or VSL) in this case would be £1.5m.

Before proceeding, one very important point should be stressed, namely that, as defined above, the VPF is not a 'value (or price) of life' in the sense of a sum that any given individual would accept in compensation for the certainty of his or her own death – for most of us no sum however large would suffice for this purpose so that in this sense life is literally priceless. Rather, the VPF is in fact aggregate willingness to pay for typically very small reductions in individual risk of death (which, realistically, is what most safety improvements actually offer at the individual level). This reflects peoples' normal approach to risks which they face in everyday life, where they trade off cost or convenience against real, but very small risks. The Treasury Green Book emphasises the point when it notes that:

> The willingness of an individual to pay for small changes in their own or their
> household's risk of loss of life or injury can be used to infer the value of a prevented
> fatality (VPF). The changes in the probabilities of premature death or of serious injury
> used in such WTP studies are generally small (HM Treasury 2003, p61).

But of course given the 'aggregate willingness to pay' definition, strictly speaking the VPF applicable to a safety improvement that will affect a relatively well-off group in society will inevitably exceed the figure for a poorer group simply because willingness to pay is ultimately constrained by ability to pay. It is essentially for this reason that most advocates of the WTP approach recommend VPFs which reflect the aggregate willingness to pay of a *representative sample* of the population as a whole. Using an overall average figure effectively amplifies the (typically lower) willingness to pay of the less well-off and somewhat deflates the (typically higher) willingness to pay of upper-income groups. In this respect, the VPF involves a modification that might be said to reflect a social or 'citizen's' value judgement being applied to individual 'consumer' values.

Before proceeding to consider the various ways in which researchers have attempted to obtain empirical estimates of values of safety using the WTP approach, two further refinements should be noted. First, so far only passing reference has been made to peoples' concern – and hence willingness to pay – for others', as well as their own safety. To the extent that people do display such 'altruistic' concern then it might seem reasonable to expect that it would be appropriate to augment the WTP-based VPF to reflect the amounts that people would be willing to pay for an improvement in others' safety. However, things are not quite so straightforward. In fact, it turns out that the legitimacy or otherwise of including peoples' willingness to pay for others' safety in the definition of a WTP-based VPF depends crucially on the nature of their altruistic concern for other peoples' general wellbeing. If this concern is 'safety-focused' in the sense that, while person A cares about person B's safety, A is in fact quite indifferent about B's ability to pay for say, a holiday abroad, a meal out or a new carpet, then A's willingness to pay for B's safety should be included in the definition of VPF. If, on the other hand, A's concern is more widely cast and includes B's ability to spend on 'other things', then A's altruistic gain from an improvement in B's safety will tend to be offset by A's awareness of the fact that B will ultimately have to make his/her own contribution by paying for the safety improvement through, for example, taxes or public transport fares – and in this case inclusion of A's willingness to pay for B's safety in the VPF would involve a form of double-counting and would therefore be unwarranted.

So, is peoples' concern for others' wellbeing typically safety-focused or more widely cast? While research concerning the nature of altruistic concern is still on-going, to date work on the empirical estimation of willingness to pay-based values of safety has tended to proceed along relatively conservative lines by restricting attention to peoples' own willingness to pay for their own safety; or aggregate household willingness to pay for the overall safety of all household members.

A second refinement of the WTP approach involves recognition of the fact that safety improvements also involve other benefits to society, such as avoidance of net output losses (i.e. the loss of the value of the victim's future output over and above his/her future consumption) or medical and ambulance costs. To the extent that people appear in the main not to take account of such factors in assessing their willingness to pay for improved safety (and there is some evidence that they tend not to (Jones-Lee et al. 1985)) then an allowance for these factors should clearly be added to WTP-based values of safety. However, such additions tend to be small in relation to the typical magnitude of aggregate willingness to pay for safety per se, at least in the case of risks of death. More specifically, the UK Department for Transport (DfT) VPF currently stands at about £1.5million, of which avoided net output losses comprise only about £100,000 and medical and ambulance costs £1,000.

6.1 Estimating the VPF

Having examined the basic principles of the willingness-to-pay approach, the next obvious question is then how one might, in practice, obtain empirical estimates of values of prevention of statistical fatalities and non-fatal injuries or illness.

Broadly speaking three types of empirical estimation procedure have been employed to derive WTP-based values of safety. These are known respectively as the 'revealed preference' (or 'implied value'), the 'contingent valuation' (or 'stated preference') and 'relative valuation' approaches.

Essentially, the revealed preference approach involves the identification of situations in which people actually do trade off income or wealth against physical risk – for example, in labour markets where riskier jobs can be expected to command clearly identifiable wage premiums. By contrast, the contingent valuation approach involves asking a representative sample of people more or less directly about their individual willingness to pay for improved safety, (or, sometimes, their willingness to accept compensation for increased risk).

The problem with the revealed preference approach when applied to labour market data is that it depends on being able to disentangle risk-related wage differentials from the many other factors that enter into the determination of wage rates. The approach also presupposes that workers are well-informed about the risk that they actually face in the workplace.

Viewed in this light, the great advantage of the contingent valuation approach is that it allows the researcher to go directly and unambiguously to the relevant wealth/risk trade-off – at least, in principle. On the other hand, the contingent valuation approach has the disadvantage of relying upon the assumption that people are able to give considered, accurate and unbiased answers to hypothetical questions about typically small changes in already very small risks of consequences that are likely to be unfamiliar and difficult to imagine.

Finally, unlike the revealed preference and contingent valuation approaches, the relative valuation approach does not involve an attempt to estimate wealth/risk trade-offs directly, but rather seeks to determine the value of preventing one kind of physical harm relative to another. Thus, for example, the DfT's current monetary values for the prevention of various severities of non-fatal road injury were obtained by applying estimates of such relative valuations to an absolute monetary 'peg' in the form of the DfT's then-existing WTP-based roads VPF (Department of Transport 1993, 1994).

6.2 Dread Risks, Multiple Fatality Accidents and Increased Exposure to Risk

Having considered the question of public and workplace safety regulation in the UK at the general level and the role of cost-benefit analysis and the valuation of safety in particular, three specific points would appear to warrant further discussion:

- Should willingness to pay-based values of safety in general – and the VPF in particular – vary from one context to another to reflect the differing degrees of 'dread' that people typically associate with the prospect of death or injury in different circumstance? More specifically, should the VPF employed in the evaluation of proposed rail safety projects be set at a higher level than that applicable to road safety given that, for most people, the prospect of death in a rail accident is even more horrendous than the thought of being killed in a road accident?

- Should the VPF applied in the evaluation of a safety programme aimed at preventing multiple-fatality accidents exceed that used in the assessment of the prevention of single-fatality cases?
- While willingness to pay-based values of safety will typically be employed in the evaluation of projects aimed at *reducing* the risk of death or injury, in some cases the question will instead be whether the non-safety benefits of a proposed project are sufficient to outweigh the costs that will result from the *increase* in risk to which the project will give rise. Do willingness to pay-based values of safety constitute the appropriate instrument by which such costs should be estimated?

While it might reasonably be supposed that psychological factors such as a sense of lack of control, involuntariness, responsibility and fear *per se* would indeed constitute grounds for setting preference-based values of safety for more highly-dreaded causes of death or injury at a significant premium in relation to corresponding values for less highly-dreaded causes, it transpires that at least for causes involving more or less immediate death, this is *not* the case. Thus, in a research project commissioned by the HSE it was found that for causes such as rail accidents, fires in public places and drowning, while there is indeed clear evidence of a substantially higher dread factor than in the case of road accidents, this is to all intents and purposes offset by the substantially lower level of the 'baseline' risk of being involved in a rail accident or a public fire or drowning and that as a result the willingness to pay-based VPF for such causes does not differ markedly from the corresponding roads figure (Chilton et al. 2006). This having been said, for causes of death preceded by a protracted period of pain and suffering (such as cancer), some would argue that there is a case for setting the VPF at a substantial premium, so that while the HSE recommends application of a uniform VPF of approximately £1.5million in 2007 prices for all causes involving more or less immediate death, in the case of cancer the HSE figure is twice this size.

Turning to accidents involving multiple fatalities, the picture is very similar. Thus, in a number of studies (e.g. RSSB 2008), it has been found that members of the UK public in the main do not regard, say, 30 fatalities in a single rail accident as being worse than 30 fatalities in separate rail accidents, so that from a social perspective there would appear to be no grounds for setting the multiple fatality rail accident VPF at a premium in relation to the single-fatality figure. This having been said, it would not be particularly surprising if senior decision makers in private sector rail companies elected to apply a 'multiple fatality' premium to the VPF, given the extensive media attention and political reaction that typically follows a major rail accident and the adverse commercial consequences of such a response.

Finally, what can be said about the appropriate way in which to value safety in situations in which a proposed project can be expected to increase, rather than reduce risk for some section of the public? In this case there would seem to be little doubt that the ethical precepts underpinning conventional social cost-benefit analysis require that the cost of the increased risk should be defined so as to reflect the minimum sum that those adversely affected would be willing to accept as compensation for the deterioration in their personal safety. In short 'willingness to accept' (WTA)-based figures should take the place of the willingness to pay (WTP)–based figures used in the case of safety improvements. But then the question is how the WTA-based VPF for a given cause of death can be expected to relate quantitatively to its WTP-based counterpart. Put more directly, if the typical individual's maximum willingness to pay for a 1 in 100,000 reduction in the risk of death in a road accident during the coming year is £15 (implying a VPF of £1.5million for a large group of similar individuals) what might one expect the individual's minimum required compensation to be for a 1 in 100,000 increase in risk?

While economists initially assumed that for small variations in risk the WTA figure would be much the same as WTP (if perhaps a little larger), there is by now a very substantial body of empirical evidence indicating that the typical individual's willingness to accept compensation for a small increase in the risk of death by a given cause will exceed his/her willingness to pay for a risk reduction of the same magnitude by a factor of between three and five (e.g. Guria et al. 2005). In short, for our individual who was willing to pay £15 for the 1 in 100,000 reduction in the risk of death in a road accident, it would not be at all surprising if his/her minimum required compensation for an increase in risk of the same magnitude was in the region of £60. In view of this, there would appear to be little doubt that in evaluating a proposed project that is expected to expose some individuals to an increased risk of death or injury then the cost of this increase in risk should be estimated on the basis of a VPF that is in the region of four times as large as the corresponding VPF used in the appraisal of risk reductions.

7 Decision Theory

While taken as a whole, decision theory comprises a wide variety of concepts and techniques, for present purposes it would seem most appropriate to focus on so-called 'Multi-Criteria Decision Analysis' (MCDA), particularly as this is the procedure that is being increasingly employed alongside CBA by UK public sector decision making agencies (e.g. Phillips and Stock 2003, Morton and Fasolo 2008).

Essentially, MCDA aims to assist a decision maker, or decision-making panel, to reach a decision concerning the optimal way in which to achieve a given objective in a well-informed, structured and coherent manner. In order to do this the MCDA process first requires the decision making panel (typically with the assistance of MCDA advisors) to establish a 'value tree' which specifies:

- The *objectives* that the panel wishes to achieve
- The *options* available to meet those objectives

- The characteristics or attributes of the options that the panel considers to be the *criteria* relevant to an assessment of the effectiveness of the options in meeting the objectives

For each available option the decision making panel is then required to *score or 'value'* each of the criteria on a scale from 0-100 in terms of the degree or extent to which the characteristic or attribute associated with that criterion is provided by the option concerned. The panel is then required to assign a 'weight' to each criterion to reflect its relative importance in meeting the panel's objectives. This weighting task – which is typically viewed as the most demanding aspect of the MCDA process – is usually undertaken in one of three ways:

- Simply making a judgement concerning relative importance
- 'Swing Weighting' which involves comparing and quantifying the relative value of a move from a score of 0 to a score of 100 on each of the various relevant criteria
- 'Trade-off Weighting' which requires the panel to determine the score, x, such that a swing from a score of 0 to a score of x on the criterion judged to be most important is regarded as being equally desirable as a swing from 0 to 100 on the criterion concerned.

The final stage in the MCDA process then involves computing a weighted sum of the scores of the criteria for each of the different options available, with the option having the highest weighted sum of scores being regarded as the most desirable. Notice that in this process an 'undesirable' criterion such as cost would be scored so that the least costly option was awarded a score of 100 and the most costly a score of 0.

8 Concluding Comments

As noted earlier in the paper, while there are marked conceptual and practical differences between the five broad avenues of approach to decision-making in the field of health and safety, in practice it has tended to be the case that decision makers have in fact drawn on more than one of these approaches in appraising prospective safety investments and healthcare programmes. Thus, for example, the HSE's Tolerability Triangle clearly draws directly on both safety standards and cost-benefit analysis. In addition, there are few if any public or private sector agencies that would rely exclusively on the results of, say, cost-benefit or cost-effectiveness analysis in reaching a major safety investment decision. Rather, the results of such analyses would typically be viewed as constituting just one input to a decision-making process that also drew on rules set as 'standard practice', as well as informed and balanced judgement. And again, as already noted, there is an increasing tendency to seek to ensure that such judgement is exercised in a structured and coherent manner by drawing on the decision-making apparatus provided by MCDA.

In short, the analytical procedures outlined in this paper are almost certainly better seen as complementary – rather than competing – tools in the allocative decision making process, at least when applied in a balanced and circumspect manner.

References

Card WI, Mooney GH (1977) What is the Monetary Value of a Human Life? British Medical Journal, 281:1627-1629

Chilton S, Jones-Lee M, Kiraly F et al (2006) Dread Risks. Journal of Risk and Uncertainty 33:165-182

Cullen WD, Uff J (2001) The Southall and Ladbroke Grove Joint Inquiry Into Train Protection Systems. Health and Safety Executive, London

DfT (1993, 1994) Highways Economic Note No.1. Department for Transport, London

Edwards (1949) Edwards v National Coal Board 1 KB704

Guria J, Leung J, Jones-Lee M et al (2005) The Willingness to Accept Value of Statistical Life Relative to the Willingness to Pay Value: Evidence and Policy Implementations. Environmental and Resource Economics 32:113-127

HM Treasury (2003) The Green Book: Appraisal and Evaluation in Central Government, The Stationery Office, London

HM Treasury (2005) Managing Risks to the Public: Appraisal Guidance. HM Treasury, London

House of Lords Select Committee on Economic Affairs (2006) Government Policy on the Management of Risk. The Stationery Office, London

HSE (1992) The Tolerability of Risk from Nuclear Power Stations. HMSO, London

HSE (1999) Reducing Risks, Protecting People. Health and Safety Executive, London

Jones-Lee MW, Hammerton M, Philips PR (1985) The Value of Safety: Results of a National Sample Survey. The Economic Journal 95:49-72

Marshall (1954) Marshal v Gotham Co Ltd AC360

Morton A, Fasolo B (2008) Behavioural Decision Theory for Multi-Criteria Decision Analysis: A Guided Tour. Journal of the Operational Research Society 59:1-8

Phillips L, Stock A (2003) Use of Multi-Criteria Analysis in Air Quality Policy, Report to Department for Environment, Food and Rural Affairs

RSSB (2005) The Definition of VPF and the Impact of Societal Concerns. Rail Safety and Standards Board Report T430

RSSB (2008) Assessment of the Value of Preventing a Fatality. Rail Safety and Standards Board Report T616

Transport Safety

Hazard Management with DOORS: Rail Infrastructure Projects

Dave Hughes and Amer Saeed

ATKINS Limited

Farnham, UK

Abstract LOI is a major rail infrastructure project that will contribute to a modernised transport system in time for the 2012 Olympic Games. A review of the procedures and tool infrastructure was conducted in early 2006, coinciding with a planned move to main works. A hazard log support tool was needed to provide: an automatic audit trial, version control and support collaborative working. A DOORS based Hazard Log (DHL) was selected as the Tool Strategy. A systematic approach was followed for the development of DHL, after a series of tests and acceptance gateways, DHL was handed over to the project in autumn 2006. The first few months were used for operational trials and he Hazard Management Procedure was modified to be a hybrid approach that used the strengths of DHL and Excel. The user experience in the deployment of DHL is summarised and directions for future improvement identified.

1 Introduction

London Overground Infrastructure (LOI) is a major rail infrastructure project that is responsible for the extension and refurbishment of the old East London Line (ELL) to deliver a new East London Railway (ELR). The LOI project is also procuring new rolling stock, 30 Class 378s, which will operate on the ELR when opened in early 2010. The ELR will contribute to the aim to provide a modern transport system in time for the 2012 Olympic Games and is a key component of the Transport for London's (TfL's) £10bn 5 year investment plan. For a major project of this scale and duration that will involve multi-disciplinary teams in a number of geographical locations, procedures and tools that support collaboration are needed. With the move to main works due to start in late 2006, a review of the procedures and tool infrastructure was conducted across the project processes (in March 2006, the project was referred to as the East London Line Project (ELLP)).

Atkins (formerly Advantage Business Group) are part of the TfL integrated project team. Their specific role is within the Safety, Quality and Environment

C. Dale, T. Anderson (eds.), *Safety-Critical Systems: Problems, Process and Practice*,
DOI 10.1007/978-1-84882-349-5_5, © Springer-Verlag London Limited 2009

(SQE) team. As part of this role, Atkins led the review of the existing procedure and tool support for Hazard Management, this review was conducted in the context of the overall TfL tool strategy. The result of this review was a recommendation to develop a multi-user Hazard Log as the basis of tool support and where necessary propose modifications to the existing procedures.

1.1 Outline of Paper

The next section provides a summary of the review of the current hazard management practices and the capabilities needed for the vision set out for the main works phase. Section 3 provides a record of the approach followed for the development, assessment and handover of the DOORS based Hazard Log Tool. Section 4 describes the Hazard Management Procedure supported by the Hazard Log Tool. Section 5 contributes with concluding remarks and future plans.

2 Hazard Management Review

Hazard management is the process of identifying, recording, analysing and subsequently implementing measures to control the effects of hazardous situations in systems where the lives of people are at risk (Leveson 1995). Even relatively simple systems give rise to large amounts of information and the need for tool support to have an effective approach to Hazard Management. On a project of this scale, which is multi-disciplinary in nature and involves contractors from many different companies, a great deal of information accumulates that is relevant to safety. It is vital this data is managed in an efficient manner, whilst maintaining the integrity of the hazard data.

For the initial phase of the project, Hazard Management was supported by a Hazard Log implemented in an MS Access database. Hazard Logs are used to record and track the results of hazard analysis and risk assessment throughout the lifecycle of the system. The MS Access based Hazard Log and associated procedure were both compliant with the conditions of Yellow Book 3 (Railtrack 2000). These had been sufficient for this early phase, during which work was conducted by a small co-located team.

2.1 Hazard Management Objectives

The manager of the MS Access Hazard Log reported that too much of his time had been spent on clerical duties maintaining the database, rather than managing the hazards. With the transition to main works, the basic data management tasks should be pushed to other members of the project team who need to review and edit the information. However, any such wider access needed to be provided in a controlled manner in order to maintain data integrity

Following a detailed review with the Project's Safety Team, a number of short-comings were identified with the existing tool support that would make it unsuita-ble for the proposed usage in the main works phase. These included problems with usability, multi-user access and version control. However, the underlying data model (which had been derived from the project's risk register) and hazard identi-fication procedure were viewed as being appropriate. It was agreed to replace the existing MS Access Based Hazard Log, by a more appropriate tool while preserv-ing compatibility with the ELLP's Hazard Management Procedure (HMP). This procedure is based on established Railway Standards (EN 50129 2003; EN 50126 1999).

2.2 Hazard Log Tool Capabilities

A workshop was conducted to define, at a high-level, the capabilities that should be offered following the support tool improvement initiative. These were to be or-ganised in terms of *baseline capabilities* (to ensure there was no loss of capability) and *enhanced capabilities* (to be adequate for the main works phase).

2.2.1 Baseline Capabilities

The baseline capabilities were derived from the original hazard log specification and current usage of the tool:

- Users shall be able to record hazards, accidents and actions in a centralised database.
- Users shall associate hazards with accidents that can be caused by the haz-ards and actions that aim to resolve the hazards.
- Users shall be able to generate reports. These shall include management summary reports and reports to support daily usage.
- Users shall be able to conduct a Qualitative Safety Risk Assessment.

2.2.2 Enhanced Capabilities

A number of enhanced capabilities would need to be provided in order for the Hazard Log to be appropriate for the main works phase. These capabilities were recorded as high-level objectives, together with supporting rationale.

Audit Trail. Wider access to the Hazard Log would lead to the need for greater accountability for its usage. An automated record of the changes performed, by whom and when should be provided. (During the early phase, this was achieved manually by providing commentary.)

Version Control. A means for creating, retrieving and comparing Baselines of the Hazard log should be provided.

Change Control. It was recognized that most of the hazards had been identified, however as understanding in the project increases during main works modifications would be proposed. A means for managing change requests from a wider user group and providing restricted access to make direct changes is needed.

Collaborative Working. The geographical distribution of users and the increase in number of users will require support for collaborative working. This will include provisions for shared access, remote working and the ability to import and export data between standard tools.

During the review of objectives, the ELLP Requirements Manager suggested that during the main works many of the actions will lead to safety requirements. A desirable objective was that it should be possible to trace between safety requirements and the actions in the Hazard Log, this would support the eventual development of a safety case.

3 Implementation of Hazard Log Tool

The implementation of the Hazard Log Tool was conducted in four phases. In the first phase, the options for tool support were discussed with the key stakeholders these included User Representatives and the TfL IT standards group. This led to the development of a *Tool Strategy*. The second phase involved conducting a detailed requirements analysis and produced the *Hazard Log Specification*. The third phase was design and implementation to produce a *Prototype Tool*. The fourth phase (which consists of four sub phases) is to test, refine and review the tool, this includes migration and validation of the data from the existing Hazard Log – this leads to a *Validated (populated) Tool*. The overall approach for the development and assessment of a Hazard Log is illustrated in Figure 1.

3.1 Options for Tool Support

The initial discussions involved a number of strategic decisions on the approach to tool support. The first was to decide whether to develop a bespoke tool or to build on a COTS product. A number of options for a bespoke tool using the '.Net' framework were considered, but discarded due to perceived difficulties in meeting the non-functional objectives. The strategy of using a COTS product was adopted with the preference to use a product that is already part of the established ELLP tool set. An investigation of general purpose tools, specialist safety tools and requirements management tools against the high-level objectives was conducted with the Safety and IT project Teams.

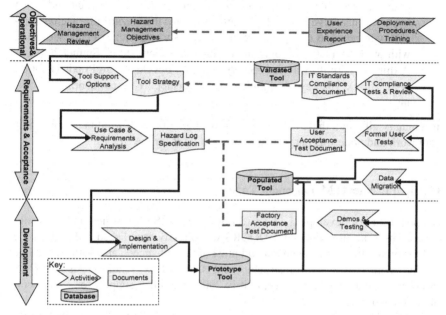

Fig. 1. Overall Approach for Hazard Log Tool

3.1.1 General Purpose Tools

In terms of general purpose tools, the two main candidates were MS Excel or MS Access. MS Excel had benefits in terms of usability and presentation of data overcoming a distinct weakness of the existing tool. Modifying the existing MS Access tool would maximise re-use. However, in both cases inherent auditing and version control capabilities were limited.

3.1.2 Safety Management Tools

For specialised safety management tools, there were three main candidates.

- The *Cassandra* Hazard Management System, developed by HVR (HVR 2008). This has been designed to support 00-56 (MOD 1996), though this has similarities with the project's hazard management procedure the risk classification matrix would need modification and relationships to safety requirements would be limited to cross-references.

- The *Adelard Safety Case Editor (ASCE)*, developed by Adelard (Emmet and Cleland 2002). This is a hypertext tool for constructing and reviewing structured arguments. ASCE is a flexible tool the main strengths being a graphical presentation that can make argument structure explicit and a rich hypertext narrative mode. The shortcoming for the Hazard Log included inability to relate to safety requirements. This shortcoming is being addressed with work on a DOORS plug-in (Taylor and Cleland 2007, Emmet 2007).
- A third possibility was the *eSafetyCase* tool developed by Praxis (Lautieri et al. 2004). The key strength here was the support for collaborative working.

In summary although these tools offered some benefits, each would require significant work and none was part of the existing tool set for the ELLP.

3.1.3 Requirements Management Tools

The possibility of developing a Hazard Log in DOORS (Telelogic 2008) was suggested. This was attractive since DOORS was already established in ELLP as the tool for requirements management and most of the enhanced capabilities would be met by existing DOORS infrastructure and 'Out of Box' features. Also DOORS was soon to be available on Citrix (Citrix 2008) providing support for remote collaborative working.

DOORS is often used to record Systems Engineering artifacts, these include interface and assumptions registers, the basic information management characteristics and the need to manage relationships to requirements are similar to those proposed for the Hazard Log. With regard to Risk Management, DOORS has been used to support qualitative risk assessment (Weinnberg et al. 2004), this normally requires some customization in DXL (Doors eXtension Language). Further, DOORS has been used to support specific hazard management systems in the Defence (Hamoy et al. 2004) and Railway sectors (Elphick and Irving 2006). Also a commercial product, ISCaDE that has customized DOORS for safety management is available (RCM^2 2006).

3.2 Use Case & Requirements Analysis

A Doors based Hazard Log (DHL) was selected as the option for further development. The high-level capabilities and the features reviewed during the options study provided input to a Use Case Analysis workshop for DHL.

3.2.1 Use Case Analyses for Hazard Management

The Use Case Analyses considered both functional and non-functional requirements. The former were based on the baseline capabilities and the latter on the enhancement capabilities.

3.2.1.1 Functional Use Case Analysis

For the functional Use Case Analysis (see Figure 2), four main User Types were
identified. **Remote User**: an occasional user of DHL who will be based off-site.
Local user: A frequent user of DHL who will be based in the ELLP offices.
Manager: a passive user of DHL who will view reports produced by a Local User. **Administrator**: An expert user of DHL, responsible for maintenance of structural and data integrity. (These User Groups were reviewed following experience
with the prototype.)

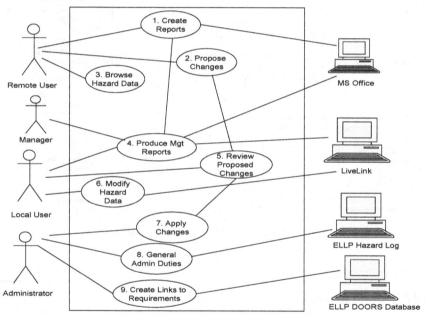

Fig. 2. System Context Use Case (Functional)

The high-level capabilities were analyzed in detail during the requirements workshop within the context of the decision to adopt a DOORS based solution. Some
example capabilities are listed below:

- *Remote Users* shall be able to navigate the relationships between hazards,
  accidents and actions.

- *Remote and Local Users* shall be able to review and approve proposed changes to the Hazard Log.
- *Local Users* shall be able to generate a report of the 'Top Hazards by Risk Rating after Mitigation' hazard as defined in the existing report table.

3.2.1.2 Non-Functional Use Case Analysis

To establish the non-functional requirements on DHL a Use Case Analysis was conducted for those actors that influence the DHL environment (see Figure 3).

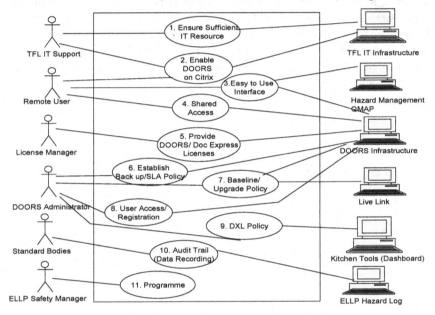

Fig. 3. System Context Use Case (Non-Functional)

3.2.2 DHL Context Model

DHL will be installed within the DOORS database used by the ELLP and will interact with eight external systems. The systems and their relationships are depicted in Figure 4.

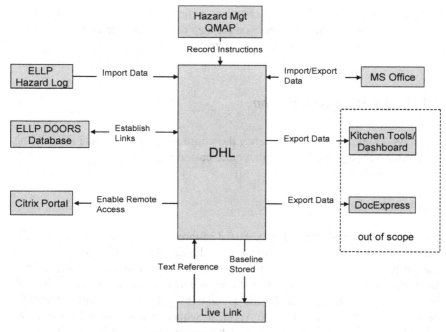

Fig. 4. DHL System Perspective

Hazard Management QMAP. A QMAP[1] (QMAP 2008) definition of the instructions for the usage of DHL in the context of ELLP HMP.

ELLP Hazard Log. The source of the existing hazard data to be imported to DHL

ELLP DOORS Requirements Database. The record of ELLP requirements to which links will be established from DHL.

Citrix Portal. A web page through which DOORS (hence DHL) will be accessed by users.

LiveLink. The document management system used in ELLP, DHL will record text references that are a unique definition of a document in Live Link and DHL users will store Baseline reports in LiveLink.

MS Office. DHL will import and export data from/to Word and Excel.

Two systems (Dashboard and DocExpress) are part of the DOORS infrastructure at the ELLP, DHL can interact with these tools to improve presentation of data recorded in DHL. However, no need was identified for this interaction to support the ELLP HMP during the requirements workshop.

The requirements analysis also identified a number of assumptions and dependencies on IT support. For example, ELLP IT Support will ensure that the re-

---

[1] QMAP is a process mapping tool, currently the usage is only to record high-level instructions.

sources available on the DOORS server are sufficient for DHL. To obtain agreement on this assumption an estimate on the size of DHL (server capacity) and the numbers of users (license utilization) was provided.

3.3 Design & Implementation

The main design activity was to define the information model for the Hazard Log and establish those features that will require customisation in DXL.

3.3.1 Information Model

The information model for DHL consisted of three entities that correspond to the existing action, hazard and accident tables of the ELLP Hazard Log (see Figure 5). The cardinality was that actions and hazards have a many-to-many relationship, a hazard can map to many accidents, but each accident can only map to one hazard. The latter restriction is needed for the qualitative safety risk assessment, basically the accident is the end event of the Accident Sequence and its definition includes risk data (see Section 3.3.2.2). The potential for a relationship to the ELLP DOORS Requirements Database is also indicated.

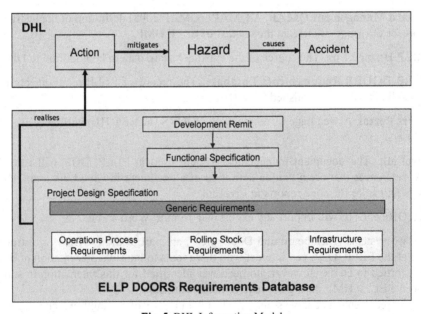

Fig. 5. DHL Information Model

The information model was implemented by defining a DOORS Formal Module for each of the entities. A detailed review of the existing attributes of the Hazard Log showed that some were redundant, for those attributes that were used in the MS Access Tool a mapping table was defined to the attributes of the DOORS Formal Modules. A number of additional attributes were defined. The relationships were implemented as link modules. Local and traceability (cross module) views were defined as the basis of the reports.

3.3.2 Customization of DOORS

Most of the capabilities needed from DHL were achievable through the configuration menus and in-built wizards in DOORS. However, there were three features that needed development in DXL. The DXL coding style needed to be compatible with deployment on Citrix.

3.3.2.1 Reporting

The DOORS Traceability Wizard can be used to collect data from Hazard, Action and Accident modules and present them in a tabular view. Though the standard reports provided the data required, the default format made such reports difficult to review or export into MS Excel. A number of customizations were developed with DXL.

3.3.2.2 Qualitative Safety Risk Assessment

The ELLP Hazard Management Procedure (HMP) defines a qualitative approach to Safety Risk Assessment. The approach is based on three risk factors (each assigned a numerical value, based on a logarithmic scale) that are combined (as a cross product) to produce a risk rating. The three risk factors are:

- **Hazard Frequency**: How often the hazard may be presented.
- **Accident Severity**: The severity of a potential accident leading from the hazard.
- **Accident Probability**: The likelihood that the hazard will lead to the envisaged accident.

This methodology has been adopted as it is better at modeling potential hazard and accident sequences.

3.3.2.3 Change Proposal System

The standard DOORS Change Proposal System (CPS) allows a change request to be associated with a Hazard. However, the approver of the change must examine the current description and proposed description manually. To assist in the review process the CPS was extended by providing a mark-up view which would highlight deletions and additions within the Tool and allow a summary report to be produced.

This is a key aspect of DHL as it provides 'controlled' remote access to the Hazards Data and a user-friendly means to review and action change requests. This provides flexibility and convenience (reducing the clerical burden) without compromising data integrity.

3.4 Assessment & Handover of DOORS Hazard Log

The progression from the prototype to a validated tool was achieved by informal demonstrations to obtain early feedback and progression through three formal gateways.

3.4.1 Prototype Demonstration

The review of the prototype was conducted three months after start of development. The review was attended by the stakeholders involved in the initial Use Case Analysis, this took the form of a presentation that walked through the key design decisions followed by a demonstration of the tool using example data. There was general agreement on the structure of the data model and views presented by the prototype.

Three key changes were suggested: (1) modifications in the mapping table between the data attributes in DOORS to the original MS Access Fields, (2) a number of additional reports and (3) enhancements on the usability and applicability of the Change Proposal System (i.e. to enable change requests on Actions and Accidents). The extension of the CPS is a good example of how prototyping can elicit additional requirements. Given that the usage of the CPS, is now predominately over the Action Module, this additional requirement had a significant effect on the utility of DHL.

3.4.2 Factory Acceptance Testing

A Factory Acceptance Test (FAT) specification was prepared and a traceability table to the Hazard Log Specification reviewed with the DHL Administrator. A formal test session was then conducted with sample data, following successful completion the (unpopulated) Hazard Log was signed off.

3.4.3 Data Migration

The existing Hazard Log already consisted of a large number of hazards, accidents and actions. For each of these data items, there were many attributes that had been populated during the preliminary hazard analysis workshops. To enter this information directly (manually) into DHL would have been time consuming and error prone. The mapping tables defined during the implementation of the Formal Modules were used to develop a number of DXL utilities to import the data from the MS Access based Hazard Log into DHL. A further set of DXL utilities were then developed to automatically create links between DOORS objects that corresponded to the associations in the Access tables.

A baseline of the existing Hazard Log was taken on an agreed date and the DXL utilities used to populate DHL. This first version of DHL was then baselined to provide an audit trail of the data migration process.

3.4.4 User Acceptance

A User Acceptance Test (UAT) specification was agreed, this was a subset of the FAT with additional tests to validate the data migration process. DHL was installed in the ELLP DOORS Database as a separate project, in a production area, by the ELLP IT Team and the appropriate user groups created.

The UAT was conducted with representatives from the user groups. Most of the test cases were passed. However, a number of issues were raised over the presentation of data in DHL, for a large volume of data. These issues had not been apparent during the FAT as only a sample of the data had been used. In particular, there was a feeling that an Excel like presentation would be more usable.

Specific detailed tests were defined and conducted for those features that were supported by the DXL scripts. This included generating several change requests and performing a number of change scenarios with users. For the Qualitative Safety Risk Assessment, after the raw values of the three risk factors (see Section 3.3.2.2) were imported, the DXL script was executed to calculate the product risk score and compared with known values. Further modifications were made around boundary cases as additional tests.

The validation of the data migration was conducted with the DHL administrator, based on a comparison of an export of the data from DHL and the MS Access based hazard log. This process was successful in providing a validated database.

3.4.5 IT Compliance Tests & Review

The ELLP IT team were involved during the development and assessment of DHL. A formal review was conducted following the successful UAT, in Autumn 2006. This covered a review of the structure of DHL and approach to DXL. A particular issue was the ELLP DOORS database had not yet been tested on Citrix. Although Telelogic confirm that DOORS 7.1 is compatible with Citrix, there was a risk the DXL utilities may introduce incompatibility with Citrix or DOORS export features. A test environment was used to confirm that the DXL utilities would work over Citrix.

Finally, infrastructure issues such as use of DOORS licenses and a back-up strategy were agreed, validating the earlier assumptions. DHL was then moved from the production to live environment and handed over to the project (now renamed as LOI) in Autumn 2006.

4 Deployment & Experience with DHL

Following handover the Hazard Log (HL) manager conducted some operational trials with a few members of the Project team and DHL was deployed on the project in late 2006. The following sections provide a summary of user experience over the first 18 months of deployment.

4.1 Procedure & Policy

In parallel with the assessment of DHL, the Hazard Management Procedure for LOI was revised, to be compliant with Yellow Book 4 (RSSB 2007). DHL was to be deployed in the context of this with the aim to achieve the following.

- The compilation of one complete record of ELR hazards in the ELR Hazard Log (i.e. DHL) presented by the construction and operation of the ELR.
- To provide a means of managing ELR hazards between the LOI stakeholders.

The Hazard Management process is illustrated in Figure 6.

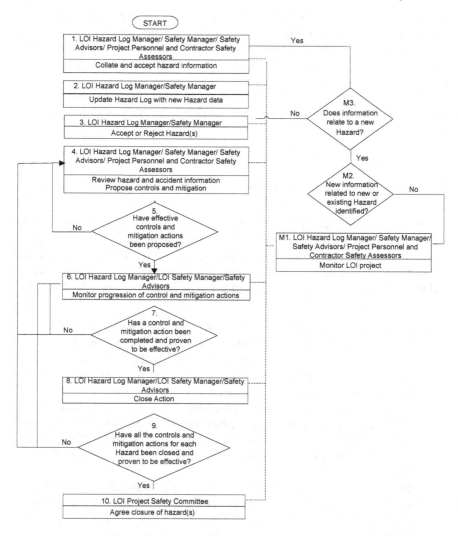

Fig. 6. LOI Hazard Management Process

The basic process is that a hazard and accident scenario (sequence of events and environmental conditions that lead from a hazard to the associated accident) will be proposed. Typically, this will be a result of Hazard Identification studies conducted by either the LOI project team or any of the stakeholders (Rolling Stock Provider (RSP), Main Works Contractor (MWC), Passenger Service Operator (PSO), Infrastructure Manager (IM), etc.). Hazards can also be raised during the project by any project team member or extended project team member by proposing them to the Safety Manager or the Hazard Log Manager. Hazards will be accepted or rejected by assessing the likelihood and severity of the scenario. The

LOI Hazard Log Manager and Safety Manager shall work with Contractor Safety teams to propose control and mitigation measures (actions) for each accepted Hazard and accident scenario. The measures are reviewed until they are deemed effective in reducing the risk to a level which is ALARP (As Low As Reasonably Practicable), they are then tracked to completion. The project is continuously monitored for any changes to design, operational procedures or for potential new hazards which will be incorporated into the DHL via the hazard management process.

4.2 User Reference & Training

For the User Types identified during the use case analysis (see Figure 2), four groups were implemented within DOORS to which individual users are assigned by the DOORS Administrator (who is responsible for the DOORS Application within TfL). Each group was configured to restrict access to specific information and to limit the extent to which information can be Read, Written, Edited and Deleted.

- *Remote User.* A regular user of the DHL who will be based off-site, e.g. Contractor Safety Teams from MWC, RSP, PSO, IM. No familiarity with DOORS is expected, so some basic training on the DHL will be given. Read-Only access to information in the three main modules (Hazard, Accident and Action), write access to the Change Proposal Modules.
- *Local User.* An occasional user of the DHL who will be based in the ELLP offices, and may or may not be familiar with DOORS, some training on the DHL will be given if necessary. This type of user corresponds to relevant members of the ELLP team. Read-Only access to information in all modules.
- *DHL Administrator.* An expert user of the DHL who will be based in the ELLP offices, is expected to be a competent DOORS user. This type of user corresponds to the role of ELLP Hazard Log Manager. Read, Write, Edit, Delete Access to all modules. Capability to configure other user access.
- *Manager.* An occasional user of the DHL who will view reports and Hazard Log content. This type of user corresponds to the roles of ELLP Safety Manager and SQE Manager. Read-Only access to information in all modules.

User training was conducted on a needs basis. When necessary, and at an appropriate time, project staff or contractor staff were briefed on how to use the remote DHL to review the database and also how to submit change proposals. PowerPoint slides were developed to aid this process and also acted as a reference after the briefing was given.

4.3 Experience

Most of the hazard and accident data already existed in the original log and was transferred over into the DOORS format during the Data Migration process. As such, it was intended that usage of the DHL would predominantly be editing the existing hazard and accident data, adding hazard and accident mitigation measures (actions) and adding new hazard and accident data when necessary.

4.3.1 Review Hazard and Accident Information

When the project began using the DHL, the majority of the work involved meeting with contractors to agree their level of contribution (Step 4, in the Hazard Management process). This included agreeing on which hazard-accident scenarios they could contribute control or mitigation measures to, in order to reduce risk, and defining what those measures would be. It became apparent that most measures which the contractors introduce to reduce risk will generally reduce risk on more than one hazard. This plays to DOORS' strengths as only one action entry needs to be made and then it can be easily linked to each hazard for which the measure reduces risk. This provides a benefit to Excel where multiple entries of the same measure would be required which brings with it issues of maintaining the integrity of each duplication.

4.3.2 Monitor Progression of Hazard Control

As the project progresses, day to day reviews of the hazards, subsequent accident possibilities and control and mitigation measures (i.e. actions) were conducted (Step 6, in the Hazard Management process). DHL was found to be good for maintaining data, manipulating it into various views and ensuring integrity as only the HL manager had change access to the 'live' data and if any errors were made they are easily rectified by viewing the history (i.e. What was changed? When was it changed? Who made the change?).

However, DHL was not so good for conducting detailed reviews. Excel is a more appropriate tool for this purpose. Therefore, for everyday reviewing and comment on the data, Excel exports were used which were easily exported from the DOORS database 'Excel output' view.

4.3.2.1 Generation of Excel Reports

Using DHL as the 'databank' and Excel exports for day to day review worked very well for two main reasons:

- View capabilities of DOORS enabled easy export into Excel which could then be printed out and reviewed and additions or edits marked up by contractors or project personnel. As these reviews were done on the Excel output, the integrity of the master data in DOORS was never at risk of being corrupted.
- The method of data storage in DOORS is significantly more robust than Excel so manipulation of the data was easy whilst maintaining data integrity.

There are three separate (formal) Modules: Hazard, Accident and Action. Each stores the data relevant to each information type and links exist to connect related entries in each module. However, by using layout DXL script (code) it is possible to 'follow the links' between the modules and display data from other modules. This is how the 'Excel View' showing each Hazard Object, all the Accident Objects it is linked to and all the actions which are linked to that Hazard is created. This 'Excel View' is a saved view in the Hazard Module and can be easily exported to an Excel spreadsheet whenever necessary. The first screenshot in Figure 7 shows the three modules containing Hazard, Accident and Action data. The links between those modules enable the 'Excel View' which is the second screenshot (here shown in four parts as scrolled from left to right). The final screenshot shows the Excel output which was predominantly used to interface with contractors and other staff members.

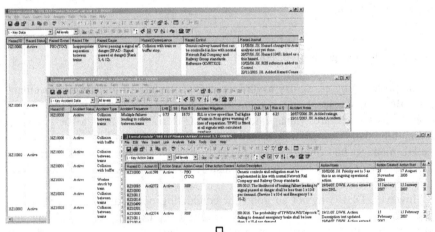

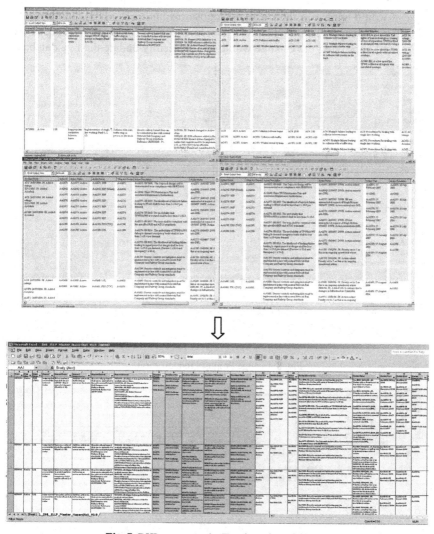

Fig. 7. DHL export to the Excel version of the log

4.3.3 Change Control

Once the initial task of identifying and inputting action data into the DHL had been established, any editing of the measures (i.e. Actions) or the Hazard and Accident data was done through the CPS. After relatively short instruction on DOORS and how to submit a change proposal members of the RSP safety team submitted many CPs with no problem whatsoever. Figure 8 below shows the Change Proposal form which users would fill in and Figure 9 shows how that proposal would appear in the Change Proposal Module. The DHL administrator and Safety Manager then decides whether to accept or reject the Proposal. Accepting and approving the Change would automatically update the live database.

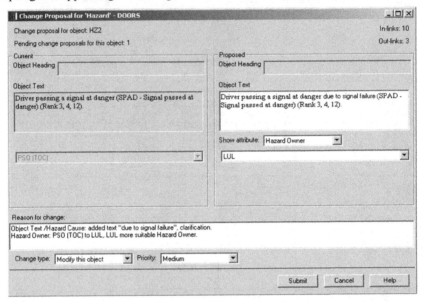

Fig. 8. Change Proposal request form

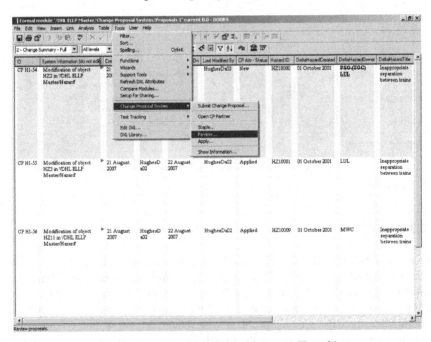

Fig. 9. Change Proposal Module (changes to Hazards)

4.4 Review of Enhancement Capabilities

Looking back over the first 18 months usage of DHL, a subjective assessment of how well the enhancement capabilities have been met is offered below, by the HL manager.

Audit Trail & Version Control. The audit trail was achieved by periodically baselining the modules after any major updates to the DHL. Any changes made after the last baseline would be stored in the history of the attributes. The CPS then provides an audit trail of all the amendments to the initial data set which was stored in the DHL (a record of the rejected change proposals with justifications is also maintained). Baselining, viewing the history and setting up and using the CPS were all easy as they are integral part of the DOORS software.

Change Control, CPS and Data Integrity. Change control and maintaining data integrity was achieved by only allowing the DHL administrator edit and write access to the DHL. If any changes or additions were required by the project team or contractors it would be by editing the Excel exports and requesting change or by submitting Change Proposal Requests using the CPS. This was found to be a major strength of the use of the DHL alongside Excel exports.

Collaborative Working. This was achieved by giving remote read access to contractor teams via Citrix and providing regular Excel exports from the DHL.

The desirable capability of linking between safety requirements and control measures (actions) has not yet been utilized. As there were no existing relations between the hazard log and requirements database, there was a substantial set of relations to be (manually) established following data migration. Due to time constraints, of the Requirements Team, the links between existing actions and safety requirements (see Figure 5) are still to be created. A typical occurrence when attempts are made to retro-fit traceability. This would have been significantly easier to do (and perceived as more beneficial) if the hazard log had been in DOORS from the start of the project rather than having to create all the links after the data was transferred.

5 Concluding Remarks

The main objective of reducing the clerical load on the HL Manager was achieved by the roll-out of DHL. By moving the responsibility of reviewing the Hazard Log data to a wider project team (including contractors), a more collective understanding of the Hazard and Accidents was achieved. This was useful in the identification of common Actions (measures) to reduce the risk associated with accident scenarios. The main project risk of wider usage was that this may lead to a reduction in data integrity. This was adequately mitigated by the detailed audit trail maintained in DOORS and the use of the customised CPS. Further, by ensuring that data was recorded in a centralised database (without duplication of objects) maintenance of data integrity was simplified.

For collaborative working the deployment on Citrix provided the basic functionality for remote working. However, there were occasional performance issues that deterred remote users for making day-to-day usage. A further weakness, in terms of usability, was the presentation of large volumes of data that was recorded in three modules. The Hazard Management Procedure was modified to be a hybrid approach that used the strengths of Excel and DHL to define a robust and pragmatic Hazard Management system.

Future development of DHL is being considered, this includes:

- Automated E-mail notifications of change requests raised on Hazards or Actions.
- Establish links between the Actions and safety requirements in the Requirements Database.

Over the last year, there have been a number of improvements in DOORS and related tools that could be used to address the usability issues.

- Telelogic DOORS Web Access™ is a product based on DOORS that provides a web-browser interface to support remote working (Telelogic 2008).
- ComplyPro2 (ComplyServe 2008) offers a 'Grid View' on DOORS data that is Excel like and may remove the need to export into Excel. This may also resolve some of the issues related to remote access on Citrix.

Acknowledgments The authors are grateful to TfL for allowing the experiences gained on the project to be shared and acknowledge the funding provided by the Atkins Defence Capability Development programme for the preparation of this paper.

References

Citrix (2008) Technologies. http://www.citrix.com/English/ps2/category.asp. Accessed 13 October 2008

ComplyServe (2008) http://www.complyserve.com. Accessed 13 October 2008

Elphick J, Irving M (2006) Railway Systems Engineering in Action, INCOSE Railway Interest Group. http://www.incose.org.uk/Downloads/RIG%20060912%20Railway%20Systems%20 Engineering%20In%20Action%20-%20Paper.pdf. Accessed 13 October 2008

Emmet L (2007) Recent developments in ASCE plugins, including DOORS and PDF Plugins. http://www.adelard.com/web/hnav/ASCE/user-group/17-Oct-2007/Recent_plugin__develop ments.pdf. Accessed 13 October 2008

Emmet L, Cleland G (2002), Graphical Notations, Narratives and Persuasion: a Pliant Systems Approach to Hypertext Tool Design. Proceedings of ACM Hypertext. http://www.adelard .com/papers/ht2002_emmet_cleland_asce_paper.pdf. Accessed 13 October 2008

EN 50129 (2003) CLC/SC 9XA Railway applications - Communication, signalling and processing systems - Safety related electronic systems for signalling

EN 50126-1 (1999) CLC/TC 9X Railway applications - The specification and demonstration of Reliability, Availability, Maintainability and Safety (RAMS)

Hamoy C, Hemer D, Lindsay P (2004) HazLog: tool support for hazard management, Proceedings of the 9th Australian workshop on Safety critical systems and software, Brisbane, Australia. http://crpit.com/confpapers/CRPITV47Hamoy.pdf. Accessed 13 October 2008

HVR (2008) Cassandra Hazard Management. http://www.risktools.co.uk/cassandra.htm. Accessed 13 October 2008

Lautieri S, Cooper D, Jackson D et al (2004), Assurance Cases: how assured are you? Proc. of the International Conf. on Dependable Systems and Networks. http://www.praxis-his.com/publications/documents/AssuranceCase_DSN04.pdf. Accessed 13 October 2008

Leveson N (1995), Safeware: System Safety and Computers, Addison Wesley

MOD (1996) 00-56 Safety Management Requirements for Defence Systems

QMAP (2008) http://www.qmap.co.uk. Accessed 13 October 2008

Railtrack (2000) Engineering Safety Management, issue 3, Yellow Book 3. http://www.yellowbook-rail.org.uk/site/the_yellow_book/volume_2/part_2.pdf. Accessed 13 October 2008

RSSB (2007) Engineering Safety Management, Yellow Book 4. Rail Safety and Standards Board. http://www.yellowbook-rail.org.uk/site/the_yellow_book/yellow_book_vol1and2_issue4.pdf. Accessed 13 October 2008

RCM² (2006), ISCaDE manual. http://www.rcm2.co.uk/products/DOORS.htm. Accessed 13 October 2008

Taylor A, Cleland G (2007), ASCE News Summer 2007. http://www.adelard.com/web/hnav/ASCE/newsletter/ASCE_News_Summer_2007.pdf. Accessed 13 October 2008

Telelogic (2008) DOORS. http://www.telelogic.com/doors. Accessed 13 October 2008

Weinnberg L, Soussan D, Swanson S (2004) Utilizing the power of DOORS to take the 'Risk' out of Risk Assessment. Telelogic Americas User Group Conference http://download.telelogic.com/download/paper/Utilizing_DOORS_To_TaketheRiskOut_DOORS_Weinberg.pdf. Accessed 13 October 2008

Dependable Risk Analysis for Systems with E/E/PE Components: Two Case Studies

Jörn Stuphorn, Bernd Sieker and Peter B. Ladkin

Causalis Limited

Bielefeld, Germany

Abstract Accurate risk assessment of safety-related systems involving software is a hard engineering problem for well-known reasons. We present two case studies in the use of Ontological Hazard Analysis (OHA), a semi-formal method for hazard identification and analysis aiding Correct-by-Construction (CbC) approaches to developing such systems. OHA controls very carefully the means of expression of safety requirements, starting with a simple semi-formal language and proceeding to more expressive requirements through formal refinement, a decades-old technique for CbC program development developed in the computer-science theory community. In the case studies, the use of OHA allows the risk assessment of the systems through known techniques, avoiding the general problems posed by non-continuity which are inherent in attempting to assess the risk of systems based on software.

1 Introduction

There is a major question of how to perform an accurate risk analysis of systems with software-based components (often subsumed under the rubric electrical/electronic/programmable-electronic, or E/E/PE systems). There is a consensus amongst senior scientists and engineers, backed by rigorous statistical reasoning, that developing systems by 'the usual methods' and testing to identify and eliminate faults cannot attain the required dependability. Other methods are needed, and again the consensus is that these methods must be rigorous, which means formal. It is important that

- the methods connect with the usual methods used by system safety engineers, and
- that they admit practical application to typical industrial examples.

Computer scientists have many formal methods at their disposal whose capabilities are well-known, but which methods are not typically used in industrial devel-

C. Dale, T. Anderson (eds.), *Safety-Critical Systems: Problems, Process and Practice*,
DOI 10.1007/978-1-84882-349-5_6, © Springer-Verlag London Limited 2009

opment, for various reasons, amongst them that they violate one of these two conditions. We relate in this paper two case studies of how a particular approach, Ontological Hazard Analysis (OHA, first proposed in under the name 'Ontological Analysis' (Ladkin 2005)) can be used for risk assessment of E/E/PE systems.

The basis for OHA is to start with a very abstract requirements specification, of a form which computer scientists are used to produce, in a semi-formally-controlled language. This initial language L must be such that

- it is a formal language, containing names for objects, and symbols for properties of those objects and relations between them, i.e., it is a subset of the language of predicate logic
- the set of all possible (non-equivalent) statements in the language is *finite*
- all users can agree on which of these statements state safety requirements, say the set S
- the safety requirements identified can be seen to constitute a sufficient set

There is some skill involved in picking this first language, and the success of the OHA method is dependent on a suitable choice. The finite set of non-equivalent statements in L must also be small enough that engineers can consider them all, and make judgements about them, in a reasonable period of time.

OHA proceeds from L and S by *formal refinement*, a well-known technique in computer science but not one common amongst system safety engineers. The language L is extended, by considering new objects, properties and relations which express structure and behavior of the system in more detail, less abstractly. Let us call this language L1. The concepts of L (objects, and especially properties and relations) must be expressed in L1. The definitions of the concepts are known as *'meaning postulates'*. The safety requirements in S have their translations into L1, producing say the set of requirements S1, and these are the safety requirements that have to be assured. It may be necessary to introduce new requirements in L1 that guarantee (logically imply) the requirements in S1. Thus the set of safety requirements in L1 is a set S1' which includes S1. This process is repeated as many times as it takes to achieve the goals, which may be

- a system architecture, at, for example a source-code level, so that code may be developed directly from the architecture
- a system architecture which allows standard methods of risk analysis to be applied

We call the successive languages *levels*. The initial language L is *Level 0*, its successor L1 *Level 1*, and so on.

The important feature of the refinement process is the traceability it enables between initial, very abstract system functional definition and, in the end if all goes well, the source-code-level design. This traceability eliminates much of the uncertainty in the development process which leads to unreliability of the risk assessment of the resulting system.

Good idea, but does it work? Many formal approaches do not pan out when applied to industrial examples. We have performed three OHAs on industrial examples. The three analyses were all very different in both style and formal techniques used, but they were all successful in reducing risk assessment to generic methods, and all used the same semi-controlled language/controlled refinement approach of OHA.

1. The first author defined a generic communications-bus architecture applicable to both CAN-bus and Flexray-based communications for road vehicles. The initial language in which the functional requirements were stated was moderately complex. The refinements were achieved through applying HAZOP to the current level, then performing a partial causal analysis of how these deviations could occur (per deviation a mini-Why-Because-Graph, called an epWBG, was created) and the vocabulary necessary for expressing these causal factors defined the next level. The analysis was moderately complex, as he says. However, the epWBGs could be easily converted into fault-tree representations, and already at Level 2 the separate mini-fault trees resulting from the epWBGs could be combined into a single fault tree, enabling the usual fault-tree risk-analysis method of assigning probabilities to the leaf nodes and working one's way upwards through the tree. Thus the goal was accomplished of taking a moderately-complex and realistic E/E/PE system and developing it to the point at which state-of-the-practice risk analysis methods could be applied. Any residual unreliability of such an analysis resides in the usual difficulties with fault-tree analysis (the accuracy of the necessary probabilistic-independence assumptions, for example) as well as in the confidence of the accuracy of the derivation of the fault tree. (We admit a certain amount of laziness here – the actual derivation of the fault tree was performed as a student project at the University of Bielefeld, where the third author teaches. Thus we confirmed that the conversion is feasible, which was the point of the exercise, but we did not necessarily arrive at a fault tree which we would trust!)

2. The second author attempted to derive a computer-based system for performing the communications between train controller and drivers necessary for operating trains according to the German train-dispatching protocol for non-state-owned railways. Train dispatching (German 'Zugleitbetrieb') is the common means of operating trains on single-track lightly-used rail lines, which are commonly not equipped with signalling systems. The protocol is defined in a document, the FV-NE, which is part of German administrative law. He started from the obvious, overriding requirement for block-based train protection, that no two different trains may occupy the same block at the same time except under certain special circumstances. The Level 0 language required to express this is astonishingly simple, and enabled a manual selection of safety requirements, which is complete in the sense that they cannot be logically strengthened. Level 1 and further levels were defined through the usual type of refinement process familiar to computer scientists, in which the extensions of the language were carefully controlled in small steps. It proved to be possible to express the entire functional operation of the system at each level in terms of a global finite-state machine, and the state machines were formally proved to refine each other,

sometimes through addition of extra requirements which then become safety requirements. The final step involved transforming the global state machine into a set of communicating state machines, one representing a driver and one a train controller, with message-passing. This was expressed in a structure called a Message Flow Graph (MFG), for which the third author has defined a formal semantics (Ladkin and Leue 1995), and thus the MFG could be formally proved to implement the appropriate global state machine. The MFG agents were then implemented as SPARK procedure skeletons with the appropriate annotations by Phil Thornley of SparkSure, and the annotation proved to implement the MFG. Thus the entire development ensured complete traceability between very-high-level safety requirements and SPARK source code. Suppose such a system were to be implemented as either an automated dispatching system, with computers replacing the human agents, or, more practically, as a support system which checks that the required steps have been performed by the human agents. Then the risk of using the system resides entirely in the hardware and communications systems used, as well as in the compiler used to compile the source code, and in human factors such as whether the system is used as intended, and there is no residual risk inherent in the logic of the program design itself. The risk of this computer-based system has thereby been reduced to that of other, generic risks, which data from other, unrelated projects may be used to assess.

3. The first two authors have performed a security analysis for a configuration control and downloading system for road vehicles with configurable components based on generic hardware, in the European Commission Integrated Project AC/DC, which involves a number of large European automobile and component manufacturers. The secure downloading of a configuration from secure manufacturer sources to a vehicle in the field is a vital component in the process which the project is attempting to define and prototype. The authors first defined a threat model, with which their project clients agreed, and then using OHA derived a complete set of attack patterns and therefrom the attack trees for this threat model. No other technique is known to us which could have accomplished this in a checkably-reliable way. The total effort involved was eighteen person-months, a non-trivial amount but still a low level of effort when compared with the consequences of a successful attack. Since this example concerns security and not safety, we do not consider it further here.

Conclusion. The field of E/E/PE safety lacks methods for performing risk analysis on systems with software-based components in such a way that one may be confident in the risk assessment. The technique OHA, based on expression of requirements in semi-controlled language and formal refinement steps, allows the risk assessment of an E/E/PE system to be based on generic state-of-the-practice risk-assessment methods, in such a way that one may be as confident in the results of an assessment as one is confident in these generic methods. The application of OHA may be straightforward or more complex, but in our case studies on industrial examples it has lain within the range of the economically achievable. We thus recommend its use.

Structure of the Paper. We have stated above the purpose and conclusions, as well as briefly described the case studies concerning the use of Ontological Hazard Analysis. This constitutes, if you like, the 'executive summary' of the work. The two following sections present some details of the first two case studies

2 First Case Study: OHA for an Automotive Communications Bus System

Bus communication systems in road vehicles became useful with the integration of increasing numbers of electronic devices. The multiplexing of these at first separated systems via a communications system enabled savings in weight, lower costs of production, and greater design flexibility.

With emerging new areas of application such as X-by-Wire, communication protocols supporting time-triggered communication are an increasingly common sight in cars.

2.1 Initial System Description

Schematically, an integrated communication bus system in a car can be depicted as shown in Figure 1. The operator of the vehicle gives input into the system using steering wheel, pedals, shift box and other selector switches, of which the states are assessed by sensors which provide input for network Nodes (NIC). These are interconnected with a network bus by which information exchange is enabled. Other Nodes process the available information and provide them to connected actuators with can then influence brakes, gear, inverter, transmission, etc.

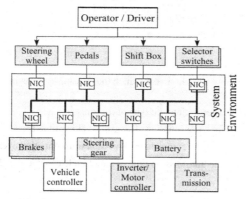

Fig. 1. Integrated Communication Bus System

For the identification of hazards to the communication bus, the system is defined to compass the nodes and the physical wiring of the network bus; all other elements are part of the environment.

2.2 Ontology of the initial system description

Based on the initial system-description three objects with ten properties and one relation are identified. To avoid misunderstanding the meaning of each element of the ontology is defined with the element in the tables below.

Table 1. Objects of the System

Object	Description
NIC	The Network Interface Controller. This is the interface between the input device and the physical network.
Wiring	The physical connection between the systems' NICs. Transmission
Transmission	The transport of information between NICs over the physical network.

Table 2.a. Properties of NIC

Property	Description
Input	The information received by the NIC
Output	The information transmitted by the NIC
Intact	The integrity of the NIC, whose absence prevents the NIC from working properly.

Table 2.b. Properties of Wiring

Property	Description
Intact	The integrity of the wiring, whose absence prevents the physical network from working properly.

Table 2.c. Properties of Transmission

Object	Description
Size	The size of the transmission
Deadline	The latest possible point in time at which the transmission can be received without loosing its value.
Period	Frequency of the generation of a type of transmission
Mode	The mode used for a transmission. This can be either time-triggered or event-triggered.
Latency	The time it takes for the complete transmission of information over the network.
Jitter	The variance in the transmission time of a multitude of same-typed transmissions.

Table 3. Relations of the System

Relation	Description
Connection(Wiring, NIC)	The feature of the NIC to be connected properly with the Wiring.

2.3 Guide-Word based Approach for Identification of Hazards

We used HAZOP's guide-word-based approach to identify deviation because of its systematic nature.

Table 4 HAZOP guide-words used and their interpretations

Guide-Word	Source	Interpretation
No	RSC01	None of the design intent is achieved
	RCC99	This is the complete negation of the design intention - No part of the intention is achieved but nothing else happens
More	RSC01	Quantitative increase in a parameter
	RCC99	This is a quantitative increase
Less	RSC01	Quantitative decrease in a parameter
	RCC99	This is a quantitative decrease
As well as	RSC01	An additional activity occurs
	RCC99	This is a qualitative increase, where all the design intention is achieved together with additional activity
Part of	RSC01	Only some of the design intention is achieved
	RCC99	This is a qualitative decrease, where only part of the design intention is achieved
Reverse	RSC01	Logical opposite of the design intention occurs
	RCC99	This is the logical opposite of the intention
Other than	RSC01	Complete substitution. Another activity takes place
	RCC99	This is a complete substitution, where no part of the original intention is achieved but something quite different happens
Early	RSC01	The timing different from the intention
	RCC99	Something happens earlier in time than intended
Late	RSC01	The timing different from the intention
	RCC99	Something happens later in time than intended
Before	RSC01	The step (or some part of it) is effected out of sequence
	RCC99	Something happens earlier in a sequence than intended
After	RSC01	The step (or some part of it) is effected out of sequence
	RCC99	Something happens later in a sequence than intended
Faster	RSC01	The step is done with the right timing
Slower	RSC01	The step is not done with the right timing
Where else	RSC01	Applicable for flows, transfers, sources and destinations

By combining the HAZOP guide-words with each element of the ontology, a comprehensive list of possible deviations is generated. As usual in HAZOP, these possible deviations now have to be interpreted for their impact and meaning in the specific application. A number of these putative deviations can easily be dismissed, as certain guide-words may not make sense when applied to certain elements.

The list of guide-words shown in Table 4 is a combination of guide-words proposed by the Royal Society of Chemistry (Hazell et al. 2001) and (Redmill et al. 1999).

Overall our system ontology for the initial system description comprises 14 elements and the set of guide-words 13 elements. The combination of elements with guide-words produced 182 possible deviations which were reduced by the interpretation process down to 59 meaningful deviations, a reduction of about 67%.

2.4 Formalisation of Deviations by Usage of Ontology

The systematic generation of deviations produces some equivalent deviations in varying wording. Such deviations do not have to be analysed more than once, but can be difficult to identify. We accomplished this by expressing the deviations semi-formally using the vocabulary of the ontology. E.g. the deviation *'Information is reversely transmitted'* can be expressed by the formula *'Output(NIC) = INVERSE(Input(NIC))'*. Equivalences are much easier to see using the semi-formal mathematical-style language.

As a side effect, this formalisation helps to identify missing elements in the ontology, which can then be included to enable the expression of further deviations. In the step from the initial system description and ontology to the first refined version, this led to an additional 3 objects, 21 properties and 1 relation. The refinement to the second refined version identified another 14 properties and 1 relation.

After three iterations of refinement the system ontology overall comprises 6 objects, 45 properties and 3 relations.

2.5 Extended Partial Why-Because Graphs

To analyse the causal factors leading to a deviation, an extended partial Why-Because Graph (epWBG) is created. Why-Because Graphs were intended for a-posteriori analysis of incidents, in which all causes of a node actually occurred (Ladkin 2000). We could say by analogy with fault trees, that the graph-relationships are all AND-related. For system development, we need to consider alternative ways in which an event can occur, and thus one needs to represent an OR-type relationship as well, as in e.g. Mackie's INUS conditions (Mackie 1974). The WBG is extended by introducing an OR relationship, and because we are only concerned with limited causal relationships among certain elements, we call the result an extended partial WBG or epWBG.

Typically the epWBG describing the causes of the occurrence of a deviation are rather small, the number of their nodes varying between 1 and 11. For example, the events that can cause the deviation *'The Network has no shielding'* which can be expressed as *"Shielding(Network) = 0"* to occur can be represented as in Figure 2.

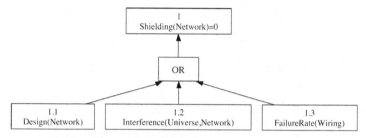

Fig. 2. epWBA of deviation 'The Network has no Shielding'

From the system definition only three events can lead to the deviation occurring: either the shielding was omitted during design; direct interference from outside the system caused the shielding to disappear; or the shielding failed by itself.

Other deviations are more complex in their causal description. The causes of the event of a network node becoming dysfunctional or broken, *'NOT In-tact(NIC)'*, are shown by the epWBG in Figure 3.

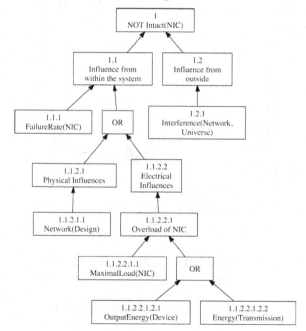

Fig. 3. NIC is not intact

2.6 Statistics of the Analysis

As shown in Figure 4, the elements in the ontology of the system description expanded most in the first refinement step. The step from 2nd to 3rd iteration also provided a more detailed system description; the missing elements were mostly properties of objects and one relation.

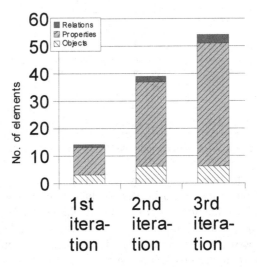

Fig. 4. Extent of Elements in System Description's Ontology

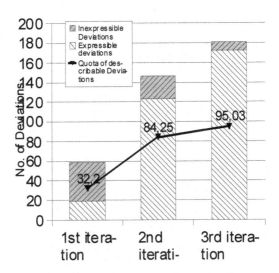

Fig. 5. Expressible and Inexpressible Deviations

In Figure 5 the overall numbers of deviations are shown, classified into deviations expressible with the system description's current ontology and those so inexpressible. The refinement step is expressly intended to be able to state these deviations. As can be seen, with advancing refinement of the system description, the percentage of expressible deviations continually improves.

2.7 Transformation of epWBGs into Fault Trees

For risk assessment of the system, it is necessary to quantify the possible failures. One common way to do this is through a fault-tree analysis. A fault tree was created by first translating the epWBGs into corresponding small fault trees, which were then combined into an overall fault tree describing all the possible factors leading to a failure. This transformation was performed by a group who were learning how to work with fault trees. The goal was not to produce a fault tree suitable for troubleshooting and system maintenance, which requires that nodes adjacent to the root-node act as decision points, but rather to produce a fault tree which could be used for risk assessment, in which leaf nodes are assigned probabilities and the probabilities are combined moving up the tree towards the root-node. Thus, when constructing the combined fault tree, certain 'classification nodes' were introduced to denote clusters of similar factors without regard as to whether these classifiers were observable. So e.g. *Human failure* was used as such a classifier and would obviously not be appropriate in a fault tree used for diagnosis.

2.7.1 Filtering of epWBGs

During the course of the analysis, several epWBGs were built which identified problems residing in the specification. As the goal of the fault tree lies in the assessment of risk for an implemented system, such specification faults were not included in the combined fault tree, for they would be eliminated before the implementation stage.

Another feature of the deviation-identification approach is the identification of trivial events such as *'The device does not exist'*. In most cases, such events occur also through failures in specification or the implementation and would similarly be eliminated before the implementation stage and were not included in the combined fault tree.

epWBGs comprising only two nodes resolve to an identity in fault-tree notation. They occur as one node in the generated fault tree.

2.7.2 Algorithm used for clustering epWBGs

As the epWBGs are formulated to describe deviations, one epWBG can describe factors involved in other epWBGs. To cluster these, the following procedure was used:

1. Choose one epWBG
2. Look at leaves
3. Select concepts in leave nodes
4. Look up concepts in HAZOP tables
5. Identify the interpretation that fits the node in HAZOP table
6. Go to the list of identified deviations and identify the respective deviation number
7. Repeat process for the epWBG for the identified deviation

The application of this procedure led to several combined epWBGs which formed the basis for the next step, the transformation into one larger fault tree.

2.7.3 Conversion of clustered epWBGs into partial Fault Trees

A typical example for the conversion from an epWBG into a partial fault tree is shown below and should be self-explanatory given the above comments.

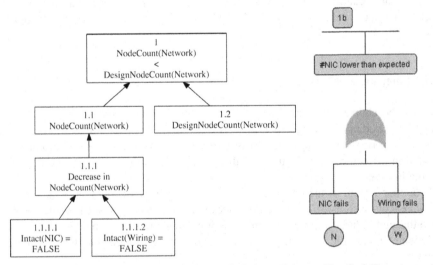

Fig. 6. epWBG formulated to describe deviation and the resulting Fault Tree

2.7.4 Combining partial Fault Trees into one overall Fault Tree

As root node for the fault tree the event *'Problem occurs'* was chosen, a nonde-script, but generic name for all system failures identified in the OHA.

Investigation of the epWBGs revealed that all failures could be classified under the topics *'Human failure'*, *'Information not transceived'* and *'No data from device'*. The resulting head of the Fault Tree is shown in Figure 7.

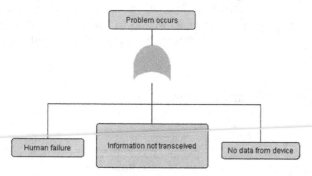

Fig. 7. Head of Fault Tree

Then the partial fault trees were sorted according to their respective classification. The resulting fault tree comprises about 150 nodes. This is of a size often encountered in industrial fault tree analyses and the risk calculation can be handled by the usual methods. The fault tree represents only a certain level of refinement of the system, however, this refinement suffices to allow an arguably realistic assessment of risk given the usual probabilistic independence assumptions in fault tree analysis. We would caution however, that such independence assumptions must themselves be carefully analysed in order to ensure they hold. Our analysis did not go this far.

3 Second Case Study: OHA of Train Dispatching

This work formalises the German train-dispatching protocol for non-state-owned railways ('Zugleitbetrieb'). Administrative law (VDV 2004) sets the requirements for how this is to be done. We derive a system expressed in SPARK source code which implements a (completed version of) this legal protocol.

Complete traceability is maintained between the abstract high-level safety requirements and the SPARK source code through formal refinement. Were the SPARK code to be implemented in communicating machines which either back up or replace the human agents of the system, then the risk analysis of the system may assume that the logic of the communications is faultless. The residual risk consists of the risks associated with the ADA compiler, the hardware used for running the code and for the communications, and human factors.

A set of safety requirements which are guaranteed to be adequate are derived by starting with a very simplistic, seemingly trivial description. The safety requirements are determined for this first level (Level 0) by enumerating all possible truth functions for two trains in the available language, and determining which of these are safety requirements.

The original Zugleitbetrieb (ZLB) relies on a single human operator (the dispatcher, or Zugleiter) to make sure that a given track section is free before allowing any train to enter that section. There are no signals and other supporting technology to locate trains. The system, as well as its derived system developed here, relies solely on messages passed between the train conductors and the dispatcher.

2.2 Ontological Hazard Analysis

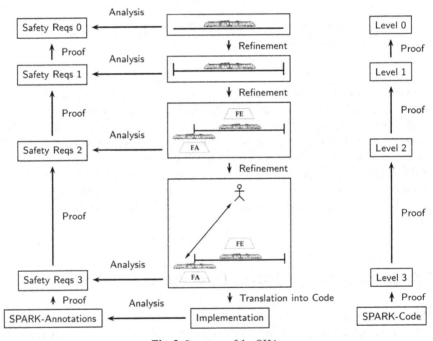

Fig. 8. Structure of the OHA

3.2.1 Starting the OHA --- Level 0

The goal of the highest specification level, Level 0 is not to provide a detailed description of train operations, but to provide a description that is so simple that we can define safety axioms to which all applications experts can assent and at the same time ascertain that these axioms are both *correct* and *complete* relative to the expressions of the language.

Fig. 9. Schematic Representation of Level 0

Table 5. Level 0 Sorts

Sort	Description
Vehicle	Any train or other vehicle operating on tracks
Block	A section of a track inside or outside a station

Table 6. Level 0 Relations

Relation	Description
inA(F,S)	Train F is in Block S
ZV(F,S)	ZV(F,S) Train F may occupy Block S under central responsibility (normal scheduledoperation)
LV(FS)	ZV(F,S) Train F may occupy Block S under local responsibility (special case)

Determining Safety Axioms. Using elementary propositional logic as well some semantic domain knowledge we are able to determine that there turn out to be only 6 safety postulates on Level 0 from consideration of a couple of dozen non-equivalent statements from a total of 256 statements before semantic reduction. We use the following shorthand notation for a train F1 and one block S: LV(F1,S) = LV1, ZV(F1,S) = LZ1, inA(F1,S) = in1; similarly for train F2. The Safety Postulates at Level 0 are shown in Table 7.

Table 7. Safety Postulates at Level 0

Safety Postulate	Description
$ZV1 \Rightarrow \neg LV1$	If a train is in a block under central responsibility it cannot be there under local responsibility
$\neg LV1 \wedge in1 \Rightarrow ZV1$	If a train is in a block and is not there under local responsibility then it is under central responsibility
$in1 \wedge ZV1 \Rightarrow \neg LV1$	If a train is in a block under central responsibility it cannot be in that block under local responsibility
$(F1 \neq F2) \Rightarrow (LV1 \Rightarrow \neg ZV2)$	If a train is in a block under local responsibility another train under central responsibility cannot be in that block
$(F1 \neq F2) \Rightarrow (in1 \Rightarrow \neg ZV2)$	If a train is in a block another train under central responsibility cannot be in that block
$(F1 \neq F2) \Rightarrow (ZV1 \Rightarrow \neg ZV2)$	If a train under central responsibility is in a block, another train under central responsibility cannot be in that block.

3.2.2 Level 1: First Refinement

Fig. 10. Schematic Representation of Level 1

The generic block of Level 0 is refined as follows, introducing the new sorts Track and Station. This leads to Table 8.

Table 8. Level 1 Sorts

Sort	Description
Vehicle	Train or other track vehicle
Block	A track section
Track	A piece of track in the station
Station	A station where messages are exchanged

On this level we then have 10 relations. Meaning Postulates define what each Level 0 sort and Level 0 relation means in terms of the Level 1 language.

Using the Meaning Postulates we arrive at 12 Safety Postulates for Level 1.

3.2.3 Level 2

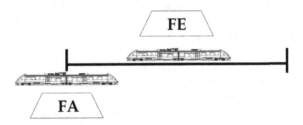

Fig. 11. Schematic Representation of Level 2

In this level no new sorts are added, but additional relations concerning 'clearances' are added, as shown in Table 9.

Table 9. Level 2 Relations

Relation	Description
FA(F,A,B)	Train F, in station A, has asked for clearance to go to station B
FE(F,A,B)	Train F, in station A, has received clearance to go to station B
AFE(F,A,B)	Train F, in station A, has been denied clearance to go to station B
KH(F,A,B)	No obstructions are known for train F to go from station A to station B

At this point we are now able to build a state-machine representing the global states of clearances which represents a train journey.

The state-machine is shown in Figure 12, which is presented as a Predicate-Action-Diagram (Lamport 1995).

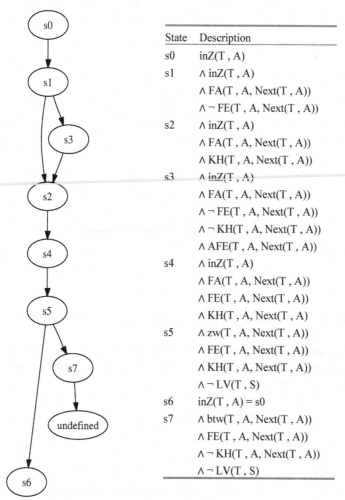

State	Description
s0	inZ(T , A)
s1	∧ inZ(T , A)
	∧ FA(T , A, Next(T , A))
	∧ ¬ FE(T , A, Next(T , A))
s2	∧ inZ(T , A)
	∧ FA(T , A, Next(T , A))
	∧ KH(T , A, Next(T , A))
s3	∧ inZ(T , A)
	∧ FA(T , A, Next(T , A))
	∧ ¬ FE(T , A, Next(T , A))
	∧ ¬ KH(T , A, Next(T , A))
	∧ AFE(T , A, Next(T , A))
s4	∧ inZ(T , A)
	∧ FA(T , A, Next(T , A))
	∧ FE(T , A, Next(T , A))
	∧ KH(T , A, Next(T , A)
s5	∧ zw(T , A, Next(T , A))
	∧ FE(T , A, Next(T , A))
	∧ KH(T , A, Next(T , A))
	∧ ¬ LV(T , S)
s6	inZ(T , A) = s0
s7	∧ btw(T , A, Next(T , A))
	∧ FE(T , A, Next(T , A))
	∧ ¬ KH(T , A, Next(T , A))
	∧ ¬ LV(T , S)

Fig. 12. Level 2 state-machine

Three simple Meaning Postulates and elementary logic leads to only two new Safety Postulates, which can be expressed informally as:

- if no obstructions are known and clearance has been given, the block can be occupied under central responsibility
- clearance for a block cannot be given for a second train, if clearance has already been given for a train for the same block in either direction.

Hazards. The new hazards identified at this level are simply the negations of the newly identified Safety Postulates:

- Clearance has been given, and no obstruction is known, but the conditions for occupying the block under central responsibility have not been met.
- Clearance has been given for two trains for the same block at the same time.

3.2.4 Level 3

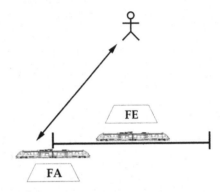

Fig. 13. Schematic Representation of Level 3

Level 3 includes the specific defined communications between trains and a dispatcher.

Message types correspond to the states in which the trains can be, and are designed according to the message types prescribed in the regulations for German non-state-owned railways (VDV 2004).

Table 10. Message types at Level 3

Message Type	Description
FA	Request for Clearance (Fahranfrage)
FE	Clearance (Fahrerlaubnis)
AFE	Denial of Clearance (Ablehung der Fahrerlaubnis)
AM	Notification of Arrival (Ankunftmeldung)

In addition, we define relations to describe sending and receiving of messages, as shown in Table 11.

Table 11. Relations at Level 3

Relation	Description
Sent(MT,T,A)	Message of type MT, concerning train T and station A has been sent.
Recd(MT,T,A)	Message of type MT, concerning train T and station A has been received.

Note that the sender and receiver of the message are implicit. Messages of type FA and AM are always sent by the specific train to the dispatcher, messages of type FE and AFE are always sent by the dispatcher.

Through appropriate Meaning Postulates, the state machine of Level 2 can be augmented to include communications. This now more complex state machine can be transformed into a Message Flow Graph (MFG), to make the communications visually clear. The MFG represents the individual agents and their changing states as vertical lines, message passing between agents as angled lines. The MFG can be formally shown to define the same global state machine as the Predicate-Action-Diagram for this level.

The MFG is used as the starting point to define the SPARK implementation and the SPARK verification conditions are determined by hand to define the MFG of Figure 14.

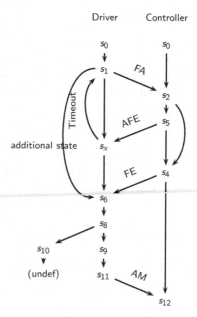

Fig. 14. The Message Flow Graph

Table 12. States corresponding to the Message Flow Graph

MFG-Trans.	Driver-State	Controller State	Global State
s0	inZ(T , A)A)	–	inZ(T , A)
s0 → s1	∧ inZ(T , A)	--	∧ inZ(T , A)
	∧ Sent⟨FA, T , Next(T , A)⟩		∧ Sent⟨FA, T , Next(T , A)⟩
s1 → s2	--	Recd⟨FA, T , Next(T , A)⟩	∧ inZ(T , A)
			∧ Sent⟨FA, T , Next(T , A)⟩
			∧Recd⟨FA, T , Next(T , A)⟩

3.2.5 The Step to Code: Implementation in SPARK

SPARK is based on a subset of the Ada language. It uses annotations to denote data and information flow and to specify pre- and post-conditions for functions and procedures.

The SPARK tools include a static code analyser that uses the annotations to prove the absence of run-time errors, such as division by zero, buffer overflows and other bounds violations before the code is actually compiled.

SPARK annotations

- strengthen specification
- 'Design by Contract'
- Allow analysis without access to implementation
- Analysis can be done early, before programs are compilable

SPARK Code Verification Tools

- Examiner

  - Checks control flow and data flow
  - Checks information flow
  - Generates proof obligations ("verification conditions") for run-time errors

- Simplifier

  - Automatic proof of large majority of proof obligations

- (Interactive) Proof Checker

  - Used to prove the remaining verification conditions
  - Used to prove conformance of Code to pre/postconditions

Properties of SPARK Code

- Unambiguous
- Bounded space and time requirements
- Free of runtime errors

Code for train dispatching has been completed by Phil Thornley of SparkSure, based on the Message Flow Graphs. Proofs have been completed that the Code fulfils the annotations, and that the annotations fulfil the Level 3 Message Flow Graph description.

Typical Example of SPARK annotations corresponding to the MFG

```
procedure Send_FA (DS : in out Driver_State);
--# global out Messages.Out_Queues;
--# derives Messages.Out_Queues from
--# DS
--# & DS from
--# *;
--# pre D_State(DS) = D_S0;
--# post To_S1(DS~, DS);
```

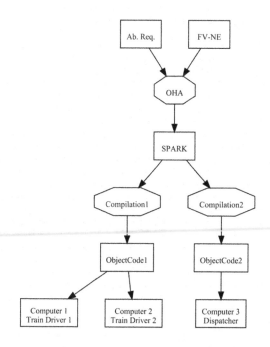

Fig. 15. Summary of Second Case Study

The uninterrupted traceability from Level 0 requirements down to the SPARK source code ensures that the source code fulfils the Safety Requirements of Level 0.

References

Hazell RW, McHattie GV, Wrightson I (2001) Note on Hazard and Operability Studies [HAZOP]. Royal Society of Chemistry, London

Ladkin PB (2000) Causal Reasoning about Aircraft Accidents. In: Koornneef F, van der Meulen M (eds) Computer Safety, Reliability and Security, 19th international conference, SAFECOMP 2000. Springer Lecture Notes in Computer Science, 1943:344-360

Ladkin PB (2005) Ontological Analysis. Safety Systems 14(3) May 2005

Ladkin PB, Leue S (1995) Interpreting Message Flow Graphs. Formal Aspects of Computing 7:473–509

Lamport L (1995) TLA in Pictures. IEEE Trans. Software Engineering SE-21:768-775

Mackie JL (1974) The Cement of the Universe: A Study of Causation. Oxford University Press

Redmill F, Chudleigh M, Catmur J (1999) System Safety: HAZOP and Software HAZOP. John Wiley & Sons, Chichester

VDV (2004) Fahrdienstvorschrift für Nich-bundeseigene Eisenbahnen (FV-NE). Verband Deutscher Verkehrsunternehmen. Ausgabe 1984, Fassung 2004

Safety in Society

Accidents – Policy and Punishment

Are there boundaries to the effectiveness of criminal sanctions in preventing accidental conduct?

Alan Fisher

Fisher Scoggins LLP

London, United Kingdom

Abstract   This paper discusses recent and impending changes in Health and Safety law, questions the utility and supposed justification of tougher criminal sanctions and appeals for greater clarity in health and safety law as to what is truly a criminal offence. It also questions the use of the 'reverse burden of proof' and warns against unintended consequences if responsible people are made to feel that they are being treated unfairly.

1 Introduction

The views expressed in this paper are the personal views of the author alone and not necessarily of Fisher Scoggins LLP. The Health and Safety at Work Act 1974 (HSWA) was a safety revolution but like all revolutions it can run out of steam and some say our approach to safety needs to be revitalised. The law's answer has been more laws and higher penalties, including corporate manslaughter offences for companies, prosecution of directors under Section 37 of HSWA and soon we will see custodial sentences under HSWA. Is it not time to take a deep breath and ask whether this will really make us any safer? Perhaps now is the time to beware of the law of unintended consequences. The over zealous criminalisation of accidental conduct may become counter productive. For instance is fear of prosecution deterring talented people from entering engineering and technology? Are businesses locating their manufacturing operations in other countries because our safety regime is seen as hostile to enterprise? Are organisations deterred from sharing safety critical experiences because of fear that the information might find its way to the regulator and result in a prosecution? Perhaps we are even failing to truly understand the distinction between an accident (which usually means human error) and criminal conduct.

C. Dale, T. Anderson (eds.), *Safety-Critical Systems: Problems, Process and Practice*,
DOI 10.1007/978-1-84882-349-5_7, © Springer-Verlag London Limited 2009

1.1 How Times have Changed!

> 'Unfortunately, health and safety legislation over the past few years has proved to be a large and very blunt instrument when targeting dangerous behaviour. When even the Health and Safety Executive and the Royal Society for the Prevention of Accidents have spoken out about the stifling effect of layers and layers of risk-assessment and health and safety preventative measures now required for the most trivial of events, it is clear that something has gone wrong.'

The above quotation from a recent House of Lords debate (Lord Taylor of Holbeach, 2008) shows that realities and perceptions about health and safety law do not always coincide. On the one hand you do not have to go far to find the popular press making ridicule of some latest 'HSE ban flowerpots' type story and then often in the same paper you see some piece saying we are letting bosses get away with murder. Indeed you can expect the full range of emotions but what is the reality? Do we really need new laws and tougher sanctions? I think both sides of the argument are prone to exaggeration – as far as I know flower pots have not become illegal and similarly the argument that we will benefit from tougher penalties is also overstated. The primary purpose of punishment is to deter unacceptable conduct. Deterrence itself assumes that the existence of the sanction will be brought to mind and thus tip the balance towards an acceptable form of behaviour rather than an unacceptable one. The concept implies a choice between two behaviours. Such a choice is not in the author's view characteristic of how most accidents occur. I have been involved in the legal aftermath of many disasters, including a number of train crashes and most recently the explosion at Buncefield. In every case that I have been involved in I have asked myself, 'What should have been done to prevent this?' Yet in virtually every case I regret that my answer was really only based on 20/20 hindsight. Some time ago I read a book called 'Human Error' by Professor James Reason (Reason 1990). On page 214 he says, *'For those who pick over the bones of other people's disasters, it often seems incredible that these warnings and human failures, seemingly so obvious in retrospect, should have gone unnoticed at the time. Being blessed with both uninvolvement and hindsight, it is a great temptation for retrospective observers to slip into a censorious frame of mind and to wonder at how those people could have been so blind, arrogant, ignorant or reckless.'* Reason is absolutely right. It is far too easy to come along after the event and say we must have tighter and tighter regulation but as the recent collapse of the world banking system shows only too well no amount of regulation (and in this I include use of the criminal law) can ever prevent all possible pathways to disaster.

To answer my own question we certainly must continue to improve our performance but I am not convinced that we need more laws and tougher penalties. Underlying all of this is the very difficult question of whether the greater deterrence that such measures promise will in fact deliver any real improvement in safety performance. So where is this paper going? I intend to consider the much discussed new offence of corporate manslaughter, followed by the impending introduction of wider powers to impose custodial sentences for breach of HSWA and to consider what I believe to be the limited scope to bring about improvements in safety performance by overreliance on deterrent sanctions. Finally I intend to discuss the question of the potential culpability of safety regulators themselves. I do however first want to put my remarks in context. I am not in any way an opponent of better health and safety. I temper my criticism by plainly stating that the HSWA has been a remarkably successful piece of legislation, it has done far more than anyone could really have expected and in the vast majority of cases it is sensibly enforced by sensible and conscientious people with the active support and enthusiasm of the people regulated by it.

2 The Spectrum of Culpability

We have to accept that we are inevitably concerned with a wide range of offenders and an equally wide range of what I will call 'culpability' indicators. Offenders range from the small owner-managed business to the multinational. Culpability ranges from purely inadvertent failure by someone who takes safety very seriously to those who quite frankly don't give a damn. In terms of frequency, most prosecutions are brought against small companies. But the headline grabbing mega-fines tend to fall on household name companies largely because they operate in areas such as transport where errors can have disproportionately high casualties.

2.1 Moral Culpability for Unintended Harm

I have always felt uneasy about the idea of accidental conduct bringing down the full weight of the criminal law. I still remember being taught at law school that the criminal law was as much concerned with the guilty mind ('mens rea') as with the guilty action. I can see a world of difference between, say, deliberately taking a guard off a machine so as to maximise productivity at the cost of increased risk, and being caught out by what is really an unforeseeable concatenation of circumstances[1] such as I believe happened to the driver who went through a red light at Ladbroke Grove, where a non-standard signal and a particular set of circumstances led to tragedy. I also think that at least part of the events at Buncefield may come into this category. Deterrence has a role at the strategic level of management. It can force entrepreneurs to consider safety and correctly resource and organise a responsible approach to risk assessment and mitigation but it cannot ensure that the final outcome of such a management process will be 'safe'.

---

[1] In the sense of the 'accident trajectory' described by Reason in his 'Swiss Cheese' model.

2.2 Indifference about Safety

Of course thoughtless people who cause accidents by showing *no concern* for the safety of others must be stopped and I would agree punished severely in many circumstances. But the blind assumption that we have become so used to, that severe penalties will result in a marked improvement in safety performance, in my view rests on shaky foundations. Fines went up dramatically following the decision in R. v Howe and Sons (Engineers) Ltd (Howe 1999) but fatal accidents continued at much the same rate as before, the most significant improvements having followed in the decade after the HSWA when prosecutions were rare and penalties modest. Those who counsel for severe penalties in the name of deterrence and thereby assume an automatic improvement in safety should in my view provide the evidence. In my submission the argument that severe penalties = greater deterrence = performance improvement needs to be proved otherwise we might just be seeking revenge not deterrence. 'So what?' you might say, 'It can't do any harm to have severe penalties.' Maybe that is right but I do not think it is a self-evident truth.

At one end of the spectrum we can find cases that cry out for custodial sentencing powers. In 2006 Mr Lin Liang Ren was convicted by a jury at Preston Crown Court on 21 counts of manslaughter following the drowning of at least that number of illegal migrant workers picking cockles on Morecambe Bay. No thought had been given to the safety of these people and a custodial penalty was rightly imposed. It is important to note that this was a prosecution not under HSWA but for gross negligence manslaughter. It should be appreciated that the debate is therefore not about whether custodial penalties should be available for cases like this but whether they should be available for lesser cases charged under the HSWA. The policy choice is not therefore between having a custodial sanction or not but whether it is appropriate to have such a sanction available for all cases that are prosecuted under the statute.

The vast majority of cases are not in fact about those who do not give a damn. They are about those who are trying to do their inadequate best. The next case I refer to is at the opposite end of the culpability spectrum from the cockle pickers case.

The former Chief Constable of the Metropolitan Police, Sir John Stevens (now Lord Stevens) gives an insight into what it is like to be on the receiving end of a HSE prosecution in his autobiography 'Not for the faint-hearted' (Stevens 2005). The Commissioner was prosecuted under HSWA following an incident on 24 October 1999 when a young constable fell through a glass skylight of a factory while chasing a suspect. Some years later Sir John found himself spending six weeks in the dock at No 2 Court at the Old Bailey. Sir John attended almost every day of the trial save for one when a particularly sensitive anti terrorist operation had to take priority. Perhaps I may quote from his book:

'When I had the first meeting with solicitors in my office, they warned me that the charges would be difficult to defend, because I would have to prove my innocence, rather than requiring the prosecution to prove their case against me ... I decided that if I was found guilty of neglecting the welfare of my officers, I would resign. I was in no doubt about that. Within a week of knowing I was going to be prosecuted, I wrote a letter of resignation which I put in my safe, directing that that it be handed to the Police authority if the worst came to the worst. Whether or not they accepted my resignation, I would have gone, because my position would have been untenable.'

Fortunately under the law as it was in 2003, the farce of Sir John standing trial was not accompanied by the bizarre prospect of him also facing a custodial penalty as would be the case if the prosecution occurred after the Health and Safety (Offences) Bill becomes law. I have no doubt that if Sir John had resigned London would have paid a high price for the HSE's misconceived decision to prosecute. But equally importantly we should consider how many people are being dissuaded from even offering themselves for important roles because of the fear of taking responsibility for health and safety issues.

My firm is immensely proud of the role we played in defeating the prosecution of Sir John but our experience also embraces the spate of rail disasters of a few years ago. I have two children both with a scientific leaning, the question of choice of career came up in our household at about the same time. The idea of engineering (not to mention railways) or anything that might involve health and safety responsibilities was nowhere to be heard. Imagine if that was the case in all households. I agree it's not research but I am still entitled to put the question, why do a job with health and safety responsibilities when there are wonderful and often much better careers on offer in accountancy and dare I say it becoming a civil servant, taking no responsibility whatsoever and eventually getting a knighthood? I regularly meet decent and responsible engineers and businessmen who believe they are being oppressed by health and safety law.

Again, reality and perception do not always coincide. There are competitive pressures that have to be balanced by regulatory control but overwhelmingly people are trying to do their best but occasionally are simply overwhelmed by the complexity involved in understanding and preventing accidents. Many are really no more than the victims of happenstance.

Unfortunately the problem we face is that the law has to be ready and able to deal with the worst offender in the worst case and that can give rise to an impression that the vast majority of responsible industry is to be tarred with the same brush. It is perhaps too easy to get confused between maximum penalties available and what actually happens in practice but on the other hand there are now literally hundreds of lawyers claiming to specialise in health and safety regulation when twenty years ago there were none, so their fears cannot just be dismissed as paranoia.

3 The New Offence and Tougher Penalties

3.1 Corporate Manslaughter

Much has been said and written about so called corporate killing. Please indulge me if I am telling you what you already know. To demonstrate the changes that have been made I first need to sketch what the law used to be.

Prior to the new Act a company could only be convicted of manslaughter on proof of the following:

- That an individual acting on behalf of the company owed a duty of care to the deceased
- That there was a breach of that duty by that individual
- That such breach caused or contributed to the death
- That the breach was 'gross' in the sense that it showed on the part of the individual a disregard for human life to the extent that it was criminal AND
- That such an individual was at the relevant time a 'directing mind' of the company, its embodiment or a relevant part.

The hurdle that the prosecution found most difficult to overcome was the final element of a 'controlling mind'. This echoes back to my opening comments about criminal responsibility requiring a mental element – in the case of a company to get a conviction you had to show that the individual in which you could find the necessary 'guilt' had a sufficient role in the company to be its 'controlling mind'. In practice this proved to be unworkable as the failed prosecution following the Herald of Free Enterprise disaster demonstrated and subsequent failed cases confirmed. The particular limitation of the old law was that you could not aggregate different failings by different individuals within the organisation and if you could find someone against whom sufficiently serious allegations could be made you then had to show that he or she was sufficiently high up in the company to be its controlling mind. This proved to be virtually impossible in the case of very large organisations. In short, as one of my partners has put it, you had to find someone who was both *'big enough and bad enough'*.

The new offence is to be found in the Corporate Manslaughter and Corporate Homicide Act 2007. Reading the title your first question might be, does this create two offences and if so how does one differ from the other? In fact there is only one new offence: in England and Wales it is called Corporate Manslaughter, and in Scotland, Corporate Homicide. The offence can be committed by a corporation, a department of government or a public authority, a police force, a partnership, trade union or employers' association.

The definition of the offence is to be found in section 1(1), *'An organisation to which this section applies is guilty of an offence if the way in which its activities* are managed or organised (a) causes a person's death, and (b) amounts to a gross breach of a relevant duty of care owed by the organisation to the deceased.'

Section 1(3) provides that, 'An organisation is guilty of an offence under this section only if the way in which its activities are managed or organised by its senior management is a substantial element in the breach referred to in subsection (1).

I want to focus on just three elements, namely (a) what is a 'gross breach'? (b) what is a relevant duty of care? and (c) who are 'senior management'?

3.1.1 What is a 'Gross' Breach?

This is to my mind a very difficult question. The starting point is that the breach must be negligent as we would understand that term in civil law, i.e. conduct falling below the standard to be expected, but how far below that standard does it have to be to be gross? The statute has left that difficult decision to the jury. Section 8(2) gives the jury some guidance, 'The jury must consider whether the evidence shows that the organisation failed to comply with any health and safety legislation that relates to the alleged breach, and if so (a) how serious that failure was; (b) how much of a risk of death it posed.'

Section 8(3) gives the jury some further guidance so that it may also '(a) consider the extent to which the evidence shows that there were attitudes, policies, systems or accepted practices within the organisation that were likely to have encouraged any such failure as is mentioned in subsection (2), or to have produced tolerance of it; (b) have regard to any health and safety guidance that relates to the alleged breach.'

Section 8(4) then says that section 8 does not prevent the jury from having regard to any other matters they consider relevant.

Of course it is right that the jury should look at the extent to which Health and Safety legislation was breached. So if the law had said for instance in the case of the Piper Alpha tragedy, that the operator must fit subsea isolation valves so that they could have turned the supply off immediately below the platform rather than at the end of a pipe miles away, and they had not done so, that would have been a perfectly legitimate indicator of a 'gross' breach. If the law had said fit such a valve, the compliance task for the operator would be easy – you just do it and if you can't do it then you have to find another way of operating your platform that does comply with the law. However the trend in regulation has been away from prescriptive rules such as this and towards 'goal setting' standards. Sections 2 and 3 of HSWA are a case in point: they are the two most widely used sections when it comes to founding a prosecution but they are 'goal setting' standards – respectively you must do everything that is reasonably practicable to minimise the risk posed to your employees and the public. When coupled with the reverse burden of proof provisions of section 40 (explained later) many have argued that if there has been an accident it is virtually impossible to say that the duty has been discharged and it is therefore a strict liability not dependent on real moral culpability. I have personal experience of appearing before a tribunal following one of the more spectacular train crashes where the party that I was seeking to recover a substantial liability against had been convicted under section 3 and the submission was conscientiously made that the conviction should be disregarded as it was no indicator of negligence but simply one of bad luck! I don't think section 3 does in fact create a truly strict liability but I do understand the views of those who argue that it does. If they are right a conviction becomes more of an 'accident tax' than an indicator of moral culpability. However that debate can be put to one side as it is self-evident that there is a significant moral difference between failing to comply with a prescriptive rule where compliance is simply a matter of fact and failing to comply with a *'goal setting'* rule where compliance involves a complex exercise of judgement.

The practical application of section 8(3) is I think going to be interesting. In the prosecution following the Hatfield disaster proceedings were taken against the then head of Railtrack and it was suggested that under his stewardship Railtrack had put the pursuit of profit ahead of its safety responsibilities. It was an allegation which spectacularly failed when the evidence was produced to show that he had a highly developed sense of 'safety culture' and had taken a close personal interest in safety related issues. So in terms of practical defence strategies if your organisation were ever unfortunate enough to be prosecuted under the new law make sure you have a 'Hi Vis' evidence trail that you can deploy to show that you have sought to implement an effective 'safety culture'.

While it is obviously a desirable thing to demonstrate to the jury that you took your health and safety responsibilities seriously on matters of sentence, this section is making such things as attitudes relevant to the determination of a critical component of the offence itself. That seems to me to be an odd way of drafting a law as whether or not the offence has been committed might depend more on form than on real substance. But it is followed by a subsection which is even more puzzling allowing the jury to consider virtually anything else!

It would appear to make admissible virtually any evidence that a prosecutor thinks might assist in getting the jury 'on side'. The only limitation I can see is that there would have to be some causal link between the 'bad attitude' or the 'anything else' and the fatality. What is or is not a causal link is a difficult question and one which could well not be understood by some juries. The area is not without its own jurisprudential difficulties, as expertly explained in a recent paper (Popat and Donnelly 2008).

3.1.2 What is a Relevant Duty of Care?

Section 3 tells us what is meant by a relevant duty. Subsection 3(1) bases the existence of a duty on the law of negligence and then identifies a number of specific relationships where a duty will attach. I paraphrase the section below:

(a) a duty owed to its employees or to other persons working for the organisation or performing services for it
(b) a duty owed as occupier of premises
(c) a duty owed in connection with:
   (i) the supply by the organisation of goods and services
   (ii) carrying on construction or maintenance operations
   (iii) carrying on 'any other activity on a commercial basis'
   (iv) the use or keeping of any plant, vehicle 'or other thing'
(d) a duty owed to a person who, by reason of being a person within...subsection (2) is someone for whose safety the organisation is responsible.

Now the first question which came to mind when I first looked at this was why is this section so convoluted? I think the answer is that it is intended to be far ranging for some and narrow for others. The 'others' are I suggest the emergency services and that would be consistent with the equally long and convoluted wording used in Section 6 from which mercifully I will spare you. As to the unlucky 'some', I do not expect 2(1)(a) to cause much difficulty in the case of a direct relationship between employer and employee. However where 'outsourced' activities and 'home workers' or 'specialist subcontractors' are involved it is sometimes difficult to ascertain who exactly is the duty holder. The additional wording added to subsection (a) clearly anticipates that this net is intended to be cast far and wide. Subsection 2(1)(b) is self explanatory. A hotel for instance would owe a duty to customers using its facilities but I can see there may be issues as to what exactly is the nature of the 'occupation' required to be an occupier. Subsection 2(2)(c) includes the supply of goods and services and by the following sub paragraphs further extends the catchment area to specifically include construction and maintenance services. In short the intention is clearly to provide a wide definition of situations where a duty can arise and the practical problem is likely to be identifying situations where there it can be confidently stated that there is no duty. I wonder if it would not have been clearer and equally comprehensive to have simply provided that a relevant duty would be any situation where there would be a duty under HSWA. The fact that this has not been done would seem to support the view that this law is intended to have an even more far reaching scope. For the sake of completeness I should mention Section 2(2) which provides the auxiliary definitions necessary to make sense of Subsection 2(1)(d) and is intended to apply the new offence to what are known in the legal trade as 'deaths in custody'.

However the important point to note is that the section is telling you where you might find a relationship which might impose a relevant duty, whether there actually is and most importantly whether it has been broken is always a matter of fact.

3.1.3 Who are 'Senior Managers'?

The Act offers little guidance but I would suspect it will be set lower in the organisation than you may think. There is a contrary view amongst my colleagues who think that some guidance can be drawn from the cases decided before the new Act.

They say that it may drop the bar down a little in the management hierarchy, but given the need for the gross breach to be '*in or about the way that the business or a substantial part of it is organised or managed*', the only acts and omissions which will be attributable to the company are those of pretty high executives who have influence over the way the business as a whole (or nearly so) is run and which direction it goes. My partner Mark Scoggins acted for some of the Defendants in the prosecutions arising out of the Hatfield derailment. In Hatfield, the Balfour Beatty 'Regional Director' of the East Coast Main Line maintenance contract had a staff of about 1,400, an annual budget of about £50m+, and his contract contributed around 25% of the entire turnover of the maintenance business. But he did not attend main board meetings. The trial judge ruled he was not a directing mind of the maintenance company despite the significant contribution his contract made to overall turnover. In effect he was 'helping to run a part of the business', not 'running the business of the maintenance company'.

Before leaving corporate manslaughter it is necessary to say something about sentencing. First of all you can't put a company in prison so no question of a custodial sentence arises but the indications are that the sentencing guidelines will require courts to impose penalties in the region of between 2% and 10% of turnover. Note that this is not profit but turnover and could amount to some very big numbers for any large corporation that is convicted.

However, please do not let me give you the impression that corporate manslaughter is the biggest threat on the radar. Save for the failure to accurately define the kind of conduct that it is or should be aimed at (which I believe should have been can be categorised as 'reckless disregard'), I think it is to be welcomed and may even have levelled the playing field somewhat between large and small organisations. My private fear is that come the next major accident – calls for prosecution will be draped across the press whether justified or not and that in turn will translate into prosecutions that are not justified in terms of moral culpability but will be successful because of the failure of the Act to properly address the level of moral delinquency required. It will then become part and parcel of a new form of witch hunting.

The new law has replaced the old law as to charges of manslaughter brought against corporations but please do not think that it also abolishes the existing law that allows individuals to be charged with gross negligence manslaughter. An individual can still be charged with gross negligence manslaughter at common law. It is a charge which seems to be used with some regularity particularly against the medical profession. You will recall that two junior doctors at Southampton were recently convicted and received suspended custodial sentences. I only have time to summarise briefly the constituents of the offence.

- There must be a duty of care owed by the accused to the deceased.
- Death of the deceased must be caused by breach of that duty of care by the accused.

- The breach of the duty of care by the accused must be so great as to be characterised as gross negligence and therefore a crime.

Exactly what makes a breach so great as to become criminal remains a difficulty and is a question for the jury who often ask the judge to explain and find that the explanation takes the matter no further – it simply remains a matter for them.

You will also know that there was a case a few years ago where Mr Lee Harper, a managing director of a small construction firm, was imprisoned for sixteen months following a fatal accident at a construction site. Details of the case can be read on the HSE website (HSE 2005).

Neither should you allow Section 37 of the HSWA to fall from your radar. Section 37 can be used to prosecute an individual director where a breach of HSWA has occurred with the 'consent and connivance' of that individual. In practice a trend has been noted by my colleagues where both the company and one or more individual directors are charged and it then 'becomes known' that the charges against the individuals will be dropped if the company agrees to plead guilty. That brings me to my second topic which is the imminent introduction of custodial penalties for breach of the HSWA.

3.2 Custodial Penalties under HSWA

The Health and Safety (Offences) Bill was given an unopposed second reading in the House of Lords on 4 July 2008. By the time you get to read this script I expect it to have become law. Introducing the Bill to the House of Lords, Lord Crocott gave a lucid testimonial to the success of the HSWA, *'The record of the 1974 Act speaks for itself. Between 1974 and 2007, the rate of injuries per 100,000 employees fell by a huge 76% and Britain had the lowest rate of fatal injuries in the European Union in 2003 which is the most recent year for which figures are available. The EU average was 2.5 fatalities per 100,000 workers; the figure in the UK was 1.1.'*

So you might ask, why is there a need to increase the penalties? There are officially three reasons. (1) To bring them up to date so that they match the offence. Not so sure about that, as the figures tend to suggest that the Act continues to work well and I seldom hear courts complaining that they have insufficient sentencing power particularly as the Crown Court already enjoys the power to give unlimited fines and the effect of the Howe decision was to encourage them to use their powers which they do not seem to have found it necessary to do. (2) It is said that it will enable more effective deterrence. This is again put forward as a self-evident fact, and if there are people who are making conscious decisions not to comply because they think it is cheaper to not comply and pay the penalty, then I would agree the penalty needs to be higher. However I question first of all whether there are many such businesses and secondly whether if there are, would they ever comply. (3) The third justification is to establish greater efficiency in the administration of justice. The logic here is that by increasing the sentencing powers of lower courts more cases will stay at magistrates' level. As I think is generally accepted, prosecution is (in most cases) the last resort and a relatively small part of the regulators work so I am not quite sure that I follow this reasoning. I think the real reason is that a number of powerful trade unions want this measure and it is politically convenient to give them what they want. Whether it is appreciated that the new powers are just as likely to be used against the worker as they are against the boss remains to be seen.

It is said that there is a history of judges complaining that they cannot imprison people for breaches of the HSWA. There is the well known example of a trader convicted in 2006 who put customers at risk by pretending to be a CORGI registered fitter when he was not. In my firm's experience we have not encountered such a case, but I presume that the Government have a large file of letters from Judges to this effect. Perhaps I will ask to see it under the Freedom of Information Act. I am sure that there are some cases where a custodial penalty is well deserved and in principle I have no issue with such penalties being available. My issue is with the well established trend for making legislation opaque as to when such sanctions are to be imposed. I have already subjected you to my views on the lack of definition of 'gross' negligence in the Corporate Manslaughter Act. Imprisonment is a serious punishment, the exact circumstances when it is to be imposed may not always be capable of being set out in detail in a piece of legislation but we seem to have come to a stage where the policy is to deliberately leave it as vague as possible.

Yet, I think there is a consensus on when a draconian penalty such as imprisonment should rightly be imposed in a safety-related prosecution. That is where there has been something that is distinctively more than inadvertent or accidental conduct. What a human factors expert would call a 'violation' as opposed to a 'slip', 'lapse' or 'mistake'. Deliberately continuing with an unsafe practice contrary to a prohibition notice would be an obvious case. Selling food believing it may be contaminated is another; knowingly permitting workers to work with blue or brown asbestos without proper equipment and training is another. Fortunately these things are comparatively rare and I would suggest that they have a common feature namely knowledge of the danger and either culpable intent or recklessness in the face of it. These are indeed areas where deterrence can work and I find it intellectually unsatisfactory that given that we are probably all in agreement with what these distinguishing factors are that it is not possible to set them out clearly in the statute itself?

In any event by the time you read this I expect that custodial sentences will be available for almost all offences under HSWA. I suspect that the responsible managers will feel even more oppressed and the true villains won't even notice until the prosecution arises. Essentially I welcome the new sentencing powers subject only to a deep unease that what today is said to be a sanction for the evil few might in certain circumstances be misused by overzealous prosecutors to do immense harm to the responsible but unlucky offender rather than few real villains who should alone be subject to it. My concern about overzealous prosecutors has recently been demonstrated by the prosecution following a fatality at the famous Gatcombe Park horse riding event. Both the CPS and the HSE publish their prosecution policies. They say that prosecution is always a last resort. In this case the Local Authority was the prosecutor on behalf of the HSE. It also published its prosecution policy, it also said that prosecution was a last resort and that the mere fact of a fatality did not determine that a prosecution would be brought. In fact that was the *only* reason that this prosecution was commenced and then continued with relentlessly even though there was not the slightest evidence of moral culpability. Eventually the prosecution was struck out as an abuse of the process of the Court (Vann 2008).

There is one further aspect of the new penalties concerning the possible infringement of the Human Rights Act that I think I should make you aware of. It was described by the Under-Secretary of State Lord McKenzie in the House of Lords debate as being a *'complex and detailed issue but one of crucial importance'*. I cannot improve on the way he put the issue so I quote what he said. '*The convention point at issue is Article 6.2, which confirms the right to a fair trial and the presumption of innocence, and its relationship with Section 40 of the 1974 Act, which reverses the burden of proof on to the defendant when the offence is subject to the statutory qualification "so far as is reasonably practicable" The difficulty with any "reverse burden of proof" provision is that it is an inroad into the presumption of innocence enshrined in Article 6.2 of the convention. Section 40 of the Act was challenged in a prosecution conducted by HSE in 2002 against a plant hire contractor, David Janway Davies, for breach of Section 3(1) of the 1974 act. The Court of Appeal ruled against Janway Davies holding that the reverse burden of proof contained in Section 40 was compatible with the convention. The Court's approach was to examine whether fair balance had been struck between the fundamental right of the individual and the general interests of the community, it being for the State to justify an inroad into the presumption of innocence "which should be no greater than is necessary, justified and proportionate". On the basis of this and other case law the government have looked carefully at the compatibility with human rights legislation. We consider that the proposals in the Bill, including the widened scope for custodial sentence are reasonable and proportionate and that section 40 continues to represent a fair balance between the rights of the individual to a fair trial and the protection of life and limb from dangerous work practices. I should stress that, where section 40 has an impact, there is first of all still an onus on the prosecution to show that there is a prima facie case, and the prosecutor would do so by referring to the reasonably practicable steps that an individual could have taken.'*

I confess that I have got a bit of a bee in my bonnet over the 'reverse burden of proof'. I certainly agree it is a complex issue and in order to avoid saying anything controversial without fully understanding how the Government reached its conclusion I asked first the HSE and then the Department of Work and Pensions to disclose under the Freedom of Information Act any documents relating to how the Government have 'looked carefully' at this issue. I had rather assumed that they would have commissioned a QC to provide an opinion and the response I received from a Mr Philip Noble at DWP seems to confirm that there is some sort of document but he won't share it with me because it is apparently said to be privileged. This I find difficult to accept as when the Freedom of Information Act was debated in Parliament an assurance was given by Lord Falconer that 'blanket' claims to legal privilege would not be made.

Mr Noble said that if I did not like his decision I could ask for it to be reviewed which I duly did while at the same time bringing to his attention the assurances given by the Government about not making inappropriate claims to legal privilege. I have not heard from him since![2]

In any event I have done my best to try and inform myself about all sides of this argument but all that Mr Noble has done is to further reinforce my belief that you have to take what Governments say about the way new powers will be used with a very large pinch of salt just like prosecution policy statements.

So at the risk of displaying my ignorance I ask you to note that the passage from Janway Davies cited by the Under-Secretary of State emphasised three elements: (a) necessity (b) justification and (c) proportionality.

I would add that the there is a fourth element that was mentioned previously namely that *it is for the State to justify an inroad into the presumption of innocence.* So has the State shown that a reverse burden of proof is necessary in the context of a *custodial* penalty under HSWA? If as we are told a custodial penalty is only appropriate in an extreme case how can the reversal of the burden be necessary? If it is an extreme case the evidence will be overwhelming. As I understand the rhetoric a custodial sentence will only be appropriate in the clearest case of wrongdoing. If so surely it follows that the State can and should be able to prove its case without any shortcuts and further that in order to uphold the moral force of the condemnation of such an offence it should do so. And further if as we are told the prosecutor will already have shown what was reasonably practicable how can it be said that a shortcut is necessary?

Justified – well if it is not necessary it would seem to follow that it is not justified.

Proportionate – sending someone to prison for accidental conduct is just about at the top end of the human rights scale – so where is the case that the use of such a shortcut is proportionate?

I am sure that if the DWP ever discloses its legal reasoning in support of the opinion it has formed these concerns will be easily resolved. I will let you know when I present this paper next February. However by then the Bill will be an Act and any chance of a proper democratic debate over these issues before this measure becomes law will have long since passed.

---

[2] Time of writing August 2008.

4 The Liability of Regulators

This brings me to my final topic namely the liability of regulators themselves. I see this as being a counterpoint to any discussion of the punishments to be imposed on those who transgress their obligations to conduct themselves in a safe way. What if the regulator himself is guilty of falling below the standards of competence imposed on those he regulates? I understand that if HSE itself transgresses the procedure is to send itself a letter! I know of no criminal sanction that is available but theoretically they could be sued for negligence.

The only case I know of where the HSE have been joined in litigation as a party allegedly jointly responsible for causing an accident was Ladbroke Grove. And yes I was the lawyer behind that. The immediate response of the HSE was to trot out the usual old stalwarts such as: they are not a duty holder and to impose a duty would stifle them in the performance of their public duties. None of these arguments in my view hold water and are no better than civil service excuses. HSE's immediate response was to try and strike out the proceedings on the basis that they could not be subject to a civil action. I am pleased to say they failed in that regard but it was something of a hollow victory as eventually the proceedings were discontinued for commercial reasons. Still I think we opened the door and left it ajar. The recent report by the Parliamentary Ombudsman into the failure of regulators revealed in the wake of the Equitable Life scandal must surely serve as a wakeup call that regulators are just as likely to make errors as anyone else. In a healthy democracy they should be more open about their own failings, to do so would further the interests of good regulation as the regulator would be seen to live in the same world as the regulated

We need to have better ways of holding regulators accountable for their own failures. Co-incidentally the same thought has occupied the Law Commission as at the time of writing they have just issued a consultation paper entitled 'Administrative Redress: Public Bodies and the Citizen' (Law Commission 2008). Don't hold your breath if you think this might be going anywhere that will make regulators more accountable to the public! It does promise an easier route to having decisions reviewed by other civil servants but at the cost of restricting access to the Courts. In a nutshell what it canvasses is a different system of civil justice for public bodies – in the case of what comes within the ambiguous description of *'truly public'* functions they propose a so called *'principle'* of *'modified corrective justice'*: this is said to reflect the special position of such bodies and afford them appropriate protection from *'unmeritorious'*[3] claims. In fairness I should say that it is a 180 page complex document. It seems to me to advocate two different systems - one for the governed (*'us'*) and another for the governors (*'them'*). It proposes a higher threshold of culpable conduct when applied to *'them'* than applies to the rest of *'us'*. If so, regulators would only be liable if their breach is not just negligent but

---

[3] One would have thought that the Courts were perfectly well equipped to protect against 'unmeritorious claims' – they tend to throw them out with costs against the claimant!

'really serious'. Even better for *'them'* they might also be excused from some of the less obviously fair rules of damages such as joint and several liability that *'us'* are subject to. One might say 'nice law if you can make it'!

In the paper there is a discussion of why we should not be concerned that exempting public authorities from the rigors of the ordinary law would reduce its deterrent effect. Apparently research indicates that the behaviour of public authorities is not much influenced by deterrence. I am not sure if that makes me sleep easier in my bed!

This is a dreadfully superficial treatment of a very serious topic tagged onto the end of a long and I fear boring presentation so I do encourage you to download the consultation paper from the Law Commission's web site and form your own views. So I will just conclude by recalling to memory what the great professor Dicey once described as an essential feature of the rule of law namely one law applying equally to all. I end where I began – how times have changed!

References

Howe (1999) R v Howe and Son (Engineers) Ltd 1 All ER 249

HSE (2005) Company director jailed following roof work fatality. HSE press release. http://www.hse.gov.uk/press/2005/e05003.htm. Accessed 13 August 2008

Law Commission (2008) Administrative Redress: Public Bodies and the Citizen. Law Commission Consultation Paper. http://www.lawcom.gov.uk/remedies.htm Accessed 13 August 2008

Lord Taylor of Holbeach (2008) Hansard, 4 July 2008

Popat P, Donnelly K (2008) Causation. Henderson Chambers Health Safety and Environment Seminar, 17 April 2008

Reason J (1990) Human Error. Cambridge University Press, Cambridge

Stevens J (2005) Not for the Faint-Heated. Weidenfeld & Nicolson, London

Vann H (2008) Gatcombe Park: Prosecution Collapses as proceedings deemed an Abuse of Process. Crown Office Chambers Health & Safety and Regulatory Law Update. http://newsweaver.co.uk/crownoffice/e_article001151041.cfm?x=b11,0,w Accessed 13 August 2008

Professional Issues in System Safety Engineering

John McDermid, Martyn Thomas and Felix Redmill

University of York, Thomas Associates and Redmill Consultancy

York, UK   Bath, UK   London, UK

Abstract   For many years the profession of system safety engineering has been emerging. This paper argues that the time has now come when it requires recognition, a voice, proper governance and leadership.

System safety engineering is an amalgam of many disciplines, in particular, software engineering, safety engineering and management, and systems engineering, and this paper shows that system safety engineering must address the most difficult aspects of all of these. But professional matters extend beyond merely technical considerations, and the paper concludes by showing why there is the need for a new professional body.

1 Introduction

This paper is concerned with professional issues in system safety engineering. As befits a paper in the Safety-critical Systems Symposium (SSS), it focuses on the issues relating to software-intensive systems, although the concerns of professionalism go much wider than that. Software is now the key to the functionality of most modern systems, e.g., being instrumental in providing perhaps 80% of the functions in a modern aircraft. Much software in such complex systems is now safety-related or safety-critical, and failures of this software can give rise to incidents if not accidents. For example, the massive altitude fluctuations experienced by a Boeing 777 flying out of Perth in August 2005 were caused by errors in fault management logic (ATSB 2007). The primary professional concern addressed here is with the development and assessment of such safety-related or safety-critical software, and the competence of the individuals engaged in these activities.

The paper starts by considering the challenges of complex software-intensive systems. It then introduces safety concerns, before going on to discuss professionalism and the possibility of establishing a 'new' professional body in the UK.

C. Dale, T. Anderson (eds.), *Safety-Critical Systems: Problems, Process and Practice*,
DOI 10.1007/978-1-84882-349-5_8, © Springer-Verlag London Limited 2009

2 The Essential Nature of Software-intensive Systems

Software-intensive systems are inherently complex. They are used in applications that have demanding requirements, e.g., controlling an unstable aircraft such as Typhoon, often with added difficulty from handling unreliable sensors, supporting a graphical user interface, having to schedule overlapping tasks, and the need to use general-purpose components. Digital systems can exist in huge numbers of discrete states – far too many to comprehend or test exhaustively.

Systems are composed from subsystems that, viewed from a narrow perspective, are systems in their own right. In what follows we use the term *subsystem* only where it is necessary for clarity.

A system's most important requirements always exist in the real world, not at the hardware or software interfaces[1]. For example, medical systems are required to deliver the right dose of drugs or to alert medical staff to a patient's condition; aircraft are required to transport passengers safely between airports; engine controllers are required to deliver power and to achieve fuel efficiency and low emissions.

Viewed in this way, a system comprises not just the technology but also all the people who work with the technology to deliver the requirements. Pilots are part of aircraft systems, just as radiographers are part of radiotherapy systems, and the operators were part of the nuclear power system at Three Mile Island (USNRC 2007). This *sociotechnical* perspective turns the interfaces between pilots and their avionics into internal system interfaces (or subsystems) and focuses attention on how the pilots are trained to respond to changes in other parts of the system, as much as on how these subsystems are designed to respond to inputs from the pilots. Training simulators and airline procedure manuals are then seen to be safety-related, and should be included in any system hazard analysis. If the humans are considered to be outside the system, it is too easy to attribute failures to 'human error' without considering whether the design of the overall system made such errors more likely to happen, or harder to detect before they led to an accident.

Transforming these real-world requirements into specifications for hardware and software systems and subsystems, and operator training, is difficult and prone to error. Accidents have occurred where the hardware, software and operators behaved as specified but nevertheless contributed to the circumstances that led to the accident. For example, one factor that led to an aircraft overrunning a runway in Warsaw in 1993 (Ladkin 1996) was that the pilots were unable to engage reverse thrust on the engines because the methods used to detect that the aircraft was on the ground determined that the aircraft was still flying in those conditions (landing in a crosswind, on a wet runway, with only one landing gear in contact with the runway). It is important that the link between the real world requirements and the

---

[1] For an excellent discussion of the implications, see Michael Jackson's books (Jackson 1996, Jackson 2001).

system or subsystem specifications is made as explicit and visible as possible, so that assumptions can be reviewed thoroughly by experts in the application domain.

System failures are system phenomena; components may fail without the system failing. For example, system operators may be able to limit the effects of a technology failure through work-arounds, as pilots are trained to do if their flight management system or an engine fails. In the case of the Perth incident, the pilots regained control of the aircraft, even though the Air Data and Inertial Reference Unit (ADIRU) gave erroneous acceleration data.

The hardware and software architecture may also recover from subsystem failures: a combat aircraft may have a low complexity *fly home* mode designed to survive damage that destroys combat capability, and an industrial plant will often have low-complexity protection systems that limit the system failures that might otherwise result from a failure of the control system.

It is almost always the right architectural choice to put most of the inherent complexity of the application into software[2]. This reduces the size and complexity of the hardware (with an accompanying reduction in components, component interfaces, power consumption, weight, volume, and random failures) and may reduce the need for human operators. Also, digital technology is often the only way of meeting the complex demands of the system's environment.

Software faults can be characterised on a scale from small to large, where a large fault is one that leads to erroneous behaviour for a wide range of inputs. Some faults may be so small that the combination of inputs and system states that lead to failure is very unlikely to occur during testing or operation of the system. Such faults are often colloquially described as *obscure*.

Almost universally, the software development process contains an extensive period of testing and error correction. By definition, large faults are more likely to be discovered (and therefore corrected) than small faults. In the usual situation, where the software contains very many faults[3] and where testing continues until the failure rate of the software during testing falls to an acceptably low rate, a relatively small number of relatively large faults will have been removed, leaving a high number of obscure faults in the fielded system. These faults may lead to failures when the system encounters conditions in operation that differ from those met during testing. Indeed data from operating system field failures suggests that about 30% of the faults seen would be expected to occur only once every 3,000 years of operation – in other words there are a lot of obscure faults.

Systems are usually required to respond smoothly to changing inputs, without sudden discontinuities in behaviour except under extreme conditions where an alarm may be raised or a protective shutdown initiated. Physical structures behave smoothly within limits – wings flex, springs extend and contract, buildings sway –

---

[2] We include custom hardware, such as Application Specific Integrated Circuits (ASICS) and Field Programmable Arrays (FPGAs), in the term 'software', as much of the complexity of modern digital systems now rests in such devices.

[3] Studies have shown typical fault densities between 5 and 30 faults per KLoC *after* the software has completed all testing (Pfleeger and Hatton 1997, German and Mooney 2001).

and this continuous behaviour has formed the intuitions of generations of engineers. But these intuitions mislead when we are dealing with digital systems, because they function by moving between very many discrete states and any of these transitions may be faulty. It is therefore unsound to infer that a system will behave predictably for inputs that lie between those that have been tested, without any further information regarding linearity or continuity of behaviour; in principle, a successful test only shows that the system works as expected under the precise circumstances of the test and, without further analysis of the system logic, no interpolation or extrapolation from test results can be justified.

Evidence that a particular development process has been followed gives very limited information about the properties of the resulting system. It is usually *necessary* to follow a rigorous process, so that claims about the delivered system can be shown to derive from properties of the system architecture or design, but the evidence provided by the process is second-order: it provides the basis on which first-order evidence from testing or analysis can be trusted.

It is possible to *reason* about system properties if this is done using appropriate abstractions, and if the delivered system can be shown to implement the abstractions accurately. Advances since 1980 in mathematically-based methods and tools have made rigorous analysis and even formal proof cost effective for some classes of industrial and commercial systems (Amey 2002). Increasingly, analysis and reasoning are seen as central to the professional development of dependable systems (Jackson et al. 2007), and the idea of evidence-based approaches to systems and software is encompassed in recent safety standards, e.g. Defence Standard 00-56 Issue 3 (MoD 2004).

3 Matters Arising from Safety Considerations

The previous section presented some of the software issues in system safety. These are critical, because almost all modern control systems are software-based and their effectiveness and dependability, including safety, are reliant on competent and professional software engineering. But, though it may be possible in some cases to design and produce software for a safety-related application without safety expertise, it is unwise to attempt it. The key reason why system safety engineering is a profession in its own right is that it is not the re-presentation of any single existing discipline but the conjunction of more than one discipline. In particular, it brings safety engineering and management together with all other disciplines relevant to the system – and this will normally include software engineering. Further, it does so in a specific way: by taking a holistic, 'systems' approach (i.e. via systems engineering).

From a safety perspective, taking a systems approach applies not only to the physical aspects of a system but also to time: to the physical aspects across the system's entire life cycle. From the earliest point in the life of a system, safety must be addressed, in the context not only of operation but also of maintenance and change, and beyond that to decommissioning and disposal. The requirement to consider the life cycle of the system, rather than that of only the project, is not common in software engineering – and the need to address safety is limited to certain specialist arenas. This latter observation is a concern because many more systems and technologies are becoming critical, e.g., when voice over IP (VoIP) is used in communication between air traffic controllers and aircraft.

System safety involves not merely attempting to make a system do what it is required to do, but, just as importantly, to ensure that it will not do anything that might be unsafe. This may seem straightforward, but its accomplishment demands a knowledge of what system states and behaviour could be unsafe, which, in turn, requires carrying out risk analysis and deriving safety requirements – which then have to be met in implementation. This may be contrasted with traditional software engineering, in which a system specification is, typically, primarily functional. Also, where there are non-functional requirements these tend not to be so demanding as in safety-related or safety-critical applications.

Though some safety requirements may be derived early (i.e. from knowing the system's objectives and specification), most can only be established as the system is being designed – hence it is problematic to integrate them into the system, as this inevitably means a series of design iterations, as new safety requirements are introduced and the design changed (and re-analysed). The derivation of safety requirements is challenging and subtle, and must be based on careful risk analysis.

If carried out thoroughly, risk analysis reveals the safety hazards that could be caused by the system, and the risks posed by them. It should also reveal how and under what conditions the hazards would mature into accidents. From this knowledge, safety requirements are derived, each with the purpose of contributing to risk reduction. It is then the responsibility of system designers – system architects and hardware and software engineers – to determine how to implement the safety requirements.

The implementation of functional requirements is straightforward: make the system perform the function. But for safety requirements it is more complicated. Almost no risk can be eliminated entirely, so, while a risk-reduction function may be defined precisely, a further question arises: by how much must the safety function reduce the risk to justify a claim that it is as low as reasonably practicable (ALARP)? Safe design, including the evaluation of whether or not the result is 'safe enough', is a great deal more complex than functional design.

Moreover, for software-based systems, there are added difficulties. Failure modes in the previous generation of control systems, based on electromechanical technology, were predominantly random, which enabled quantitative risk analysis, based on probability theory, to be employed. But software does not fail randomly. It fails systematically, and the probability of failure – and, thus, the degree of risk – cannot be derived either accurately or with high confidence. Additionally, the multiplicity of logical paths through a software-based system means that the likelihood of unintended interactions between subsystems is high – which is difficult to detect and also a potential cause of both system failures and accidents.

The dominance of software-based control systems therefore gives the opportunity to introduce new hazards, and to introduce new causes of hazards, which must be identified by risk analysis and mitigated in design.

On top of all this, problematic though it can be, design for safety cannot be assigned an unlimited budget. Systems must be cost-effective or they won't find a market. Design compromises are necessary for the production of a system that is both adequately safe (i.e., whose risks have all been reduced ALARP) and capable of being marketed at a profit. Achieving safety is thus a balancing act – but the balancing must be done as part of the development process, for the goal should be to prevent accidents in the first place, or at least to make them sufficiently improbable that the risk is acceptable, rather than merely to prevent their recurrence.

Because the causal factors in many accidents include operators (e.g. pilots, radiographers) making false assumptions about their systems, both system design and risk analysis should be informed by knowledge of human capabilities (both physical and cognitive) and by 'domain knowledge'. This is knowledge, not only of what a system is required by its specification to do, but also of what its intended users expect it to do, how they will operate it, to what extent they are likely to take it beyond its design constraints, and what the effects of such excursions would (or could) be. But, for system designers, even such attention to the domain of operation needs to be in two stages. First, they must acquire sufficient information to enable them to query the initial specification, cater for risks that are inherent in the application or the industry sector, and place safety constraints on system users. Second, because it is only the complete system design that provides the basis for a detailed risk analysis, it is when this has been developed that the finer points of users' background, training, beliefs about the system, and intentions for using it must be analysed for the hazards that they may create.

As well as safe design and development, system safety requires operational decisions. It cannot be achieved merely by following rules. For one thing, all circumstances cannot be covered by rules. Indeed, all circumstances cannot be predicted. When something occurs outside of the rules, the operational professional must make decisions; more so when occurrences are outside of what's predicted; and even more so when they are beyond previous experience. Further, because safety depends on it, decisions cannot be avoided, unsafe (or potentially unsafe) situations cannot be ignored. Indeed, as system safety engineering improves, the reliance on operators is likely to increase. The engineers will have dealt effectively with all the predicted problems – with the operators left to respond to those that were not predicted. This is one of the reasons that there is a growing interest in system resilience (Hollnagel et al. 2006).

From this it may be deduced that the engineering and management of operational safety requires (at least) three stages of professionalism. First there is the competent and thorough creation of rules to govern a defined situation or range of situations. Second, there is the prediction, using risk analysis, of what might, or is likely to, occur under defined circumstances. Third, there is the need for sufficient understanding of a system and its applications to be competent to cope with all possible circumstances. This includes thinking quickly and behaving flexibility in order to manage potentially unsafe system behaviour that is unexpected and even unprecedented. Each of these responsibilities is considerable and demands the highest level of professionalism. They may be discharged by different people at different times, but the combination of the three amounts to a professional discipline that extends across all of the traditional engineering professions.

So system safety engineering embraces system design and development – including software engineering – but is not limited to it. It extends across the entire life of a system, from concept to disposal, and addresses safety at each stage. It employs risk analysis as an indispensable tool, but only as a tool. When an analysis has provided its results, they must be used with discretion in decision-making processes on which the public safety is dependent. At each stage of system safety engineering, a high level of professionalism is essential.

4 Professional Issues in Software-intensive System Safety Engineering

As has been shown above, professional system safety engineers face particular challenges. They must specify and design very complex systems and then develop them using methods that ensure that the systems have the required properties, with a very high degree of confidence that can be justified by objective evidence.

In almost every case, the evidence cannot be obtained by only testing the final system; some degree of analysis will also be necessary. However the final system will be far too detailed and low-level for analysis to be practical, unless it can be supported by powerful abstractions. This is a particular issue when the system contains software, as this enables unprecedented levels of complexity. In general, the assessment of the contribution to safety of the software elements of the system needs to address:

- Requirements validity – the soundness of the safety requirements (this is mainly an issue for safety engineering and validation testing);
- Requirements satisfaction – that the software meets its safety requirements;
- Traceability – that safety requirements can be traced from the highest level to the implementation, and vice versa;
- Configuration consistency – that the evidence provided relates to the system as deployed;
- Non-interference – that non-critical elements of the system do not interfere with the critical ones and undermine their safety (or evidence about their safety);
- Integrity – that components exhibit basic integrity properties, e.g., no divide-by-zero, no buffer overflows.

A subset of these principles underpins the Civil Aviation Authority (CAA) software standard SW01 (CAA 2000), and will be addressed in guidance being produced, in the context of Defence Standard 00-56 Issue 4, by the MoD-funded Software Systems Engineering Initiative (SSEI).

Focusing on requirements satisfaction, as the National Academy study, cited earlier (Jackson et al. 2007), argues, critical properties, i.e., derived safety requirements, should be specified as unambiguously as possible and shown by analysis to be satisfied, using evidence from testing of the necessary environmental assumptions and from the analysis of the delivered system. This approach provides a 'benchmark' for a safety argument that is strong enough to justify claims for very high dependability. Thus the study identifies good principles, but there remain difficulties in practice, as few systems are 'new' and the safety engineer will need to deal with, for example, COTS and legacy subsystems (Redmill 2004).

Most current standards for developing safety-critical systems have merits, e.g., IEC 61508 (IEC 1998-2000) is one of the few to address the issues of data in safety-critical systems. However there are shortcomings in many of them because, for example, they:

- Place too much emphasis on process, as if adherence to a recommended process could justify claims for the dependability of the resulting system;
- Imply that claims can be made for failure probabilities that are far too low for it to be possible to provide any credible evidence that such claims are justified.

Of course some documents, such as DO-178B (RTCA and EUROCAE 1992), are careful to separate the failure-rate targets from claims about the software. However, the above are very serious issues for safety engineering as a profession, showing a lack of consensus, and one of the roles that a professional body would have to adopt is that of raising awareness and understanding of such fundamental issues in the community.

The combination of strong software engineering, strong safety engineering, and a systems approach are too often lacking in engineering education and, as a consequence, less widely practiced than is desirable. We need to promote of a class of engineering that combines them, so that the established science and accumulated experience of system safety engineers can be documented as current best practice and used as the basis for forming the system safety engineers of the future.

5 Reasons for a New Professional Body

The issues presented above, and the system complexities that they generate in the fields of both software and safety engineering, extend throughout engineering (electrical, electronic, aeronautical, chemical, civil, mechanical, etc.), and it follows that their management, and the expertise and skills required for it, are called for in every engineering discipline. Yet, because they are not in the traditional mainstream of any, no engineering discipline engages fully with these issues.

Moreover, the problems thrown up by this deficiency are neither small nor trivial. The volume of safety-related systems, and, in particular, those that are software-intensive, is already considerable and is increasing, and the impact of the safety implications is growing commensurately.

Further, the discipline of system safety engineering is not confined to the development stages of a system's life cycle. Crucial though it is in development projects, particularly in system design, it is just as important in maintenance and change, and beyond them to decommissioning and, in many types of system (such as nuclear-based systems), to disposal. For example, the Boeing 777 incident mentioned in the Introduction arose following a maintenance change to the software, exposing a hitherto masked fault.

There is therefore need for a professional body whose business it is to address these matters. This need has existed for some time, but the relatively low number of professionals in the field of system safety has meant that, until now, it has been difficult to achieve a 'critical mass' able to bring about change. But now, a number of changes have occurred, among them:

- The number of safety-related systems has increased;
- The visibility and importance of safety in the public eye have also increased;
- The number of engineers engaged in system-safety development projects, and in work on the later life-cycle stages of safety-related systems, has increased;
- The increased demand has exposed a lack of adequately qualified and experience safety engineers;
- The demand for system safety engineers has exposed the need for (and the absence of) defined or certified education and training;
- The demand has also exposed the need for certification of the competence of system safety engineers.

All of these, and other, matters have led to the beginnings of a movement in the system safety engineering community, not only for recognition of their profession, but also for a professional body to provide a number of requirements essential to it.

In the sphere of governance, the requirement is for leadership of the profession, the setting of strategy, the definition of relevant policies, and, in general, the provision of a voice of the profession.

A professional body is also required to contrive and provide ways of sharing best practice, defining and maintaining a core body of knowledge for the profession, defining competence requirements for various categories of system-safety professionals, and promoting system-safety education at universities and other institutions and training via reputable and accredited course providers.

It is also important that a professional body should have the authority to define a code of conduct essential to its professionals, and, because it is crucial to achieve safety in advance rather than as the result of costly accidents, to enforce it.

Indeed, the demand of modern system safety engineering for assurance of adequate safety in advance of the deployment of a system can on occasions throw up significant difficulties, both technical and ethical, for system safety engineers. Claims for the achievement of adequate safety must be based on evidence and, in software-based systems, convincing evidence is not always readily derived. The vast numbers of possible logical paths through software make exhaustive testing impossible and this, in turn, means that evidence of system behaviour cannot be complete. Thus, there is debate in the domain about the means of obtaining evidence to support claims of low hazardous failure rates of safety-related functionality. There is need for a professional body to take the lead in defining policy on this matter and, if necessary, to sponsor studies to facilitate the derivation of credible policy.

System safety engineering is a sub-set of other engineering disciplines and is not accorded the attention that it requires by any of them. Yet, as shown in this paper, it is important to modern systems and to modern society, and it carries requirements whose fulfilment is becoming more and more pressing. There is a real and urgent need for a system safety engineering professional body to provide leadership and governance of the discipline.

6 Conclusions

A growing number of systems are safety-related or safety-critical, so effective system safety engineering is crucial to UK industry and society. Whilst there are, in some domains, good practices in system safety engineering, and many professional activities, e.g., those run by the Institution of Engineering and Technology (IET), professional activity in the UK is fragmented. This fragmentation mans that the community does not effectively address all the issues relevant to the profession.

Software is a key determinant of function in many systems, and often has a major role in ensuring safety in complex systems such as aircraft and trains. Again there are good practices in safety-critical software engineering, but these are not widespread. More of a concern is the fact that there is little 'barrier to entry' to the field and there is no 'unified body' to encourage and support good practice.

A group of practitioners and academics, including the authors, has been discussing the formation of a 'new' professional body for system safety engineering in the UK, It is intended that this body would take on the broad remit of system safety engineering, and one of its important tasks would be the concerns relating to professional practices in the development and assessment of safety-critical software set out above.

References

Amey P (2002) Correctness by construction: better can also be cheaper. CrossTalk Magazine, The Journal of Defence Software Engineering. http://www.praxis-his.com/pdfs/c_by_c_better_cheaper.pdf. Accessed 9 October 2008

ATSB (2007) In-flight upset event 240 km north-west of Perth, WA. ATSB Transport Safety Investigation Report: Aviation Occurrence Report – 200503722. Boeing Company 777-200, 9M-MRG, 1 August 2005

CAA (2000) Regulatory Objectives for Software Safety Assurance in ATS Equipment (SW01). Civil Aviation Publication (CAP) 670 Part B, Section 3. Civil Aviation Authority

RTCA, EUROCAE (1992) DO-178B / ED-12B – Software Considerations in Airborne Systems and Equipment Certification. Prepared by RTCA SC-167 and EUROCAE WG-12

German A, Mooney G (2001) Air Vehicle Software Static Code Analysis – Lessons Learnt. In: Redmill F, Anderson T (eds) Proceedings of the Ninth Safety-Critical Systems Symposium. Springer-Verlag, Bristol, United Kingdom

Hollnagel E, Woods D, Leveson N (2006) Resilience Engineering – Concepts and Precepts. Ashgate, Aldershot, UK

Jackson D, Thomas M, Millett L (eds) (2007) Software For Dependable Systems: Sufficient Evidence? Committee on Certifiably Dependable Software Systems, Computer Science and Telecommunications Board, Division on Engineering and Physical Sciences, National Research Council of the National Academies. The National Academies Press, Washington DC. http://books.nap.edu/openbook.php?isbn=0309103940. Accessed 9 October 2008

Jackson M (1996) Software Requirements and Specifications. Addison-Wesley and ACM Press

Jackson M (2001) Problem Frames: Analysing and Structuring Software Development Problems. Addison-Wesley, Boston, Massachusetts

IEC (1998-2000) IEC 61508: Functional safety of electrical / electronic / programmable electronic safety-related systems (E/E/PES). International Electrotechnical Committee, Geneva

Ladkin (1996) Report on the Accident to A320-211 Aircraft in Warsaw on 14 September 1993. Main Commission Aircraft Accidents Investigation, Warsaw. Translated by Peter Ladkin. http://www.rvs.uni-bielefeld.de/publications/Incidents/DOCS/ComAndRep/Warsaw/warsaw-report.html. Accessed 9 October 2008

MoD (2004) Ministry of Defence Standard 00-56 Issue 3: Safety Management Requirements for Defence Systems. MoD

Pfleeger SL, Hatton L (1997) Investigating the Influence of Formal Methods. IEEE Computer 30:33-42

Redmill F (2004) Analysis of the COTS Debate. Safety Science 42:355-367

USNRC (2007) Fact Sheet on the Three Mile Island Accident. http://www.nrc.gov/reading-rm/doc-collections/fact-sheets/3mile-isle.html. Accessed 9 October 2008

New Challenges

Certification of FPGAs - Current Issues and Possible Solutions

Iain Bate and Philippa Conmy

Software Systems Engineering Initiative, Department of Computer Science, University of York

Heslington, N. Yorks., UK

Abstract This paper looks at possible applications of Field Programmable Gate Arrays (FPGAs) within the safety critical domain. We examine the potential benefits these devices can offer, such as parallel computation and reconfiguration in the presence of failure and also the difficulties which these raise for certification. A possible safety argument supporting the use of basic reconfiguration facilities of a reprogrammable FPGA to remove Single Event Upsets (SEUs) is presented. We also demonstrate a technique which has the potential to be used to identify areas which are sensitive to SEUs in terms of safety effect, thus allowing optimisation of an FPGAs design and supporting our argument.

1 Introduction

Programmable logic devices such as FPGAs are being increasingly used in the high-integrity and safety-critical domains. However, at present there is a lack of consensus of how FPGAs can be safely deployed and certified. One issue is whether the device should be treated as hardware or software during the certification process. Another issue is the difficulty in determining the safety effect of Single Event Upsets, leading to cautious and pessimistic design decisions. In addition, advanced features of FPGAs such as parallelism and reconfiguration in the presence of failure (available on some of the devices) are not being fully exploited. This paper aims to highlight and discuss some of these difficulties and offers potential solutions, either using existing methods or via further research.

This paper is laid out as follows: Section 2 provides an overview of FPGA features and possible scenarios for use, Section 3 describes safety and certification issues relating to FPGA use, Section 4 presents fragments of a safety argument for the use of cell scrubbing (the most basic form of reconfiguration) and a failure analysis technique which can be used to support that argument, Section 5 presents related work and Section 6 presents conclusions.

C. Dale, T. Anderson (eds.), *Safety-Critical Systems: Problems, Process and Practice*,
DOI 10.1007/978-1-84882-349-5_9, © Springer-Verlag London Limited 2009

2 Overview of FPGA Features

There are numerous different types of FPGA currently available from many manu-facturers. In order to avoid confusion this section describes what is meant by the term FPGA for the purposes of this paper. An FPGA is a programmable logic de-vice. At its heart it may have hundreds of thousands of individual logic cells, which can be connected and programmed to perform many different computa-tional tasks. Data is typically input and output via I/O blocks on the edge of the cells (see Fig. 1). Some FPGAs employ Antifuse devices on interconnects, and some use Static random access memory (SRAM). Antifuse routing devices can only be programmed once, whereas SRAM is reprogrammable. Antifuse devices are smaller, and so offer more routing flexibility than SRAM. They are also less susceptible to Single Event Upset (SEU) failures (Nallatech Ltd. 2002). However, any errors that occurred during configuration cannot be fixed in an Antifuse de-vice and the logic cells are still at risk from SEUs.

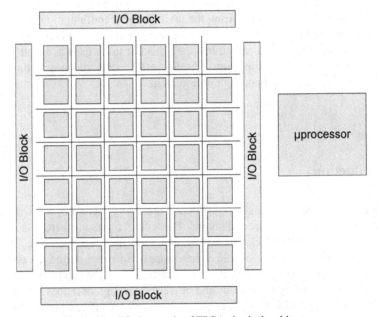

Fig. 1. Simplified example of FPGA physical architecture.

Some FPGAs may include additional dedicated devices such as static memory, multipliers and even traditional sequential microprocessors. This assists with tasks that the FPGA hardware is not well suited for. It also means that an FPGA can be used for multiple tasks (e.g. using the microprocessor for one system and the FPGA logic cells for another), thus reducing overall requirements for equipment, power and also costs.

In order to configure an FPGA, a developer must first produce an electronics hardware description written in a high level Hardware Description Language (HDL) (such as Handel-C and VHDL). This is converted into a synthesizable form (e.g. a netlist) which will then be transformed by place and route algorithms to determine how it will be configured on the FPGA. Note that the term 'programming' is sometimes used to describe the FPGA configuration/re-configuration process even though the code is different in nature. Obviously, issues such as source level design, coding and testing need to be considered for the HDL development process, but most software practices are oriented towards traditional sequential programming. HDL descriptions will need to be treated differently in some instances, e.g. when considering reasonable coverage metrics for a concurrent program.

2.1 Possible Applications of FPGAs

There are many possible uses for an FPGA within a safety critical system. Rather than attempt to enumerate all of these, this section lists some templates of use, and some different approaches to the design and configuration of FPGA devices. These are used as a basis for discussions of the potential benefits of FPGAs, consequential certification issues and possible solutions. Note that all these approaches could be used in combination with one another, for example IP Cores could be used within a highly configurable monitoring device. A further list of possible uses of FPGAs can be found in (Nallatech Ltd. 2002).

2.1.1 Monitoring System

One possible use of an FPGA is as an external monitoring device. For example, the FPGA might monitor the output from a sensor or an application for anomalies. It could also act as a voting unit for a multi-lane application. One advantage of this is that it is conceptually different to a traditional microprocessor so will have different failure characteristics to it, thus avoiding some common mode failures.

If an FPGA is used in this way then there are some obvious considerations, such as the failure rate or trustworthiness of the device (who monitors the monitor? Is it trusted to take full authority?) and who it should report a failure to.

2.1.2 Legacy Device Simulation

Another possible use of an FPGA is to simulate a legacy micro-processor. This means certified applications and code originally written for an older processor which can no longer be sourced can still be used. Obsolescence is a particular issue in the aviation industry where it can be extremely costly and complex to certify and retrofit a new system. Potentially, new applications could also be written for the simulated processor.

However, there are some potential issues with simulation. For example, whilst the execution timing will be predictable it may be slower or different to the original. Also, an FPGA implementation will have different failure characteristics to the original, and be particularly susceptible to SEUs.

2.1.3 Highly Parallel Calculations

FPGAs are by their nature able to perform many parallel computations. This makes them ideally suited for certain types of calculations such as fast Fourier transforms (Choi et al. 2003), at which they perform better than alternatives running on traditional processors (Bondhugula et al. 2006). However, by increasing parallelism, power dissipation is also increased. Therefore methods such as those in (Choi et al. 2003) have been developed in order to try and reduce this.

Another possible form of parallel computing is to have multiple applications running on the device, either within the logic cells or by using the extra peripheral devices for other applications.

Both of these uses of an FPGA can cause difficulties for a safety analyst. In terms of failure analysis of a single application with multiple threads potentially running on different types of hardware there are concerns about data and clock synchronisation, as well as some issues of overall complexity. In addition, if multiple applications are sharing the device an analyst will need to consider cross contamination of data and other interference in accessing shared resources.

2.1.4 Reconfigurable Applications

Another aspect of FPGAs is that some are re-configurable both prior to operation and during operation (unless they are Antifuse devices). Much research has been undertaken into exploring different types of reconfiguration e.g. (Hanchek and Dutt 1998, Emmert et al. 2000). These papers have a common aim – moving and/or changing the connections between logic cells in order to avoid a broken connection or cell. Many different methods have been proposed with various trade-offs required, such as some cells being set aside as backups and the main functions being paused (missing cycles), if reconfiguration takes place during operation. Despite these disadvantages, using dynamic reconfiguration can potentially increase the robustness of a system to failure and hence enhance safety.

2.1.5 ASIC Replacement

One other use of FPGAs is as an alternative to designing and manufacturing an Application Specific Integrated Circuit (ASIC). An ASIC chip is custom designed for a specific purpose. Using an FPGA in this way is cheaper than manufacturing bespoke chips if only a small volume of chips is required. It is also quicker to produce a working system. One example of this type of use is bespoke processor design such as that described in (Glavinic et al. 2000). Another example is given in (Kumar et al. 2006) for a low-cost cipher breaking system.

An FPGA suffers from different failures to an ASIC (it has more circuits which are sensitive to SEUs – see section 3.1). This may be beneficial (as a conceptually different implementation) or disadvantageous (the FPGA may not be as tolerant to certain environmental conditions as an ASIC). A further downside is that the FPGA will be significantly slower than a dedicated ASIC.

2.1.6 Use of IP Cores

Semiconductor Intellectual Property Cores (IP Cores) are reusable units of circuit design. These can be used in multiple designs and have the advantage that they provide Off The Shelf (OTS) solutions for many common functions. However, like all OTS solutions there are some disadvantages. Whilst the IP Core netlists are provided, they can be too large to easily assess for failures or unwanted behaviour. Also the IP Core may not provide the exact functionality required leading to additional work to integrate it into a design, and analysis required to ensure unwanted functionality is not triggered.

3 FPGA Safety Analysis and Certification

The previous section described how FPGAs are configured and gave multiple examples of how they may be deployed, summarising some of the related pros and cons. This section discusses in more detail difficulties that may be encountered when attempting to certify and analyse an FPGA (some of which are a direct consequence of exploiting potential benefits). We also suggest possible solutions.

3.1 Single Event Upsets

Single Event Upset (SEU) is the term used to describe a temporary flip in the state of a logic cell. It can be caused by events such as a burst of radiation or by other more gradual physical failures e.g. corrosion (Isaac 2004). A cell affected by an SEU will require resetting or reconfiguring to return it to the desired state. An example of an SEU might be that one configuration bit for a multiplexer is flipped from 0 to 1. This would mean that the wrong mux output is selected, leading to many possible issues such as the incorrect output at the board level. Another example might be an SEU within a 4 input LUT. In this situation the incorrect value will only be output for one particular combination of inputs. Thus the error may never be activated. A categorisation of SEUs can be found in (Graham et al. 2003).

A permanent state error in a logic cell is known as a Single Event Latchup (SEL), this could be fixed by a power cycle or may ultimately be permanent. Two other events of concern are Single Event Functional Interrupts (SEFI), which temporarily interrupt the normal operation of an FPGA, and Single Event Transients (SET), which are brief voltage pulses which may have the same effect as an SEU but the cells revert to their desired state without intervention.

In most cases it is impractical to manually analyse the effect of a single event of any type within an FPGA due to the complexity and size of its internal structure. As a result safety analysis is often performed only on the inputs/outputs of the board and techniques and pessimistic approaches, such as Triple Modular Redundancy (TMR), are used to mitigate against possible failures and their effects. This is expensive in terms of cost, weight and power and may not even be necessary if the effects are limited (Graham et al. 2003). Therefore, if the impact of an SEU can be more effectively managed (either through better safety analysis or reconfiguration) there are potential savings. In addition it may be possible to use FPGAs for more critical systems.

3.2 Related Standards and Guidance

It is assumed that if an FPGA is to be used in a safety-critical or safety-related system (e.g. automotive, manufacturing, military, or avionics) it will be, at the very least, subject to some safety analysis to determine how it could contribute to system hazards. Depending on the domain it may also need to be approved or certified prior to use. One difficulty with an FPGA is determining which guidance or standards are most appropriate to help with this, as it combines both electronic hardware and software features. Therefore guidance for hardware will address issues such as hardware reliability and vulnerability to environmental factors, but guidance for software development may be needed to address the depth of rigour needed during the FPGA configuration and design process. A recent online discussion between experts came to no consensus on this issue (HISE Safety Critical Mailing List 2008).

3.2.1. 00-56 (Issue 4)

The U.K. defence standard 00-56 (Ministry of Defence 2007) provides guidelines for managing safety in military systems. The most recent version of this standard requires that an As Low As Reasonably Practicable (ALARP) approach be taken when reducing the risks associated with a safety related and safety critical system. This involves identification of hazards, assessment of their risk and identification of appropriate strategies for risk reduction which are commensurate with that risk. It also requires that a safety case be developed which presents an argument and evidence that safety requirements have been met.

However, as discussed in the previous section the application of common manual techniques for identification of hazardous failures (such as Failure Modes and Effects Analysis (FMEA)) to an FPGA is impractical. Hence the risk of some failures may be over estimated. Some internal analysis is highly desirable in order to determine the effect of internal failures. A possible method for performing an FMEA style analysis internally to an FPGA is discussed in section 4. Associated with this is the need to link identified failures back to the system level.

3.2.2 IEC 61508

IEC 61508 (IEC 2000) is a general standard which applies to programmable electronics and electronic devices. Section 2 of the standard is dedicated to hardware, whilst section 3 concentrates on software. Both these sections are applicable for an FPGA, which means that the configuration design process, and all related tools will be subject to the same scrutiny as would be expected for the development of normal software.

3.2.3 DO-254/DO178B

DO-254 (RTCA/EUROCAE 2000) provides guidance on Design Assurance of Airborne Electronic Hardware. DO-178B (RTCA/EUROCAE 1992) provides guidance purely for design assurance of software. These standards are listed together here as, from discussions with industrialists, both are being used to assist in the certification of FPGAs within military systems. They are used either in conjunction or separately. There are two problems with this. Firstly, there is no consensus as to the most appropriate guidance to use, or combination thereof. Secondly, these are often used (in the authors' opinion) erroneously in the assumption that they are equivalent replacements for the now superseded military standard 00-54 (Ministry of Defence 1999) which applied to programmable electronics. The idea behind their use is to support a 00-56 style safety case with evidence gathered using the recommended processes in the DO-254/DO-178B guidance. However, using these standards would not assist with the ALARP risk assessment process required by 00-56. The DO-254 and DO178B Design Assurance Level (DAL) assignments are based on assessments of affect to the workload on flight crew and to the safety of occupants (passengers), generally an inappropriate assessment for a military situation. The level of rigour and processes applied to the software/hardware is based on the DAL. Therefore, at the very least, a reinterpretation of the DAL assignment guidance would be needed to help satisfy 00-56 requirements.

3.2 Tools and Languages

As discussed earlier, the tools used during the FPGA configuration process will need to be demonstrated to be fit for purpose. Section 2 described the process used to turn an HDL file into a configuration file for use on an FPGA. The tools used to convert the HDL into a netlist are comparable to a compiler in how they behave, therefore compiler guidance is applicable.

Place and route tools take the netlist and will link sections together in order to meet particular performance criteria. This can mean a lot of trade-offs between different criteria such as power dissipation, timing, and the ability to reconfigure certain sets of cells. It is difficult to provide a single re-usable argument to demonstrate that the algorithms used for place and route will always provide an optimal solution, since techniques such as Genetic Algorithms (GAs) can be used. These will attempt to meet a set of criteria (described as a fitness function) and use randomisation during their application. They are designed to simply reach a solution, rather than the best solution. Hence an approach for demonstrating the place-and-route has been applied successfully would be to demonstrate that the output is acceptable on a case by case basis. This can be done statically by resource analysis, using well established methods.

Depending on the behaviour or trustworthiness of the compiler or language it may be necessary to make restrictions on HDL constructs used, similar to a programming language subset. One aspect to this is to avoid certain coding constructs which may be ambiguously defined in the language standard and hence there is no guarantee of how a compiler will behave when it is used. Another aspect is to avoid constructs which are often the cause of errors, for example using an assignment statement in an 'if' statement, using dynamic memory, or using a variable before it has been initialised. Further examples of features which make verification difficult can be found in (Ada HRG Group 1998); findings in this study are reflected in subsets such as SPARK Ada and Ravenscar, and many of the findings are relevant to HDL constructs.

Some work on HDL restrictions has been undertaken e.g. (Stepney 2003, Isaac 2004) but these are not routinely being used during FPGA development. The Alliance CAD tool, which uses a VHDL subset, has been used to design a predictable hard real-time processor (Glavinic et al. 2000). This tool was said by the authors to significantly impact on the way they had to design and implement their software. Therefore it would seem there are legitimate concerns as to how the use of a sub-set would impact FPGA development.

3.3 Lack of Exploitation

Section 2 listed some of the potential uses and benefits of FPGAs. Unfortunately some of these are not being exploited fully due to difficulties during certification.

This paper concentrates mainly on the ability to reconfigure an SRAM based FPGA when a failure such as an SEU or broken interconnect is found. This is potentially very powerful, as the safety of the containing system could be better guaranteed, e.g. even in inhospitable conditions which lead to an increased risk of SEUs such as high altitude. There are a few difficulties with using it in a safety-critical device though. First, certification guidance tends to recommend analysis processes which are suitable only for a static configuration, i.e. it is assumed that the structure and layout of the logic cells does not change. There is a (reasonable) fear that re-arranging the interconnects or moving logic to different cells would mean performance requirements are no longer met and potentially hazardous failures are introduced. Second, during a reconfiguration the output from the FPGA device may be interrupted, at least for portions of the device, thus potentially interupting a stream of safety critical data. Finally, once a reconfiguration has taken place there is an issue of ensuring the restarted application is in sync with current input data and other lanes.

There are a few possible ways to ensure safe operation whilst still using reconfiguration. First, reconfiguration need not necessarily mean complex reconnections and movements of cells. At the most basic level 'scrubbing' can be used, in other words resetting and reloading an FPGA with the same data to ensure SEUs are removed. A combination of scrubbing and TMR, in which only one lane at a time is scrubbed, can provide an uninterrupted service whilst also protecting against SEUs (Garvie and Thompson 2004). Another alternative is that only a few different static configurations are permitted to be used, and each of these is analysed separately, as is the reconfiguration process. However, given that it is currently difficult to analyse a single configuration internally this may be time consuming. The semi-automated technique discussed in section 4 provides one potential method to assist.

Finally, the incidence rate of SEUs needs to be addressed. In terms of estimating the occurrence of SEUs, a sceptical approach is suggested by (Isaac 2004): *'As a general rule, the System Safety Engineer should assume these devices only have a reliability of $1x10^{-4}$ (best case from a safety viewpoint) when perform-ing safety analyses. If this is not assumed, then the higher reliability number (e.g. $1x10^{-24}$) will be used by program management'*. However, this is based on the dif-ficulty in assessing the effect of an SEU, and as discussed in section 3.1, an SEU may not cause a failure or have a safety effect even if it occurs. If better analysis and more mitigating strategies during coding were available a pessimistic stance may not be required. It is of note that work such as (Kowalski et al. 2005, Morgan 2006) has shown that the incidence of SEUs in trials is relatively low.

4 Possible Solutions

This section first describes a safety argument fragment which could be used to demonstrate that scrubbing cells to mitigate against SEUs is acceptably safe within a suitable system. Then we describe the type of analysis which could be used to assess the affects of SEUs, thus underpinning one strand of the argument.

4.1 Safety Argument for SRAM FPGA Scrubbing

Section 3.3 noted that there is a lack of exploitation of the reconfiguration ability of SRAM FPGAs (Antifuse FPGAs do not support this). Reconfiguration can range from simple scrubbing (resetting of logic blocks) to complex on the fly alterations of interconnects and movement of logic. This paper only examines the former as a starting point for exploitation, but a future aim is to look at complex reconfiguration due to its potential for providing greater safety support, particularly in situations where a system is in a highly degraded state.

A top level argument fragment is shown in Fig. 2 (expressed using the Goal Structuring Notation (GSN) (Kelly 1998)) in order to set the context. Items in the argument which are yet to be defined are represented in curly braces {}. The top level goal is fairly typical (**SysSafeGoal**) and states that the system containing the FPGA is acceptably safe. The argument has then been divided based on the system architecture, i.e. each component in the system is examined in turn for its contribution to hazards (**StratArchDirected**). The overall combination of effects is examined, e.g. for unanticipated interactions which could undesirable effects (**GoalSumParts**). It is assumed that a list of hazards, a definition of acceptably

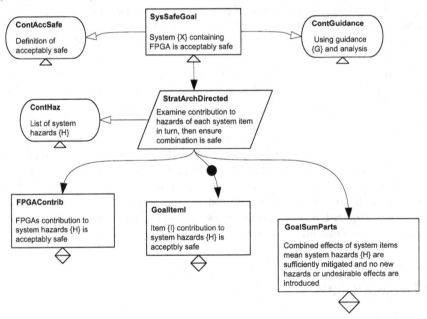

Fig. 2. Top level argument.

safe and appropriate safety guidance have all been determined for System {X} (**ContHaz, ContAccSafe, ContGuidance**). The FPGA contribution has been partially instantiated (**FPGAContrib**), all other items are yet to be defined (**Goalltem**).

Fig. 3 shows a safety argument fragment arguing that the incidence and effect of SEUs is sufficiently low in the FPGA (**FPGAReconfigSEU**). This would be part of the FPGA contribution thread of the overall argument. The definition of 'sufficiently safe' would be based on a combination of the probability of the SEUs occurring and ensuring that the effect of those that did occur was limited. For example, it could be shown that the effect of an SEU was to only contribute to a hazard which had been categorised with a low safety effect, or it could shown that an SEU which could contribute to a hazard graded highly (e.g. catastrophic) would be quickly detected and removed. At present board level analysis means that the worst possible effect of an SEU must be assumed. This argument attempts to dig deeper and look at the internal behaviour of the FPGA, theoretically supporting a higher confidence in its dependability. Internal safety analysis opens the possibility of optimising the FPGA logic design to mitigate only against significant SEUs.

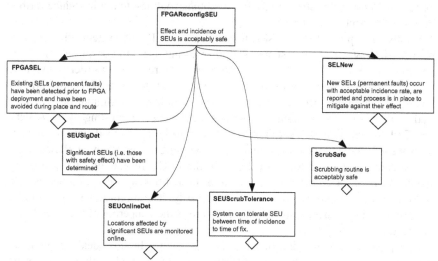

Fig. 3. Argument Fragment for FPGA Scrubbing.

The first sub-goal states that existing permanent SELs are detected prior to FPGA deployment and are avoided during place and route (**FPGASEL**). Since they are permanent they can be identified offline.

The goal **SEUSigDet** states that significant SEUs are detected prior to deployment. In other words the FPGA configuration has been examined in order to determine where an SEU could cause a safety effect. A possible method for doing this is shown in section 4.2.

The goal **SEUOnlineDet** states that those locations which could be adversely affected by an SEU are actively monitored for errors during operation. There are numerous methods for detecting an SEU online. For example, in (Zarandi et al. 2007) the authors describe a method for detecting LUT SEUs using error detection and correction codes; this would impact on the complexity of the logic design however. Another common method is to use replication (e.g. TMR) and compare results. As discussed earlier, TMR can be a crude and expensive method for mitigating against SEUs, hence our suggestion that detection is only targeted at areas of concern. Similarly, if the design has to be made more complex in order to detect SEUs it would be sensible to only apply design changes on areas of concern. Note also that SEU significance would need to be re-assessed on any altered logic, i.e. throughout the design process.

The goal **SEUScrubTolerance** refers to the ability of the system to cope with an SEU from the time of its occurrence until it is fixed. This includes operation from the moment the SEU occurs, its detection, and also a pause in operation whilst the scrubbing routines are run. Note beneath this goal there would need to be evidence of an assessment of the likelihood of SEUs offset against the time taken to fix it.

The goal **ScrubSafe** examines the scrubbing mechanisms and ensures they are acceptably safe. In other words, the scrubbing routines do not introduce further faults and do remove SEUs.

Finally, it is possible for a SEL to develop in an FPGA system after deployment (**SELNew**). If one is discovered (either during operation or during a maintenance check) then a new logic configuration may be required in order to avoid it, i.e. a new place and route. At present we assume that this type of reconfiguration would be determined offline, even though in principle reconfiguration could be used online. As the argument stands, evidence supporting **FPGASEL**, **SEUOnlineDet** and **SEUSigDet** would need to be renewed if new permanent faults were found, but the other strands of the argument should not be affected.

One concern is that a SEL develops and the FPGA repeatedly runs scrubbing routines to no effect, interrupting operation. In addition it is possible that a SET could trigger the scrubbing routines unnecessarily. The monitor system could be optimised to detect these issues, although there is the concern that this could also be affected by an SEU!

It is possible that no significant SEUs are found. In this ideal situation no scrubbing routines would be required, and hence the related goals would not be needed.

4.2 Failure Analysis of FPGA circuits

This paper has advocated the use of internal analysis of an FPGA in order to determine the safety impact and significance of SEUs, however the internal logic of a configured FPGA is extremely large and complex. One semi-automated method of performing safety analysis which may assist is FPTC. This technique annotates design components with failures and assesses how they affect other components

(Wallace 2005). Each component can either be a source of a failure, propagate a failure (i.e. pass it on), transform a failure (e.g. a late failure on input may lead to an omission on output), or be a failure sink (i.e. it has no output effect). In order to use this method each component has to be considered in turn as to how it would respond to a set of input failures, which failures it can ignore and which failures it can generate (note that it is up to the analyst to determine the appropriate level for dividing the design into components.). This part of the process cannot be animated. However, once the failures are known these can be fed into a tool which will calculate the flow of failures and hence it can be shown how they will affect a design. The analyst can use these results to assess the acceptability of a design and alter it if necessary. Full failure annotations will only need to be generated for any new or altered components.

4.1.1 FPTC Example

As a simple example consider a latch with a clock (flip flop) as shown in Fig. 4. These items are found within all FPGAs. The latch has two inputs, the clock signal (clk) and d0 (a binary value), and the output q is set to the value of d on the clock signal.

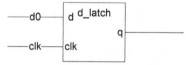

Fig. 4. Latch example.

The following table describes how the latch could be broken down into components for FPTC and shows their respective failures. Once this assessment has been undertaken, the results for each component need to be converted into the correct format for the FPTC tool.

Table 1 FPTC Latch Example Components and Failures

Item	Failures	Comment
d0	Value, *	The value of d0 may be either correct (indicated by a *) or incorrect.
clk	Early, Late, *	The clock signal may arrive early or late or at the correct time.
d_latch	Value, Stale_value, *	This corresponds to the value of q in Fig. 4. If the value of d0 is incorrect then this will be propagated to the latch output. More interestingly, if the clock signal is late then q may not have been updated by the time it is read and hence the transformed failure is "stale_value". If the clock signal is early then it is possible that d0 will not have been updated and hence the failure is also "stale_value".
Sink	None	This has been added as an end point for the tool.

The format for the FPTC failures attached to item d0 is shown in Fig. 5. On the left hand side of both expressions is a set of empty brackets, this indicates that no failure is expected on the input, i.e. d0 is a failure source. On the right hand side one expression lists the value fault and the other lists no fault (expressed by an asterisk). More sophisticated annotations can be used if multiple faults are expected.

$$() \rightarrow (\{\text{fault value}\}), ()\rightarrow(\{*\})$$

Fig. 5. FPTC annotations for d0.

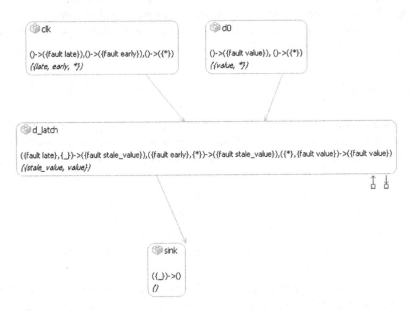

Fig. 6. Screenshot showing the latch example in the FPTC Tool.

Figure 6 shows each component and their respective failure transformations and propagations using an FPTC tool developed in the Eclipse modelling framework (Paige et al. 2008). Each component shows its failure annotations, with the resultant output failures in italics at the bottom. The failure types are fully customisable by the analyst, but it is up to them to ensure that each possible recipient component has a match to an input failure as the tool provides no warnings at present (it is perhaps debateable as to whether it should).

4.1.2 Scaling the Analysis

In the simple example in section 4.1.1 the only output failures were stale_value and value, as we would expect, and the analysis is of limited value. However, the value of this technique is its scalability and when more complex networks of components are linked together the results are much more difficult to predict manually. Each logic cell in an FPGA is identical in terms of architecture, although once configured different behaviours are offered. For example, the LUT in a cell may be configured to perform a different operation (e.g. AND/OR), and the interconnects will be configured based on the input configuration file. There are a limited number of operations though, and failure analysis of each can be performed in isolation and then automatically linked together based on a particular FPGA configuration file. It is then possible to follow the failure effect of an SEU from its original location to an output source, and hence assess its safety effect. We are currently working on implementing this functionality.

One further use of FPTC could be to use it to automatically assess multiple configurations, either offline or to dynamically assess a proposed reconfiguration online. This would work by embedding the FPTC functionality into the system containing the FPGA (perhaps onto the FPGA itself) and running it on a proposed reconfiguration. Obviously, there are many caveats with such an approach, not least of which being how to automate a trustworthy assessment of adequate safety. There are other issues too such as how to ensure safe operation during the time taken to run the assessment, particularly if multiple possible reconfigurations are rejected. Therefore, whilst online assessment is a possibility, it is unlikely at present. Instead we anticipate that this technique would be of use to a safety analyst during the design process and to assess offline reconfigurations, such as those needed to avoid permanent short/open circuits that have developed during the FPGAs operational deployment (**SELNew** in our safety argument).

5 Related Work

This section briefly describes some existing methods which are used detect SEUs and assess their significance. We compare these with our approach.

In (Sterpone and Violante 2005) the authors use a graphical tool which shows which cells can be affected by an SEU. They then compare this with a TMR architecture (the redundancy is via circuits replicated on the same FPGA) to determine if the SEU can affect more than one lane. If it can then it is assumed to be significant. The authors note that *'the choices done during place and route operations influence greatly the impact of SEUs affecting the FPGAs configuration memory'*. Our proposed FPTC analysis approach differs from theirs in that the safety effect of an SEU will be determined, rather than simply assuming it leads to undesired behaviour. It is also applicable to different architectures (not just TMR).

Emmert et al. describe 'Roving STARs' (Self-Test Areas) which robustly check for latchups (Emmert et al. 2000). They reconfigure the FPGA cells around any latchups detected and by moving the STARs around during operation they can cover the entire FPGA. However, this technique only detects permanent errors (rather than SEUs) and all latchups are avoided once found, hence it is pessimistic.

The testing technique described would be suitable for supporting the goal **FPGASEL** in our safety argument.

Another method for examining the effects of SEUs is via fault injection and testing, i.e. a configured and correctly operating FPGA file has a bit flip inserted to simulate an SEU and the effects are observed. An example of this can be found in (Graham et al. 2003) where the authors used two FPGAs, one with a correct configuration file and one with a file with a fault injected. Both were executed and the results compared. Where results differed they determined the altered bit to be SEU sensitive. Again, there is a problem here that these results are very pessimistic and do not assess the safety effect of the SEU.

6 Conclusions

This paper has described a number of different possible applications of FPGAs within safety critical systems, and also described some of the potential benefits they can offer. It has also discussed some of the difficulties which can be encountered when certifying a system containing an FPGA, particularly if they are using some of its advanced features. The paper has focussed on the issue of reconfiguration and the effects of SEUs. We presented a safety argument fragment demonstrating how FPGA scrubbing could be used to mitigate against significant SEUs. This is the most basic form of reconfiguration available on certain SRAM FPGAs. More complex forms of reconfiguration which have the potential to increase the robustness of a system containing an FPGA (e.g. to reconfigure the device when permanent open/short circuits are discovered) are an area for further examination.

At present FPGA analysis techniques which look for the effects of SEUs do not focus on their possible safety impact and hence pessimistic assumptions have to be made that any SEU which affects the output has a detrimental safety effect. We have described a method which we believe can be adapted to allow the safety effects to be properly assessed and hence allow optimisation of the FPGA design and configuration to mitigate against SEUs only where necessary. This potentially could lead to various savings in terms of cost, weight and resource usage (e.g. less redundancy being required). However, the research is currently in its early stages.

Acknowledgments The authors would like to thank the U.K. Ministry of Defence for their support and funding.

References

Ada HRG Group (1998) Guide for the use of the Ada programming language in High Integrity Systems, ISO/IEC

Bondhugula U, Devulapalli A et al (2006) Parallel FPGA-based All-Pairs Shortest-Paths in a Directed Graph. Proceedings of the 20th IEEE International Parallel and Distributed Processing Symposium. Rhodes Island, Greece, IEEE

Choi S, Govindu G et al (2003) Energy Efficient and Parameterized Designs for Fast Fourier Transform on FPGAs. IEEE International Conference on Acoustics, Speech and Signal Processing

Emmert JM, Stroud CE et al (2000) Dynamic Fault Tolerance in FPGAs via Partial Reconfiguration. IEEE Symposium on Field-Programmable Custom Computing Machines

Garvie M, Thompson A (2004) Scrubbing away transients and Jiggling around the permanent: Long survival of FPGA systems through evolutionary self-repair. Proc. 10th IEEE Intl. On-Line Testing Symposium

Glavinic V, Gros S et al (2000) Modelling and Simulation of a Hard Real-Time Processor. Journal of Computing and Information Technology 8:221-233

Graham P, Caffrey M et al (2003) Consequences and Categories of SRAM FPGA Configuration SEUs. Military and Aerospace Programmable Logic Devices International Conference

Hanchek F, Dutt S (1998) Methodologies for Tolerating Cell and Interconnect Faults in FPGAs. IEEE Transactions on Computers 47:15-33

HISE   Safety   Critical   Mailing   List   (2008)   Are   FPGAs   Software? http://www.cs.york.ac.uk/hise/safety-critical-archive/2008/0138.html. Accessed 17 September 2008

IEC (2000) Functional safety of electrical/electronic/programmable electronic safety-related systems. IEC 61508

Isaac TA (2004) Firmware in Safety Critical Subsystems. International System Safety Conference, Providence, Rhode Island, USA

Kelly T (1998) Arguing Safety - A Systematic Approach to Managing Safety Cases. University of York. D. Phil.

Kowalski JE, Gromov KG et al (2005) High Altitude Subsonic Parachute Field Programmable Gate Array. http://klabs.org/mapld05/presento/154_kowalski_p.ppt. Accessed 17 September 2008

Kumar S, Paar C et al (2006) Breaking Ciphers with COPACOBANA - A Cost-Optimized Parallel Code Breaker. Cryptographic Hardware and Embedded Systems. Yokohama, Japan

Ministry of Defence (1999) Requirements for Safety Related Electronic Hardware in Defence Equipment (00-54) (now deprecated). Ministry of Defence, UK

Ministry of Defence (2007). Safety Management Requirements for Defence Systems, Part 1 Requirements (00-56). Ministry of Defence, UK

Morgan KS (2006) SEU-Induced Persistent Error Propagation in FPGAs. Department of Electrical and Computer Engineering, Brigham Young University. MSc.

Nallatech Ltd (2002) Improved Availability and Reduced Life Cycle Costs of Military Avionics Systems

Paige RF, Rose LM et al (2008) Automated Safety Analysis for Domain-Specific Languages. Workshop on Non-Functional System Properties in Domain Specific Modeling Languages

RTCA/EUROCAE (1992) Software Considerations in Airborne Systems and Equipment Certification, DO-178B/ED-12B, RTCA/EUROCAE

RTCA/EUROCAE (2000) Design Assurance Guidance for Airborne Electronic Hardware, DO-254/ED-80, RTCA/EUROCAE

Stepney S (2003) CSP/FDR2 to Handel-C translation, University of York Report YCS-2003-357:57

Sterpone L, Violante M (2005) A New Analytical Approach to Estimate the Effects of SEUs in TMR Architectures Implemented Through SRAM-Based FPGAs. IEEE Transactions on Nuclear Science 52:2217-2223

Wallace M (2005) Modular Architectural Representation and Analysis of Fault Propagation and Transformation. Proceedings of the Second International Workshop on Formal Foundations of Embedded Software and Component-based Software Architectures, Elsevier

Zarandi HR, Miremadi SG et al (2007) Fast SEU Detection and Correction in LUT Configuration Bits of SRAM FPGAs. 14th IEEE Reconfigurable Architecture Workshop, associated with IPDPS

What is Clinical Safety in Electronic Health Care Record Systems?

George Davies

CSC Ltd

Solihull, UK

Abstract   There is mounting public awareness of an increasing number of adverse clinical incidents within the National Health Service (NHS), but at the same time, large health care projects like the National Programme for IT (NPFIT) are claiming that safer care is one of the benefits of the project and that health software systems in particular have the potential to reduce the likelihood of accidental or unintentional harm to patients. This paper outlines the approach to clinical safety management taken by CSC, a major supplier to NPFIT; discusses acceptable levels of risk and clinical safety as an end-to-end concept; and touches on the future for clinical safety in health systems software.

1 Introduction

There is mounting public awareness and perceived concern that the number of adverse clinical incidents within the National Health Service (NHS), where individuals come to harm, is increasing. In recent years the National Patient Safety Agency (NPSA) in the UK has identified that approximately ¾ million clinical safety incidents occur every year in the NHS and according to the latest published figures those incidents probably contributed to the severe harm of a patient in 1% of the reports to the organisation (NPSA 2008).

Often, once scrutinised, a large proportion of incidents are considered to be avoidable and have occurred as a result of misdiagnoses, poor communication or poor decision making; 13% of all incidents reported are defined as being part of the treatment or procedure undertaken, over 73,000 incidents, and 5% of reports are ascribed to diagnoses and to documentation incidents respectively.

In some well known cases there has been malicious intent and these incidents, though thankfully rare, also contribute to the number of incidents recorded.

A contributing factor in making poor decisions, or choosing inadequate or inappropriate diagnostic processes, is missing, incomplete, or inaccurate information.

Further contributory factors are the lack of awareness of the clinician about the available care options they can exploit on behalf of a patient and, once made, there

C. Dale, T. Anderson (eds.), *Safety-Critical Systems: Problems, Process and Practice*,
DOI 10.1007/978-1-84882-349-5_10, © Springer-Verlag London Limited 2009

remains a lack of awareness about the potential for those activities to interact in a manner that is not expected. A recent study comparing critical incidents within Emergency Departments suggests many factors that lead to harm but organisational operational differences and human error relating to the lack of knowledge or verification of tasks are common root causes (Thomas and Mackway-Jones 2008). This is readily demonstrated by the number of incidents where unexpected drug/drug and drug/ conditions interactions have been the major contributory factor to the incident (9% of the overall total).

Large health care projects like the National Programme for IT (NPFIT), building a National Care Record Service for patients using the NHS in England, are increasingly claiming that safer care is one of the benefits of the project and that health software systems in particular have the potential to reduce the likelihood of accidental or unintentional harm to patients (NHS CFH 2008).

Systems are being introduced into health care services that are increasingly used to inform, and direct, the care process. Specific disease management systems and decisions support systems are having, and will increasingly have, a major impact on the way care is delivered.

It is inevitable that users from technology savvy generations now becoming care professionals begin to use, and rely on, these sophisticated systems and that greater trust will be invested in the information provided by the system. That trust, coupled with the proliferation of systems, will result in information being challenged on fewer occasions than is currently the case. In the technology-rich future the potential for unexpected system events to lead to the harm of a patient or a population of patients must therefore be increased.

It is in this context that programmes like NHS Connecting for Health are introducing Clinical Safety requirements and developing specific standards for safety with leading standards bodies from around the world.

It is in this context that clinical safety is defined to be 'the freedom from the unacceptable risk of harm resulting from unexpected system events'. Clinical safety management must be the result of a systematic and proactive process for identifying those events that may lead to harm.

Once identified and classified those events, or hazards, and the associated risk can be managed in systems where clinical safety assurance forms an integral part of the development process.

2 What is considered Harm?

The concept of harm is one that is well understood in other safety critical systems. In public transport for example users of any service have a reasonable expectation that they will be conveyed along their journey in a manner that does not result in injury or death.

In many countries that expectation is matched by a personal responsibility to behave so that harm is avoided where a risk is obvious. In transport for example that could include sitting not standing; not opening doors before vehicles have stopped; or not distracting the staff whilst they operate the vehicle.

The problem for health services is that a similar expectation, whilst it may be assumed amongst service users, may not be so clear. For example in delivering palliative care to patients with terminal diseases the outcome is about dignity and support for the remaining period of life, yet where death is inevitable.

In healthcare there are few absolute guarantees that the care process will lead to recovery, a longer life, or an increase in the quality of life despite these being the principal objective.

In this environment expectations often exceed reality and the concept of harm is considered against a set of commonly agreed criteria. These criteria are not well researched, have no empirical basis, and are based upon a subjective perception of the objective of a care process.

They range in severity from death of a population of patients, to general inconvenience for a single patient. The key feature of these criteria is that the patient is the focus of the harm and not the service using the system.

This differentiation between harm and service interruption is one that is not made by many users of these systems. Administrative inconvenience, even administrative chaos, has a serious impact upon the business of delivering care; however, the accepted purpose of clinical safety is to prevent harm to patients and there exists a tension between the expectation of the service for an error free information service and the acknowledgement of a clinical safety incident.

Evidence from the CSC NHS Account safety incident management process is that a large number of issues are raised as having a clinical impact but those incidents are frequently shown not to represent a risk of harm to the patient (CSC 2008).

3 Clinical Safety Management

ISO/TS 29321 is a developing standard that takes the best practice from a number of existing standards dealing with safety in health services. ISO14971 is a well established standard dealing with the 'Application of risk management to medical devices'.

The concept of a 'medical device' is well understood and is considered to be a piece of equipment with functionality that allows the delivery of care or achievement of a diagnosis. That existing standard is therefore only applied to the software that controls devices like Computerised Tomography (CT) Scanners, Ultrasound Scanners etc. and not the health systems software now being deployed to manage care.

The new standard places an expectation on the supplier of software systems to manage clinical risk in a proactive and systematic fashion. For clarity a supplier is not limited to the software developer but can also include a deploying agency.

A clinical safety management system has a set of assets that are common with safety management systems in other industries. These assets usually comprise:

- A safety policy;
- A corporate governance framework for safety;
- A safety approach which has a number of safety products;
- A safety assurance organisation; and,
- Safety relationships.

In order to be successful in managing the risk associated with health systems software the management system needs to be well understood and employed across the organisation.

4 The CSC Clinical Safety Approach

Clinical risk management must begin at the start of the process of designing and developing a health software system. The definition of need and requirements is a key stage in the management of this risk, and yet it is a stage that is often forgotten in the modern world of health software systems development.

The key relationship between the identification of requirements and the recognition of associated risks may be missed because it requires a different relationship between commissioner and supplier. The traditional relationship is usually one where requirements are defined by the commissioner and passed as a completed piece of work to the supplier who interprets and produces designs.

In a world where clinical risk management is fundamental that relationship changes from a passive one to one that is active and collaborative. Commissioners have not traditionally had to consider their requirements beyond meeting the immediate or future business need. Suppliers have not had to consider a particular requirement beyond meeting those expressed business needs.

This is well demonstrated by the development of the Clinical Safety Management process within NHS Connecting for Health. The original Output Based Specifications (OBS) focused strongly on business imperatives and value for money but it quickly became clear that the impact upon clinical safety was going to be fundamental if the benefits of the programme were to be realised. In an unpublished report commissioned jointly by the NPSA and NHS CFH, and undertaken by Mark Bolt of DNV in April 2004, the most telling finding was that 'NPfIT was not addressing safety in a structured pro-active manner that others would' (Fernandez 2008).

The suppliers to the progamme may have been naive by accepting commissions that represent a high clinical risk and yet occasionally will use the 'clinically unsafe' argument to seek changes in requirements that suit the development of the solution rather than the needs of the commissioners.

Once the requirements have been agreed the CSC safety management approach leads to the process of functional hazard identification. Hazards are those events, usually unexpected, that should they occur may result in harm to a patient.

There are a number of approaches to identifying hazards. The one that CSC has found to be most successful taps into the innate skill of clinicians to use scenario planning. Clinicians use a number of scenario planning techniques to identify conditions, consider treatments and plan for positive outcomes.

The one most successfully used in hazard identification to date has been 'what if' scenario assessment. The clinical subject matter expert, with appropriate clinical safety training, considers the design of a product and asks a series of what if questions.

Examples include 'What if the system is unavailable?' 'What if a record cannot be found for the current patient?' These are extended to cover the entire functional requirement and design.

Once identified, hazards need to be assessed. The assessment has two functions. The first is to explain the implication of the hazard by applying a risk classification. The second is to compare the hazard against a set of socially acceptable criteria. All systems have a level of residual risk which needs to be clearly stated and must meet socially acceptable norms. The comparison against those criteria will drive the mitigation strategy for each hazard.

Where a risk is assessed as representing a high risk of harm, the mitigation must be systemic and will require a design rethink. Where the assessment results in a very low risk this is considered to be within the zone of acceptable risk and any mitigation may be limited to specific training of the end user to avoid the likelihood of the hazard occurring in normal use.

5 The Current CSC Experience

CSC has been undertaking clinical safety assessments on the NHS account since January 2005, when the requirement was first introduced by NHS Connecting for Health. In those early assessments much was made of the fact that the product being deployed was a 'Commercial off the Shelf' product that had been through little or no redesign prior to implementation.

The CSC solution landscape has three principal product groups. Each of these groups provides systems with particular functionality designed to support care in a number of different ways.

- Generic patient administration for secondary and acute care (e.g. hospitals and community organisations);
- Specific patient administration for individual functions within secondary and acute care (e.g. theatres, care of children, mental health); and,
- Clinical management of patients.

In addition there is also an infrastructure to host those products in centralised data centres, and to interface previously disparate systems both within the care organisation and to the National Care Record Service.

Each of these product areas and the infrastructure have now been through several cycles of formal safety assessment as the products have been reconfigured to support greater integration and to encompass more functionality to support more and more business functions.

The overall safety assurance for the NHS is provided by a specialist team at NHS Connecting for Health led by an eminent practitioner, Dr Maureen Baker, who was originally seconded from the National Patient Safety Agency and is now recognised as the National Clinical Lead for Safety for the Care Record Service.

Completion of the safety assurance allows CSC to seek Clinical Authority to Release. Once achieved the solution elements are offered to care organisations where local configuration and testing take place prior to any product 'going live'.

CSC is leading the development of a completely new product that will provide integrated clinical management functionality for patients across all care sectors and professional groups. Products do already exist with elements of that functionality; however, the underlying design principles are frequently defined by other, non UK style health systems.

That design heritage can itself be a source of clinical risk where the underlying principle is as much about managing resources as it is about managing clinical conditions. The premise behind designing a new product is that the focus can be on patient centric, condition based care management.

6 Acceptable Levels of Residual Risk

CSC frequently remind users of the health software systems that clinical safety assurance is not about declaring a product 'safe' per se. The freedom from unacceptable risk of harm obviously implies that there is an acceptable risk of harm.

That residual risk is defined by CSC as those hazards where the risk classification is 'Very Low'. The CSC Clinical Safety Management System recognises that for those risk assessed at that level, communication of the risk to users is a fundamental component in maintaining the clinical safety assurance. CSC will not specifically fix those issues where a Very Low risk has been identified and they will be placed into the process where all such fixes are considered.

7 Clinical Safety as an End to End Concept

A complication faced by all of the suppliers to the National Care Record Service is the concept of an end to end assessment of clinical risk. This is meant to ensure that risk is assessed across the whole range of care activities, even where the solution is not being employed.

This has meant that the suppliers have had to implement clinical safety incident management systems that, in the case of CSC, are invoked through the normal (technical) incident management process.

The benefit to the customer of this approach is the simplicity with which incidents that may have clinical impact can be raised and assessed. Where this approach does have a disadvantage to CSC is the number of incidents where a clinical risk is suggested and the level of that perceived risk.

In a recent 60 days reporting period some 437 incidents were raised where a clinical risk was stated (by the customer). In 95% of those incidents the level of risk was suggested to be high, severe, or very high. After formal assessment the number of risks still considered to be above low, and thus requiring immediate remediation, was 3 (less than 1%).

As an average CSC has seen that over 50% of all incidents raised by the users where a clinical risk is suggested will result in a formal assessment of no clinical risk. The suggested reasons for this apparent discrepancy between expectation and assessment are three fold:

- The users raising the incidents are often not clinicians, so are making judgements about the potential for harm without the required clinical knowledge;
- The users raising the incidents are often not trained in, or have a general understanding of risk; and,
- The users may not be using a formal classification of risk and are making a subjective judgement.

8 Managing Customer Expectations

One of the most difficult aspects of managing clinical safety as a supplier is the management of the customer expectations. The principal assumption of the NHS is that each supplier is now in a position to guarantee the safety of each and every product deployed as part of the solution.

Society seems to view health care as a sector with, in general, a low tolerance to risk. This low tolerance may be fuelled by an interest in the media in the delivery of care and especially where the perception exists that the care does not deliver against those expectations as discussed earlier.

It is in this environment that the assessment of any clinical risk is made. The assumption that any incident must have a serious consequence if it impacts directly on the care of a patient combined with an over-estimation of the likelihood of a hazard arising means that the previously discussed judgement of users becomes all the more understandable and perhaps reasonable.

Formal assessment of the clinical risk using the standards most often results in the risk classification being lowered, although in at least one case during the described period one risk was raised from very low to medium and an immediate action precipitated to 'make safe' in the short term and to mitigate the hazard for the solution across the rest of the estate.

The expectation of safety also extends, in the mind of the customer, to eliminating risk even where the risk lies in the underlying business process and where normal professional practice will mitigate completely any such potential.

Dr Baker the NHS CFH National Lead for Clinical Safety has reminded all on many occasions that clinicians cannot abrogate their professional responsibility to the system.

The final assessment logic where risk is suggested and for which, as suppliers, there is a need to be clear is as described:

1. The system is not producing data to support our financial reporting;
2. If we do not produce the relevant financial reports we will not be given all of our funding; thus,
3. If we do not get all of our funding we will not be able to offer the level of care and therefore patients will be harmed.

The ISO Standard makes it very clear that this does not represent a clinical risk in the current understanding of the term.

9 The Future for Clinical Safety in Health Systems Software

LORENZO Regional Care as a newly developed product is the first where the formal assessment of risk has been integral to the design and development of the product. The approach taken has led to a recognition both at CSC, and with the user community that to be effective Clinical Safety Management for health software systems is a collaboration between good design and development techniques, effective testing and skilled and aware users.

Prior to deployment NHS organisations are asked to appoint their own Clinical Safety Officers. These people will (and do) have a close working relationship with the supplier's Clinical Safety team and the hand over process, normally one focused on technical availability and functional stability will now be as much focused on clinically safe operation.

References

CSC (2008) Monthly report of the Clinical Safety Officer (unpublished)
Fernandez J (2008) CfH says patient safety work has progressed. E-Health Insider. http://www.e-health-insider.com/news/3685/cfh_says_patient_safety_work_has_progressed. Accessed 23 October 2008
NHS CFH (2008) Clinical safety. NHS Connecting for Health Office of the Chief Clinical Officer. http://www.connectingforhealth.nhs.uk/engagement/clinical/occo/safety. Accessed 23 October 2008

NPSA (2008) Patient safety incident reports in the NHS: National Reporting and Learning System Data Summary. Issue 9: - ENGLAND. National Patient Safety Agency
Thomas M, Mackway-Jones, K (2008) Incidence and causes of critical incidents in emergency departments: a comparison and root cause analysis. Emergency Medicine Journal 25:346-350

Safety Assessment

Back to Basics: Risk Matrices and ALARP

Glen Wilkinson and Rhys David

Atkins Defence and Safety Assurance Services Ltd

Farnham, UK   Farnham, UK

Abstract Risk matrices are tools for comparing risks relative to one another (e.g. within a single system) and hence being able to 'rank' them relative to each other for the purposes of risk mitigation and the allocation of safety resources. Risk matrices are not tools for determining the tolerability, or otherwise, of individual or 'single risks'.

However, the current trend of using risk matrices to determine whether individual risks are tolerable, and hence subject to ALARP arguments, stretches the risk matrix concept beyond its breaking point, and is thus leading to potentially misinformed decisions by senior managers regarding the true level of risk present, and hence whether risk reduction options are either needed or are reasonably practicable, across a range of projects for which they have responsibility.

1 Risk Matrices

Risk matrices tend to be activity or 'system-centric' and hence do not explicitly consider the risks to an individual, whereas the legal guidance set out by the UK Health and Safety Executive (HSE) is derived from the standpoint of understanding and assessing the total risks to individuals from all systems/activities to which they are exposed, in the course of a typical working year.

It is common, but not universal practice, when using the HSE Tolerability of Risk (TOR) threshold (HSE 2001), for analysts to apply these limits only to either 'single risks' or the accumulated risks from a single system or activity. Consequently the accumulated risk to individuals from all the risks of all the systems/activities they are exposed to in a typical working year is rarely understood.

If every possible accident for a system or an activity falls below the TOR threshold, then the risk for a system is often judged to be tolerable. Sometimes multiple thresholds may be defined, e.g. intolerable, tolerable, and broadly acceptable, with the location of each risk estimate relative to the thresholds determining the management level that is authorised to give approval.

The total risk presented by the system of interest is a parameter that should be understood by risk managers and risk acceptance authorities, but it is seldom calculated and presented explicitly. Instead, there may be an implicit assumption that

C. Dale, T. Anderson (eds.), *Safety-Critical Systems: Problems, Process and Practice*,
DOI 10.1007/978-1-84882-349-5_11, © Springer-Verlag London Limited 2009

if all of the separate risks are tolerable, then the total risk must be tolerable. This assumption may be founded on different views, including the following:

- The risk thresholds were calculated taking account of the actual or likely number of separate risks;
- There are a small enough number of separate risks that aggregating them is unlikely to move the 'worst case' risk estimate sufficiently to place it in a higher risk category;
- The highest risk category of any of the separate risks represents the system risk category.

There is no 'correct' definition of what constitutes a 'single risk'. Different analysts may each define different 'safety issues' as 'single risks' (e.g. Aircraft Loss, Controlled Flight Into Terrain (CFIT) and CFIT due to Human Error). At the level of the project, this is acceptable, providing that safety issues are being recognised and managed. However, for a senior manager with responsibility for safety, this lack of consistency makes it impossible to have a consistent comparative view of risks across multiple projects within an organisation.

Where senior managers need to compare exposure to possible loss across multiple systems/facilities/operations, they require metrics which can be directly compared. This would give managers improved appreciation of the context or implications of 'single risks' and might be presented in terms such as:

- Exposure to Loss (calculated in terms of predicted equivalent fatalities per person-year exposed);
- Exposure to Loss (calculated in terms of number of predicted events in each severity category, per person-year exposed);
- Exposure to Loss (calculated in terms of predicted equivalent fatalities per system year or per fleet/inventory year);
- Exposure to Loss (calculated in terms of number of predicted events in each severity category, per system year or per fleet/inventory year).

In many cases safety requirements are not known or are expressed in terms of the system. Therefore, attempts are made to map individual risk requirements onto the system, so that ToR threshold values may be used to derive appropriate 'surrogate' system requirements. This has to take account of many factors which are difficult to understand or estimate and which may be beyond the control of a project. These include:

- Risk exposure time for an individual (e.g. proportion of the working year);
- Number of people exposed to the system risk (e.g. including visitors, transients, general public);
- Simultaneous sources of risk beyond the system of interest (e.g. other equipment being used at the same time, other co-located systems, other non-equipment based activities).

2 Individual Risk and ALARP

Taking account of the factors above is a process of 'risk apportionment' from an individual risk budget but often with no consistency or overall control. The result is frequently inappropriate apportionment and even allocating of a whole year's 'risk budget' to a single system that is used only infrequently.

If 'single risks' are compared with risk tolerability criteria defined for overall risk (e.g. total individual risk per working year), then they will seem to be much more acceptable than they should be. If there are several 'single risks', then each may separately seem to be 'broadly acceptable' whereas the individual is exposed to an overall risk that should be judged only 'tolerable', or even 'unacceptable'.

Furthermore, if ALARP arguments based on Cost Benefit Analysis (CBA) are made for 'single risks' without appreciating the aggregated risk, too low a Gross Disproportion Factor (GDF) will be used and incorrect decisions may be reached to reject risk reduction measures as being 'grossly disproportionate'. It is therefore recommended that where ALARP arguments based on CBA are made, they must be based on the aggregated/accumulative risk, compared against the appropriate criteria for overall risk.

It is noted that comparing the aggregated risk (if known) against overall risk criteria will provide a GDF that should be used for CBA on any safety improvements that are being considered. It is the absolute position of the overall risk that determines the GDF, rather than that of a 'single risk'. It is the incremental improvement in the aggregated risk that is of interest, rather than the change in the 'single risk' issue. These incremental improvements may be the same, but they could be different if one safety improvement affects more than one 'single risk'.

Risk assessments are sometimes based on a large number of 'single risks', often because the assessment is done for each separate hazard. Several hazards may lead to or cause the same accident type and they therefore share many of the important factors in the accident sequence (e.g. preventative controls, recovery controls and escalation controls).

4. Conclusions

With the current trend of using risk matrices as a way of determining whether individual risks are tolerable and hence subjects to the rigours of ALARP, there is a very real risk that senior managers are unable to compare risks across a range of projects to determine where their highest priority risks truly lie, such that they can efficiently allocate safety resources to risk reduction activities.

Additionally, the current trend of determining ALARP argument for single risks, which a risk matrix determines to be in the tolerable range, is incorrect. ALARP should be applied at the level of the aggregated/accumulative total risk from a system/activity, but must be done within the context of the UK HSE Tolerability of Risk framework for individual risk.

Risk assessment at the level of the individual is the only way to truly understand the total level of risk that an individual is exposed to throughout a typical working year. Obviously this requires a risk assessment of all the individual systems/activities that a 'most-at-risk hypothetical person' is exposed to, but the next step of assessing the level of accumulated risk from all those systems/activities is the key step in understanding the level of risk that senior managers are really approving.

Without taking this next step and assessing the accumulative individual risk, and then taking ALARP decisions at this level, the duty holder will potentially make misinformed decisions on risk reduction and the allocation of safety resources to reduce risk to a level that is both tolerable and ALARP.

References

HSE (2001) Reducing risks, protecting people. Health and Safety Executive. HSE Books, Sudbury

Safety Case Development as an Information Modelling Problem

Robert Lewis

IntelleQ Ltd.

Worthing, UK

Abstract This paper considers the benefits from applying information modelling as the basis for creating an electronically-based safety case. It highlights the current difficulties of developing and managing large document-based safety cases for complex systems such as those found in Air Traffic Control systems. After a review of current tools and related literature on this subject, the paper proceeds to examine the many relationships between entities that can exist within a large safety case. The paper considers the benefits to both safety case writers and readers from the future development of an ideal safety case tool that is able to exploit these information models. The paper also introduces the idea that the safety case has formal relationships between entities that directly support the safety case argument using a methodology such as GSN, and informal relationships that provide links to direct and backing evidence and to supporting information.

1 Background

The development of safety cases for large complex projects needs careful consideration and planning so that the structure and presentation of material can be easily understood and maintained. Consider large-scale systems such as those found in Air Traffic Control (ATC) where there are complex interactions between the operational procedures of air traffic controllers and functionality provided at ATC workstations, flight data servers and remote systems, for applications such as radar surveillance and air-to-ground radio communications. Typically a safety case for a large ATC system can result in a multi-part document of at least 500 pages with some 400 referenced documents, each of which in turn may have numerous subsidiary references. The text must convey all safety arguments and all the detailed inter-relationships between claims, arguments and evidence. For system stakeholders, reading a document of this size and complexity is very difficult and time consuming. In addition, different system specialists and safety reviewers will require a different focus on the safety material; for example, an air traffic controller

C. Dale, T. Anderson (eds.), *Safety-Critical Systems: Problems, Process and Practice*,
DOI 10.1007/978-1-84882-349-5_12, © Springer-Verlag London Limited 2009

would be interested in the safety arguments related to air traffic operations whereas a maintenance engineer may wish to focus on safety issues concerning equipment failure rates, repair and replacement; a safety auditor might be interested in historic records showing how safety requirements have been derived from hazard analysis (e.g. from HAZOP workshops).

The extraction of discipline-significant content from documents for a large safety case is not straightforward. Navigation through documents and locating specific information is difficult because of the manner in which the information is presented. Safety arguments tend to be buried in large blocks of text and related tables and references, so that navigating through the argument thread can take many minutes. To understand a complete argument thread with supporting evidence may take hours of intensive research. Producing a coherent and consistent safety case argument for such systems with so many entities with complex inter-relationships is clearly becoming extremely difficult using a traditional 'document-centric' approach. Searching through the argument structure using search functions in text processors like Microsoft Word or Adobe Acrobat seems crude and inefficient. For the safety case author there are also significant problems maintaining such large documents and great care is necessary when inserting text to ensure references (particularly those related to argument structures) are correctly maintained.

The Defence Standard 00-56 (MOD 2007) states that for a safety case to be convincing it must show that it provides a structured argument, supported by a body of evidence that is compelling and comprehensible. Putting together a comprehensible safety case where material (particularly evidence) is created from so many different sources and formats including design specifications, descriptions of user operations, maintenance records and human factors assessments is becoming increasingly challenging.

This paper considers how information modelling techniques applied using advanced tools in the future may allow safety cases to be presented in a purely electronic form and looks at the challenges this presents.

2 Development of an electronic safety case

Tim Kelly has highlighted the many benefits from using a graphical approach based on the Goal Structuring Notation (GSN) to present safety case arguments, compared to expressing arguments in plain text (Kelly and Weaver 2004). The use of GSN is now a well accepted technique to show the relationships between safety arguments, safety requirements, objectives and supporting evidence. Use of tools, such as Adelard's ASCE (Adelard Safety Case Editor), which supports GSN-based argument structures, is clearly a very useful step in supporting the construction of a graphical safety case argument. Also the ability to manage safety case statements at an 'atomic' level as supported by Requirements Management tools, such as DOORS, the requirements management tool produced by Telelogic, also brings many benefits. These tools however are still focused on producing the final safety case in the form of a document.

Different approaches to integrating existing tools have been proposed. Cockram and Lockwood introduced the concept of an electronic safety case (eSafety Case) (Cockram and Lockwood 2003) using a tool that integrates a graphical presentation of GSN with hyperlinks to textual statements. A technique using XML as a means of Electronic Data Interchange (EDI) along with Microsoft Visio for the graphical front-end for constructing GSN diagrams is proposed by Alan Eardley, Oleksy Shelest and Saeed Fararooy (Eardley et al. 2006). These are examples of building a more comprehensive integrated toolset for the creation of complex safety cases.

This paper considers taking a look into the future and postulates on the design of the ideal electronic safety case tool by considering aspects of information modelling that consider the organization, retrieval, acquisition and maintenance of safety-significant information. What features would we like to see in our ideal safety case tool of the future? The first step is to break with the idea that the safety case exists purely as a document. A safety case is really a complex set of entities that have both formal and informal relationships. The formal relationships concern the entities that directly support the safety argument. These entities are the claims, arguments and evidence on which the safety case is based. GSN is an example of how the formal elements of the safety argument can be depicted graphically. There are also informal relationships between many of entities within the safety case. For example, there is a relationship between the operational tasks that a user wishes to accomplish with a system and the specific system functionality that is used. For example, in the Air Traffic Control domain, the controller will use functionality that provides a radar display to monitor the aircraft track and air-to-ground radio communications functionality to issue a clearance to a pilot. There are therefore complex relationships between ATC procedures and ATC system functionality. There are many different forms of informal relationships in a safety case, such as: the mapping of system functions on to the hardware elements of a system; the mapping of software tests on to specific functionality; the relationship between HAZOP workshops and functionality analyzed. There are also relationships between system requirements and clauses in regulatory standards.

Radjenovic et al have developed an information model for high-integrity real time systems and shown that there are many benefits throughout the system development life-cycle from having a well defined architectural model (Radjenovic et al 2004). They state, 'Information analysis captures and defines the domain knowledge and data requirements that are essential for implementing systems in the domain'. There is a growing awareness that information modelling is an essential aspect of good system engineering. Therefore there is good reason to assume that appropriate information models can also bring benefits to the development and presentation of information for complex system safety cases.

3 Features of an ideal safety case tool

Let us now consider the features we would like to see in an ideal electronic safety case tool. The safety case tool should certainly allow all of the types of relationships mentioned above to co-exist. This implies that the safety case information has many of the properties of a database. However, before we expand on the database aspects, consider basic features of the ideal safety case tool that will be necessary to allow both the creation of the safety case material and support its review and navigation by the safety case stakeholders and by other key third parties, such as regulators.

- It should provide a web of information that supports an argument-centric structure. In other words, the tool should assist with the construction of the safety case argument by managing entities such as claims, arguments, goals and evidence.
- It should provide means to create relationships between atomic items of information (textual, graphical and possibly multi-media) in a formal structure.
- There should be means to check that the formal structure is complete, consistent and correct, for example, that all claims are supported by goals and goals are supported by solutions (e.g. evidence, such as test reports).
- There should also be means to provide informal relations between information, such as between user operations, functionality, subsystems, software (i.e. Computer Software Configuration Items, CSCIs), requirements, hazards, test specifications, and test results.
- There should be means to navigate the information both by textual query and via graphical notation. For example, to select an item of evidence in a solution block in a GSN diagram and expose information on the test results and test design, or to 'click' on a hardware element in a system diagram and identify the functions it supports and its main interfaces to other elements, or to identify hazards related to the failure modes of a hardware element.
- It should be possible for the argument structure and evidence artefacts to be selectively viewed by different criteria, such as by discipline, by system functionality, by associated hazard. For example, 'list all software CSCIs that contribute to hazard X', 'list all safety requirements that mitigate hazard Y'.
- All changes to information should be controlled and subject to the principles of configuration management.
- There should be an audit trail to allow changes in argument structure and related information to be traceable, i.e. to show clearly how the argument structure has changed over time and why.
- For security reasons, access to read and change the safety case information should be strictly controlled by the tool.

For this ideal Safety Case tool to be appropriate for the management of safety information it is important both that the entities used within the safety case are identified and that the relationships between these entities defined. The entities supported by the tool should also be directly related to the system domain, and recognised and understood by the system stake-holders.

3.1 Formal relationships within the Safety Case

Let us first consider the formal relationships that need to exist within the safety case to support the safety argument. GSN, as already stated, is a well established methodology for this purpose and is now strongly promoted by the European Organisation for the Safety of Air Navigation for use with Safety Cases for ATC systems (Eurocontrol 2006). They state, 'the logical approach of GSN, if correctly applied, brings some rigour into the process of deriving Safety Arguments and provides the means for capturing essential explanatory material within the argument framework'. However the important principle of GSN is that when applied rigorously the top level claims of the safety case are systematically decomposed down into lower level arguments supported by evidence and defined argument strategies. 'In GSN, premises and conclusions are represented as goals. Premises can be supported by evidence, which is represented as solutions in GSN and/or decomposed into further premises (goals).' (Weaver et al. 2003)

Figure 1 provides an example of part of a safety case argument from a hypothetical safety case supporting the claim that all operational capabilities for an ATC system have been subject to human factor hazard analysis. Note that it is not the purpose of this paper to describe fully all the features of GSN but to introduce the concept that GSN defines important relationships in the safety case between certain types of information entities. Consequently, some of the less used features of GSN are omitted from this example.

In this figure the main entities of the GSN representation of a safety argument are depicted, namely 'goals', 'strategies', 'contexts' and 'solutions'. The top level goal represents the argument claim; the lower level sub-goals represent the various premises that contribute to the argument. The top level claim 'All Human Factor related hazards have been identified' is supported by a strategy to 'show that all ATC Operational Capabilities have been subject to human factor hazard analysis'. The strategy is supported by a set of goals (premises) showing that human factor hazard analysis has been applied to each ATC operational capability in turn and supported by a solution (evidence), for example, a HF hazard identification workshop report.

Each GSN graph should be drawn according to a set of rules that restrict the types of relationship that can be constructed. Many of these rules are already applied by tools such as Adelard's ASCE, to ensure that the resulting graph is meaningful and consistent with the GSN principles. Figure 2 expresses these relationships in terms of an Entity Relationship Model (ERM) – as used to model the relationships in a database.

This shows that one or more goals are required to 'support' a claim. That a goal is created to be 'appropriate' for a Strategy; that a goal is 'solved' by one or more

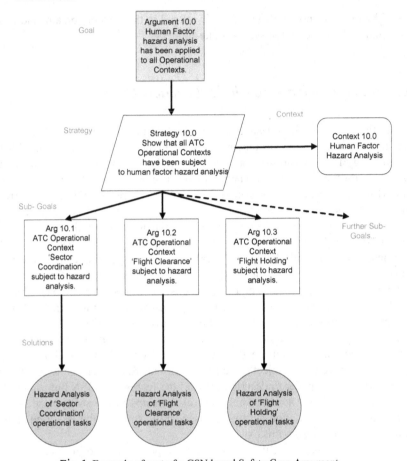

Fig. 1. Example of part of a GSN based Safety Case Argument

solutions (i.e. items of evidence). This is a very simplified view of the entity-relationship model for full GSN implementation but serves to demonstrate that it is possible to define rules for the relationships between the GSN entities.

By modelling the relationships behind the entities that form the GSN graphs it is possible to develop a safety case tool that can apply checks while the GSN graphs are being developed. For example, a tool can check that every goal is supported by a solution (i.e. evidence), and that every defined strategy is applied. It can check whether inappropriate entities are connected, for example, that evidence blocks are never connected to other evidence blocks.

In fact, if the safety case tool ensures that GSN entities obey the rules of the notation as defined by such entity-relationship models, there is no reason why the tool cannot also support complex database-type queries. For example, a tool could provide means to locate a claim tree argument by context using queries; an SQL (Structured Query Language) query might look like:

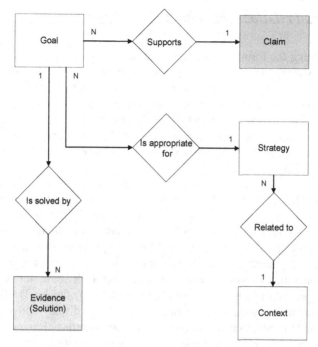

Fig. 2. Entity-relationship model of GSN Example

'SELECT claim trees FROM safety case claims WHERE context is "Human Factor Analysis"'.

This would select the set of claim trees from the total set of safety case claims and list those that are concerned with Human Factor Analysis.

If we also consider allowing our hypothetical ideal safety case tool the ability to assign attributes to GSN entities, we can start to have some quite rich queries. For example, evidence for human factor analysis could have an attribute 'risk' that classifies the risk identified by a particular HF Hazard Analysis activity. Then queries could be formed, such as,

'SELECT Hazards FROM Human Factor Hazard Analysis WHERE Risk > 3'

By presenting the safety argument in GSN format and supported by a tool that builds a database of the entities and relationships, we can significantly improve means to navigate and comprehend the whole safety case. At the same time, we can apply checks to the argument to test for consistency and completeness of the GSN, i.e. that claims are appropriately addressed by arguments decomposed into goals (i.e. premises supported by solutions – i.e. evidence).

3.2 Informal relationships within the Safety Case

Besides defining the formal safety argument using, say using GSN, a safety case for a large system, such as for a major ATC system, also has to describe many other relationships such as: a) the complex human interactions with the system, b) the functionality provided by the system applicable to these interactions and c) the safety analysis that has been applied. Typically, hazard analysis will need to cover both hazards arising from human error (e.g. an ATC Operator fails to follow a procedure) and hazards arising from equipment failure (e.g. radar main display fails to show an aircraft track).

The Failure Hazard Analysis (FHA), a key element in every safety case, needs to depict complex interactions between the use of system functionality and potential hazards and consequences. In the ATC domain, the FHA typically will need to depict complex interactions between human initiated operations, system functionality and various potential failure modes. Figure 3 provides an example of part of such a relationship model that might be required to model hazard analysis applied to an ATC operation to issue a clearance to an aircraft. It shows the relationships between the procedure to issue a clearance (as initiated by the Air Traffic Controller), the functionality used (i.e. the radar surveillance display and work station flight data) and the potential hazard (i.e. to issue an 'incorrect clearance').

If all entries in the FHA are modelled in a consistent manner then it should be possible to build a rational database and thereby provide means to navigate through this information using database-type queries – such as,

'SELECT Hazards FROM FHA WHERE Mitigation = 'Training'

This example would select all entries in the FHA where there are hazards that are mitigated by Air Traffic Controller training. The ideal safety case tool should also allow all such relationships to be viewed and explored graphically.

Figure 4 shows a further example of a relationship model associated with supporting evidence for the FHA. A Hazard and Operability Study (HAZOP) is typically attended by representatives of different disciplines. In this ATC example, a HAZOP for a complex system will be attended by Air Traffic controllers, system engineers, human factors specialists and safety engineers. Each HAZOP (organised as a set of workshops) will assess a particular area of functionality and operational usage and may identify one or more hazards from failures from functionality or from human error. A report from a HAZOP workshop provides evidence in the safety case to show that particular areas of functionality and operational usage have been covered by this form of safety analysis. Through the evidence that supports the FHA, it is possible to support a safety claim that areas of functionality and operational usage have been adequately covered by hazard analysis.

Consider the types of queries that a safety auditor or regulator might wish to make to explore the completeness of this supporting evidence. An example query might be:

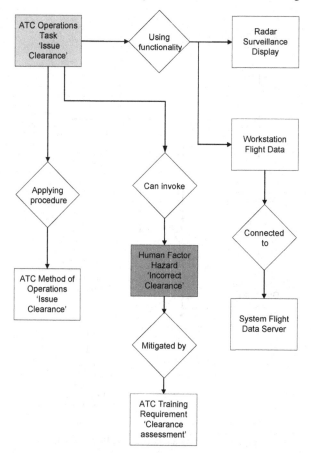

Fig. 3. Modelling part of ATC Operations Hazard Analysis

SELECT HAZOP Report FROM HAZOP workshops WHERE Method of
Operation = 'Issue Clearance'

This would search for evidence that a particular ATC Method of Operation has
been subject to a hazard analysis workshop using the HAZOP methodology.

4 Conclusion

This paper has explored just a few of the many relationships that exist between
entities within a safety case for a complex system. Apart from the formal relationships that define the basic argument structure, e.g. as can be represented by GSN,
there are many other types of relationship that provide supporting information, e.g.

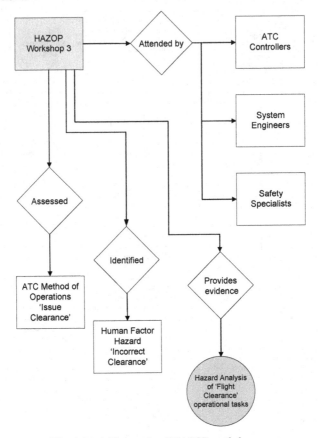

Fig. 4. Modelling a related HAZOP workshop

to define the way the system is used and functions or to define the forms of hazard analysis undertaken or related (direct and backing) evidence. Currently all of these complex relationships are defined within documents using detailed tables and cross-references that are difficult both to maintain and read.

If all of the entities and relationships that will be used to develop the safety case are well defined then it should be possible to construct an electronic safety case tool that can interact with a rational database. This would provide a much richer means to explore safety information and to check its consistency. An electronic tool as described would bring many benefits:

- There would be a more efficient means to access information related to argument threads.
- The consistency and completeness of information could be checked by the tool.
- Adding and revising information should be faster than using a document-based approach.

- It would be possible to create new powerful queries that yield valuable information about the safety case and arguments that are currently not possible with a document-based safety case.

There will clearly be significant hurdles to overcome to reach a point where an electronic tool will be acceptable as a means to formally present a safety case to stakeholders. Regulators will need sound assurance that the electronic tool has appropriate integrity. However, as systems become yet more complex a move to using more electronic tools seems inevitable. The call goes out to safety tool developers to meet this challenge. In the meantime there are still major benefits from developing the information models that will support the safety case in advance of writing the safety case. Such models will help identify key tables and cross-references that will need to be defined and maintained during the safety case lifecycle.

References

Cockram T, Lockwood B (2003) Electronic Safety Case: Challenges and Opportunities. In: Redmill F, Anderson T (eds) Current Issues in Safety-Critical Systems. Springer, London

Eardley A, Shelest O, Fararooy S (2006) Electronic Data Interchange System for Safety Case Management. Proceedings of the 3rd International Workshop on Computer Supported Activity Coordination, Paphos, Cyprus

Eurocontrol (2006) Safety Case Development Manual

Kelly T, Weaver R (2004) The Goal Structuring Notation – A Safety Argument Notation. Proceedings of the Dependable Systems and Networks Workshop on Assurance Cases, Florence, Italy

MOD (2007) Defence Standard 00-56, Issue 4. Ministry of Defence

Radjenovic A, Paige R, Conmy P et al (2004) An Information Model for High-Integrity Real Time Systems. Second RTAS Workshop on Model-Driven Embedded Systems, Toronto, Canada

Weaver R, Fenn J, Kelly T (2003) A Pragmatic Approach to Reasoning about the Assurance of Safety Arguments. Proceedings of the 8th Australian workshop on Safety critical systems and software, Canberra, Australia

Safety Process Measurement – Are we there yet?

Stephen Drabble[1]

QinetiQ

Bristol, United Kingdom

Abstract This paper examines why it is difficult to produce accurate predictions of system safety engineering effort, particularly for safety critical and safety related systems. Given the wide range of costs associated with developing safety critical and safety related systems, how does the professional system developer, ensure that allocated safety resources are sufficient to meet the needs of the customer and satisfy business drivers, i.e. the project is delivered on time, to cost, to schedule, the company makes a profit and company reputation is enhanced.

This paper attempts to highlight the benefits of safety process measurement (for the developer and the acquirer), such as a fair Return On the Investment (ROI) in safety resources and the potential exposure to business risks of not measuring systems safety engineering effort. The paper goes on to look at some of the measurement challenges that need to be overcome and what safety engineering activities could be measured.

1 Introduction

The cost of safety activities associated with developing Safety Critical and Safety Related systems are difficult to predict and range from 1- 15% (possibly more in some domains e.g. Nuclear) of total development costs, with anecdotal evidence suggesting the norm is approximately 12% (Caseley 2003). It would seem intuitive that the more complex systems, cost more to develop.

Given this wide range of costs associated with developing safety critical and safety related systems, how does the professional system developer ensure that allocated safety resources are sufficient to meet the needs of the customer and satisfy business drivers, i.e. the project is delivered on time, to cost, to schedule, the company makes a profit and company reputation is enhanced?

---

[1] Please note the opinions expressed in this paper are those of the author only and do not necessarily reflect the views of QinetiQ.

C. Dale, T. Anderson (eds.), *Safety-Critical Systems: Problems, Process and Practice*,
DOI 10.1007/978-1-84882-349-5_13, © Springer-Verlag London Limited 2009

2 Why Measure Safety Process?

2.1 Background

It simply makes good business sense for both the developer and acquirer to identify and manage (safety) risks.

The Health and Safety Executive (HSE) emphasizes the need for measuring performance in order to maintain and improve on the existing health and safety track record (HSE 2000).

In today's global, fast paced, competitive markets, organisations are continually challenged to reduce overhead and operating costs and increase profit margins. Organisations that fail to keep pace and fail to identify business risks and opportunities will simply go out of business.

Important organisational, business decisions need to be made to allocate scarce resources and budgets to deliver a system that meets the customer capability requirements, meets National and International legal requirements (where appropriate) and is delivered on schedule and on or under budget (how many systems have been delivered on schedule and on budget?).

For the developer, it's all about ensuring that the business risks are managed and that a fair Return On the Investment (ROI) in safety resources is achieved. For the acquirer, its about reducing acquisition risks to an acceptable level, by ensuring that the developer is capable of delivering a safe system that will achieve successful certification on time and on budget.

The objective of an organisational safety process measurement capability would be to accurately predict safety engineering effort, leading to cost effective utilisation of scarce safety resources and a reduction in exposure to business risks.

Failure to implement effective safety management could result in expensive retrofits to fix design flaws, loss of operational capability (e.g. grounding of a fleet of aircraft), lower productivity, retraining costs, fatalities and harm to system operators, maintainers and other parties.

The US Department of Defense Safety Program estimated safety losses to the US Navy, Air Force, Army, Marine Corps and Defense agencies to be $10 to $20 billion per year (NSC 2008).

In other words, there is a need to measure actual progress against predicted effort to understand, control and manage project risks.

Tom Demarco (Demarco 1986) said[2]:-

'You cannot control what you cannot measure.'

---

[2] The quotation 'you can't manage what you can't measure' is most often attributed to either WE Deming or P Drucker.

2.2 Safety Resource Allocation

2.2.1 Over allocation

Over allocation of safety resources and budget can lead to an over engineered system and puts pressure on profit margins which may lead to a financial loss.

There is an implicit assumption that the organisation has sufficient human resources to meet project commitments. If those human resources are not already available within the organisation, they will have to be recruited as permanent members of staff or use external contractors, or sub-contract that work to another organisation. In all cases, project costs will be increased and ability to meet the existing project schedule will be challenged as it takes time to recruit new members of staff or subcontract work outside the organisation.

2.2.2 Under allocation

Under allocation of resources and budget can lead to failure to complete all safety activities on schedule, delaying entry into service of the developed system.

In this case the customer may refuse to pay and the regulator may refuse to certify the system until all safety activities have been completed. The undesirable end result is the allocation of additional resources and budget to complete safety activities to the satisfaction of the customer and regulator. Once again profit margins will suffer and company reputation with both customer and regulator may well be damaged.

Under allocation of resources may lead to the late completion of safety analysis, missing the opportunity to influence the system design. This could lead to a developed system that fails to meet customer or legal requirements and has to be re-engineered before it can be accepted into service; all at the developer's expense.

There is a danger that under allocation of safety resources could lead to the system entering operational usage before all safety engineering activities had been completed, potentially putting the system users and other third parties at risk.

3 What are the Measurement Challenges

3.1 Safety seen as Project Cost rather than Benefit

As organisations strive to improve productivity and reduce costs, opportunities are sought to make savings (without affecting product quality) wherever possible.

System safety activities are seen as a project cost rather than offering perceived benefits to the various stakeholders. Typically, the successful outcome of system safety engineering activities is the absence of accidents. How do you measure the absence of something ?

Given the drive to reduce organisational operating costs and increase profit margins it would seem likely that system safety engineering activities would be a likely candidate for consideration for budget cuts.

System safety engineering budget cuts may prove difficult to defend without objective data of the project benefits of system safety engineering activities (e.g. identification of resources, costs and schedule required to achieve certification).

Once system safety engineering cuts are in place, the system project manager and the safety engineering specialists will be in the challenging position of satisfying safety engineering commitments with fewer resources and a smaller budget.

3.2 Influence of Domain Safety Standards

In many industries, safety critical and safety related systems will require certification by the regulator before they are allowed to enter service (Storey 1996). As part of the certification process, the system operator will have to provide evidence to the regulator, which shows why the system is safe to use, operate and maintain. In the UK, a safety case is required for military systems, offshore installation and rail and nuclear systems and it's the safety case that sets out the safety justification for the system. The UK MoD definition of a Safety Case (MoD 2007) is:-

'The Safety Case shall consist of a structured argument, supported by a body of evidence, that provides a compelling, comprehensible and valid case that a system is safe for a given application in a given environment'

Safety specific sector standards heavily influence safety activities during the systems engineering lifecycle. Sector specific standards provide a 'road map' of development methods and safety analysis techniques to meet the defined acceptance criteria.

It is worth noting that none of the industry safety standards (prescriptive or evidence based) mandate safety process measurement.

3.2.1 Prescriptive Standards

The majority of sector specific standards are prescriptive[3] and mandate specific development methods and techniques. Certification of the final system is dependent on showing compliance with the evidence requirements of the appropriate

---

[3] Examples of prescriptive safety standards include UK Defence Standard 00-56 Issue 2 (MoD 1997) and DO 178B (RTCA 1992).

standard. Some standards permit the use of alternative methods and techniques, subject to agreement with the regulator. However, additional time and effort will be required to reach agreement with the regulator and there is always the possibility that agreement on the use of the alternative methods may not be achieved. Indeed, its still unclear to both the certification authorities and industry how to approach the use of alternative methods and techniques to show compliance with the safety objectives of a sector specific safety standard (CAST 2000). Consequently, there is little or no motivation to offer alternative means of compliance with prescriptive safety standards, because to depart from the *'norm'* is perceived (perhaps not unreasonably) to represent a significant project risk of failure to achieve certification. It is not surprising then, that companies tend to use established methods and techniques as their route to successful certification.

3.2.2 Evidence/Goal Based Standards

Some sector specific standards are evidence or goal[4] based. These standards set out *'What'* is required, but not *'How'* to do it. In other words, the developer gets to select the development method and safety analysis technique. They still have to present a *'structured argument, supported by a body of evidence that provides a compelling, comprehensible and valid case that a system is safe for a given application in a given environment'* (MoD 2007).

Evidence or goal based standards offer the opportunity to select the most effective and efficient safety analysis techniques to provide the body of evidence that supports the safety argument that the *'system is safe'*. The objective of selecting effective and efficient safety analysis techniques is to:-

- Make best use scarce resources
- Deliver safety engineering outputs on or ahead of schedule and within or under budget
- Safety analysis influences system design

Justification of the selected technique will need to be provided in the safety case and often more than one technique will be required to ensure all credible hazards and accidents have been identified. Whilst a wide range of techniques are available, selection will be influenced by the project lifecycle phase, industry sector requirements and company and individual experience in the technique.

Despite the freedom to select the most appropriate safety technique and method, there is little evidence that developers are taking the opportunity to depart from the *'norm'* and continue to use established techniques and method. Perhaps that is not surprising for a number of reasons:-

---

[4] Examples of goal based standards are UK Defence Standard 00-56 Issue 4 (MoD 2007) and CAA SW01 (CAA 2008)

- Evidence/Goal based standards lack guidance on interpretation and application of the standard. A problem for both the developer and regulator.
- Evidence based standards allow the use of methods and techniques found in other standards, providing appropriate justification is provided.
- Developer proposed techniques and methods may not achieve agreement with the regulator.
- Existing safety practitioners are skilled and knowledgeable in satisfying the safety objectives of existing prescriptive standards. To use alternative methods would require hiring new recruits or re-training existing safety staff. In either case, it's a cost to the developer, with little perceived gain.

3.3 Additional Resources required for Data Collection and Analysis

Organisational resources will be required to implement a measurement frame-work. Consequently, project management staff with responsibility for delivering a system on budget and on schedule will need to be persuaded that metric data collection and analysis will repay the investment in resources and budget. Project management staff will also have to be re-assured that the act of collecting and analysing data does not present any new project risks.

3.4 Integrating and Coordinating Project Efforts

Integration and co-ordination of safety engineering efforts with other project development activities is not always achieved. Consequently, safety engineering tends to lag other systems engineering development, diminishing the ability of safety analysis to influence the evolving system design. In other words, the opportunity to 'design in' safety functionality is often lost.

3.5 Safety not addressed by Existing Capability Models

3.5.1 Capability Maturity Models

Historically, the ability of software developers to deliver large complex programs on time and on budget has been at best poor. The US Department of Defense (DoD) commissioned a report to assess performance of 17 major DoD software contracts and found that the average 28 month schedule was missed by 20 months, one four year project was not delivered for seven years and no project was on time.

In 1984 the Software Engineering Institute (SEI), was established to address the DoD's need for improved software capability, which began by looking at the reasons why software performance was poor. The SEI found that US development organisations did not possess or use a defined, shared development model (Humphreys et al. 1991). As a result, the Software Process Maturity Model was developed for DoD and industrial organisations.

In 1991 the SEI and the MITRE Corporation produced the Capability Maturity Model (CMM), which could be used by a developer to *'benchmark'* their own or-ganisational capability and maturity against the CMM. Acquisition organisations could also use the CMM to evaluate potential bidders for new contracts and de-velop a risk management strategy, based on the outcome of the evaluation.

CMM has now been superseded by a multi-disciplinary model Capability Ma-turity Model Integrated (CMMI). The CMMI was developed to extend the model beyond Software Engineering and now includes Systems Engineering and Inte-grated Produce Development CMMs.

Maturity models set out a common framework and vocabulary against which developer organisations can measure their own performance against industry *'best practice'* encapsulated in the maturity model. Process weaknesses are identified and corrective action plans developed to measure progress and achievement against the plan. The objective is to focus on those process areas, critical to busi-ness success and continually improve performance and effectiveness in those areas.

There are of course cost implications for any organization considering invest-ing in a process improvement framework based on a process maturity model. The business case needs to be made to ensure an appropriate Return On Investment (ROI) is realised for the significant investment of resources and budget. There are a number of publicly available reports (many on the SEI website) that outline the costs and benefits of CMMI-based process improvement (CMU 2004).

3.5.2 +SAFE

CMMI is a generic framework and does *not* specifically cover safety engineering aspects such as specialised safety processes, skills, techniques and competencies. However, the Australian Defence Materiel Organisation (DMO) recognised this and produced an extension (+SAFE) to the CMMI of two Process Areas to pro-vide an explicit and focused basis for appraising or improving an organisation's capabilities for providing safety critical products (CMU 2007). +SAFE was devel-oped for standalone use, is not based on any one safety standard and is not fully integrated with CMMI.

+SAFE has been used to evaluate organisational safety engineering capability producing positive results, in line with expectations (Bofinger et al. 2002).

4 What to Measure?

Once the business case has been made to measure safety performance, it is then a case of deciding what and when to measure.

4.1 Competencies

The IET define competency as *'the ability to perform activities to the standards required in employment using an appropriate mix of knowledge, skill and attitude'* (IET 2008). Therefore, we need to understand and document what those activities are, the standards to be met, what we mean by appropriate knowledge, define the skills required and elaborate on what we mean by attitude.

It is important that organisations identify and document personnel attributes, to enable objective and consistent assessment of existing staff, against safety competency criteria. The assessment results will assist in identifying roles and responsibilities for which staff are already competent and recognise where additional training and mentoring is required to enhance effectiveness and competency. The same assessment framework could be used when interviewing new staff.

Consideration also needs to be given to *'soft skills'* such as communications skills, team working – the ability to work with other disciplines both internally and externally and working off site with customers.

4.1.2 Available Guidance

The HSE Guidance for managing competence for safety related systems (HSE 2008, 2007a, 2007b) is applicable to all industry sectors and describes the core competencies, for all staff at all levels of responsibility, to enable the organisation to meet the UK requirements for competence in safety related systems in general. This guidance is not industry sector specific and therefore organisations will need to identify supplementary qualifications, skills and experience which are applicable to the industry sector in which they will be working.

The IET has published guidance aligned with the HSE competency assessment model (IET 2007).

4.1.3 What is Competency

Competency then is more than qualifications; it includes awareness of legislation, domain knowledge, effective application of safety skills in that domain, good communications skills and appropriate behaviour and attitudes. The objective of the HSE guidance (HSE 2007a) is to identify Suitably Qualified and Experienced

Personnel (SQEP) appropriate for their roles and responsibilities. Competency frameworks offer a range of benefits, such as satisfaction of safety legislation, identification of continuous professional development needs, competency assessment for new recruits and demonstration of safety competency and capability to potential customers.

4.2 Safety Culture

What is safety culture? There are numerous definitions of safety culture; the Advisory Committee on the Safety of Nuclear Installations (ACSNI) definition (ACSNI 1993) is:-

'The safety culture of an organisation is the product of individual and group values, attitudes, perceptions, competencies, and patterns of behaviour that determine the commitment to, and the style and proficiency of, an organisation's health and safety management. Organisations with a positive safety culture are characterised by communications founded on mutual trust, by shared perceptions of the importance of safety and by confidence in the efficacy of preventive measures.'

The Confederation of Business Industry's definition (CBI 1990) is a little more short and snappy:-

'The way we do things around here'

The critical element of a positive safety culture is leadership from the senior management team, i.e. management commitment to create and encourage a positive safety culture. Without leadership from the top, 'buy in' from all employees will be difficult to achieve. Employee mistrust of management statements and actions may well lead to an unwillingness to fully report all safety incidents or near misses, especially if they believe reported safety incidents will not be recorded or investigated. Senior management words must be backed up by effective action, employees must be empowered to take corrective action without fear of retribution.

Companies often refer to a positive safety culture when indicating that employees are following company health and safety rules and procedures and report incidents in accordance with those rules and procedures. However, this simply enforces the opinion that a safety culture exists, but it may only be a reactive system, i.e. waiting for an accident to occur, someone suffers harm as a result and then its reported and investigated. If the resultant corrective action is ineffective, the same incident may re-occur, someone may suffer harm and the opportunity to learn from the experience has been lost. With a reactive approach to safety management, there is little opportunity to improve health and safety performance. A positive safety culture would adopt a proactive approach to the safety management, by setting safety improvement targets and measuring performance against those targets.

There are a number of ways in which safety culture can be evaluated across organisations. Perhaps the most common is by using a safety culture questionnaire or by staff interviews. A Safety Culture Maturity Model[5] (Fleming 1999) was developed for the Offshore oil industry, which uses five stages of maturity, (very similar to the SEI CMM and CMMI), where organizations become more mature as they progress up the levels, by building on their strengths and removing their weaknesses, learning from experience and moving from a reactive to proactive positive safety culture.

Some industry sectors are more proactive and already measure safety culture, such as the Offshore Technology, Aviation and Railway sectors. Following the Southhall (Uff 2000) and Ladbroke Grove rail crash (Cullen 2001) Public Inquiries, the HSE commissioned a review of safety culture and safety climate literature for the development of the safety culture inspection toolkit for the measurement of safety culture in rail organizations (HSE 2005).

4.2.1 Safety Culture – Critical Success Factors

Leadership from the top of the organization, CEO down to the shop floor worker, is the key to promoting a positive safety culture. Senior management must demonstrate their commitment to safety both by what they say and what they do. Increased safety culture maturity will be assisted by improved two way communications between management and employees, active involvement of employees and full and comprehensive reporting of incidents and accidents in a *'no blame culture'*. Industry sectors that do not already measure safety culture would benefit from the experience of other sectors that are already measuring safety culture.

4.3 Safety Engineering Activities

4.3.1 Review of Safety Techniques

The safety engineer has a large number of safety tools, techniques and methods available for selection. This would appear to offer the safety engineer the option of selecting the best tool, techniques and method to meet his needs.

The chemical and process industries identified 40 techniques used for hazard identification (Gould et al. 2005). The report used a coarse assessment of the resources (time/cost) for each technique on a scale of 1-3, with one being quick and inexpensive and three being time consuming and expensive.

---

[5] Safety Culture Maturity is a Registered Trademark of the Keil Centre Ltd, 2003.

The information presented was not extremely useful as the scoring mechanism was too coarse to be meaningful and in practice, the number of commonly used techniques is much smaller than presented.

Eurocontrol identified 500 plus safety techniques and methods (EUROCONTROL 2005) available for selection. The 500 plus techniques were narrowed down to 21 that were either currently in use or judged to be of value for further consideration.

Further analysis of the most commonly used techniques, perhaps by industry sector, would be much more useful. In addition, new and emerging techniques should also be assessed for effectiveness against the established techniques[6].

4.3.2 Empirical Effort/Costs

Given that that the safety engineering community, across all industry sectors, will already have completed a range of techniques, across numerous projects, advice was sought through mailing lists for examples of papers, publications, case studies that discussed empirical costs/effort associated with System Safety Engineering activities. Reference to industry best practice, benchmarking, safety analysis technique selection process, applicable domain standard, chosen development lifecycle and automated safety analysis was requested.

The exam questions to be answered were, *'Why do we do what we do?'* 'What are the motivating factors?' *'How can we improve on what we already do?'* The idea was to learn from the experience of others across industry sectors with the objective of getting better at estimating safety engineering costs and resources and look for opportunities for process improvement in the safety domain.

Unfortunately, the response to the request was very disappointing, with a few respondents interested only in the outcomes, with no offers of empirical evidence whatsoever.

I did make it clear in the original request that I understood that information of this type might be commercially sensitive and for that reason it maybe more appropriate to mention safety engineering effort in terms of man-hours rather than financial costs of safety engineering tasks.

These are some of my personal thoughts on why the response was poor:-

- Commercial sensitivity – Information supplied could be used by a competitor. That said, some data already exists (King et al. 2000). Data could have been supplied anonymously.
- Motivation – Responders only saw the risk of supplying information to a public mailing list. The intention was to make the results available in the public domain for all interested parties which was in the original request for information.

---

[6] An example of emerging techniques is System Theoretic Accident Modeling and Processes (STAMP), STAMP-based Analysis (Leveson, Dulac 2005)

- Motivation – Lack of time to respond. Busy workload, schedules to meet, deliverables to make.
- Motivation – Why do we do what we do? Because the industry sector standard mandates safety engineering activities.
- Empirical data not collected. Past experience on previous project used to estimate effort
- Empirical data not readily available. Data embedded with other project data and would need time and effort to gather the data.

5 Conclusions

It makes sound business sense for both the developer and acquirer to identify and manage (safety) risks.

There is no doubt that there are some obstacles to be overcome to convince organisations of the benefits of implementing a measurement framework for safety engineering activities. However, if safety engineering activities are not measured, then there is little scope for efficiency improvements on what organizations do today.

Sector specific safety standards heavily influence safety activities during the systems engineering lifecycle. Currently, there is little or no motivation to offer alternative means of compliance with prescriptive safety standards, because to depart from the *'norm'* is perceived to represent a significant project risk of failure to achieve certification. Evidence based standards offer the opportunity to evaluate alterative techniques and measure. Yet despite the range of method, system developers appear to be staying with established techniques and not taking up the opportunity to evaluate potentially more effective and efficient techniques.

Whilst there is some limited evidence of measurement of safety competencies, safety culture and safety capability maturity, it is certainly not common across the safety engineering community.

It was not possible to compare and contrast safety engineering efforts and associated costs, due to the lack of access to empirical data.

References

ACSNI (1993) Human Factors Study Group: Third report – Organising for safety. HSE Books
Bofinger, Robinson, Lindsay (2002) Experience with Extending CMMI for Safety Related Applications. Proc. 12th International Symposium of the International Council on Systems Engineering (INCOSE'02), Las Vegas, Nevada
CAA (2008) CAP 670 Air Traffic Services Safety Requirements, Part B, Section 3, Systems Engineering, SW01 Regulatory Objectives for Software Safety Assurance in ATS Equipment. Civil Aviation Authority
Caseley P (2003) Safety Process Measurement – A Review. Defence Science and Technology Laboratory (DSTL)
CAST (2000) Guidelines for Proposing Alternate Means of Compliance to DO-178B. Certification Authorities Software Team Position Paper CAST-5

CBI (1990) Developing a Safety Culture – Business for Safety. Confederation of British Industry, London

CMU (2004) CMMI ROI Tutorial, V1.1. Carnegie Mellon University. http://www.dtic.mil/ndia/2005cmmi/monday/reitzig.pdf. Accessed 15 October 2008

CMU (2007) +SAFE, A Safety Extension to CMMI-DEV, V1.2, CMU/SEI-2007-TN-006

Cullen (2001) The Ladbroke Grove Rail Inquiry. Health and Safety Commission (HSC)

Demarco (1986) Controlling Software Projects: Management, Measurement, and Estimates. Prentice Hall

EUROCONTROL (2005) FAA/EUROCONTROL ATM Safety Techniques and Toolbox, Safety Action Plan-15, Issue 1.0

Fleming M (1999) Safety Culture Maturity Model. UK HSE Offshore Technology Report OTO 2000/049. HSE Books, Norwich, UK

Gould N, Glossop M, Ioannides A (2005) Review Of Hazard Identification Techniques, HSL/2005/58

HSE (2000) Successful Health and Safety Management. HS(G)65. Health and Safety Executive

HSE (2005) A review of safety culture and safety climate literature for the development of the safety culture inspection toolkit. Health and Safety Executive Research Report 367

HSE (2007a) Managing competence for safety related systems, Part 1, Key Guidance. http://www.hse.gov.uk/humanfactors/comah/mancomppt1.pdf. Accessed 15 October 2008

HSE (2007b) Managing competence for safety related systems, Part 2, Supplementary material. http://www.hse.gov.uk/humanfactors/comah/mancomppt2.pdf. Accessed 15 October 2008

HSE (2008) More information on competence. Health and Safety Executive. http://www.hse.gov.uk/humanfactors/comah/competenceinfo.htm. Accessed 15 October 2008

Humpheys W, Synder TR, Willis RR (1991) Software Process Improvement at Hughes Aircraft. IEEE Software 8:11-23

IET (2007) Competence Criteria for Safety-related System Practitioners. The Institution of Engineering and Technology

IET (2008) Using competence frameworks for CPD. The Institution of Engineering and Technology. http://www.theiet.org/careers/cpd/competences. Accessed 15 October 2008

King S, Hammond J, Chapman R et al (2000) Is Proof More Cost Effective Than Testing? IEE Transactions on Software Engineering 26(8)

Leverson N, Dulac N (2005) Safety and Risk Driven Design in Complex Systems of Systems, 1st NASA/AIAA Space Exploration Conference. Orlando USA

MoD (1997) Defence Standard 00-56, Issue 2. UK Ministry of Defence

MoD (2007) Defence Standard 00-56, Issue 4. UK Ministry of Defence

NSC (2008) Acquisition Safety. US Naval Safety Center. www.safetycenter.navy.mil/acquisition. Accessed 15 October 2008

RTCA (1992) DO-178B/ED12B, Software Considerations in Airborne Systems and Equipment Certification. Radio Technical Commission for Aeronautics

Storey N (1996) Safety-Critical Computer Systems. Addison-Wesley

Uff J (2000) The Southall Rail Accident Inquiry Report. Health and Safety Commission (HSC)

Safety Standards

Software Testing and IEC 61508 – Project Case Study and Further Thoughts

Wayne Flint and Ian Gilchrist

IPL

Bath, UK

Abstract This paper describes the testing activities carried out by IPL during the development of a system to the safety standards mandated by IEC 61508 (IEC, 1998). The system has been evaluated as SIL 1, and was coded in C++ with about 115 KLoC (thousand Lines of Code) produced, tested and delivered to the customer. Details are provided of the project's background, purpose, phasing, specification/design documentation and corresponding testing activities. The paper concludes with some thoughts on the testing activities adopted by the project and further reflections on the current relevance of the testing activities recommended by IEC 61508.

1 Highway Systems and the NASS Project

The client, the Highways Agency (HA), has responsibility for managing, maintaining and improving the motorway and trunk road network in England. To help with the task of avoiding congestion several computer systems are already in place. The current system used to control roadside equipment and monitor road conditions is called NMCS2 (National Motorway Communication System 2). An ATM (Active Traffic Management) project is in place on M42 near Birmingham in the West Midlands. Following its success, the innovative scheme is currently being extended on to the motorways around the city. The aim of ATM is to make best use of existing road space to increase capacity and ease congestion by controlling traffic according to actual and predicted road conditions.

In 2002 the HA went out to tender for the development of a new subsystem called the Network ATM Supervisory Subsystem (NASS), to form an additional element within the existing NMCS2 and future ATM systems. NASS takes real-time actual traffic flow data, combines this with historical traffic flow data, and then predicts future flows. If congestion is predicted, NASS will evaluate a number of predefined traffic control plans to avoid or minimise the predicted conges-

C. Dale, T. Anderson (eds.), *Safety-Critical Systems: Problems, Process and Practice*,
DOI 10.1007/978-1-84882-349-5_14, © Springer-Verlag London Limited 2009

tion, selecting the optimal plan. NASS will then issue requests for the settings of roadside signals and message signs to implement predefined traffic control plans.

The NASS contract was awarded to IPL in late 2002. The first milestone was a 'proof of concept' (PoC) system, which came in at about 20 KLoC and completed Factory Acceptance Tests (FAT) in December 2003. The second phase was for the production of a demonstrator system to be supplied to Traffic Engineering consultants working for the HA. The purpose of this system was to allow those consultants to refine the rules and algorithms internal to NASS for its safe and efficient functioning. This was delivered in April 2005, and was approximately three times the code size (60 KLoC) of the initial PoC system.

The current/third phase of NASS was delivered to the HA's West Midlands Regional Control Centre (RCC), located at Quinton, in March 2007 where it has been integrated with other Traffic Control and Signalling Systems. At this point NASS could be used to directly request sign and signal settings thereby influencing drivers using the West Midlands motorway network with a view to reducing/mitigating congestion. Due to the target environment for NASS having evolved during its development it is likely that closer integration with existing user interfaces will be necessary prior to making this step. Once this is achieved new variants of NASS could be produced and installed at other RCCs (there are seven in total) covering England's motorway network. See Table 1 for a summary of the phases of the NASS project to date.

Table 1. NASS project development phases

Phase	Name	Purpose	Delivered	Approx. code size
A	Proof of Concept	Prove NASS concept	Jan 2004	20 KLoC
B	Demonstrator	Testbed for refinement of NASS rules	Apr 2005	60 KLoC
C	NASS V.1	For live use at West Midlands RCC	Mar 2007	115 KLoC

2 System Safety and IEC 61508

The use of IEC 61508 was decided on by the HA as a result of consideration of the hazards involved. At the start of the NASS project, IPL engineers assessed that the safety level appropriate for the project was SIL 1. This relatively low grading reflects the fact that NASS does not directly control any hazardous equipment, but is involved in issuing requests for traffic sign and signal settings – which may have safety consequences when acted upon.

3 NASS Software Design

IPL started work in early 2003. Having agreed the system requirements in detail for the PoC phase, software design followed a method based on use of UML (Universal Modelling Language). The design hierarchy led to the identification of sub-systems, which in turn comprise software components, which can be either executables or libraries (DLLs, Dynamic Linked Libraries). Further OO design decomposition leads to the identification of classes, for which module specifications were created ready for coding and testing by programmers. The call specifications detailed public and private methods with code flow shown in pseudo-code, and class test plans.

The initial (PoC) phase design had 19 software components (6 executables and 13 libraries) to make up the active NASS elements, comprising a total of 94 classes. The current phase delivery has grown to 8 executables and 15 libraries, comprising a total of about 280 classes. The NASS system runs on Windows, and code production was undertaken using MSVC++ V6.

4 Testing Strategy

The IEC 61508 standard calls [7.3.2] for validation planning, and furthermore [7.7.2.6] requires that 'testing shall be the main validation method for software'. Accordingly the NASS project team together with the HA drew up a test strategy which included a formal (i.e. under independent QA monitoring) approach to testing each and every entity at each every identifiable stage of the project. Each entity has its own test plan, which details as appropriate the configurations, inputs and expected outputs which, when run successfully, will give the required confidence in the correct working of the entity under test. At the higher levels the test plans were contained in a separate (version-managed) document; at the lower levels test plans were included in the design specification. Table 2 summarises the relationship between the principal design documents and the corresponding test specifications.

Table 2. Hierarchy of principal requirements and design documents

Design Document	Informs test plan for:
Existing NMCS Documentation	System Interaction Test
NASS System Requirements Spec (SRS)	Factory and Site Acceptance Tests
Architectural Design Spec (ADS)	System Integration Test
Sub-system Design Spec (SSDS)	System Integration Test
Component Specification	Component Test (in the design spec)
C++ Class Specification	Module/Unit Test (in the design spec)

Throughout IEC 61508 [e.g. 7.9.2.4] there are demands to the effect that test results should be generated to show that tests have been run and 'satisfactorily completed'. This put quite an onus on the team to ensure that not only were they using tools that would make the various testing activities as easy and repeatable as possible, but also that the tests should, as far as possible, be self-documenting.

5 Code and Module Testing

Following classical 'V-model' lifecycle principles and IEC 61508 [7.4.7 Software Module Testing] the first task for the IPL software engineers after programming the classes was to test them. For this purpose the IPL tool Cantata++ was used. This was partly because the engineers were familiar with it, and also because it gave all the functionality needed to test to the IEC 61508 SIL 1 standard. The basic requirement is to test every class in isolation and to demonstrate code coverage to the levels of 100% entry-point (every function/method called at least once) and statement. In fact, IPL took the reasonable decision to additionally test to 100% condition coverage. This is more work than the basic project SIL demanded but was felt by the developers to give a useful additional level of confidence.

Since every class had a number of external interfaces, not all of which could be stubbed, the Cantata++ 'wrapping' facility was vital in allowing such isolation testing to be completed as planned. Stubbing involves the replacement of an external function with a programmable simulation having the same interface. Wrapping allows for the 'real' external code to be included in the test build, but with the option to intervene at the interface in order to, for example, check values being passed out or alter values being returned to the code under test.

6 Integration Testing

Cantata++ was also used for the next level up of testing, namely component testing. This formed the first level of integration testing, and was aimed at verifying the correct working of each NASS executable or DLL against specifications defined in the appropriate level of design. The testing involved calling public interfaces of the component under test, and stubbing or wrapping calls to external functions. Since NASS has its own database the component tests included 'real' database code so that testing included the option to initialise the database and check that updates to the database were as expected.

The project created and has maintained a fairly elaborate regression test facility which has allowed for nightly builds and re-runs of each class and component test in the entire system. This has served very well to enhance confidence in the change impact analysis system by ensuring that changes in one class are completely and properly compensated for in other affected classes and tests.

After testing the components the project test strategy called for sub-system testing. Since 100% coverage had already been achieved during unit testing, integration testing could be allowed to live up to its name – namely testing the integration of the software units. The team, with the agreement of the HA, determined that 100% entry-point coverage was suitable to demonstrate the completeness of the integration tests. This is in fact exactly in line with the 61508 requirement [7.4.8.3] to demonstrate that, 'all software modules ... interact correctly to perform their intended function...'

7 System Level Testing

Following sub-system testing the team carried out a further series of System Integration tests which were formally documented by IPL QA staff. These tests mainly served as a dry-run to gain confidence before going into the customer-witnessed Factory Acceptance Tests. For the most recent delivery of the project FATs took twenty days to run, much of which time was occupied by reconfiguring of the system between each successive test run. It was noteworthy that the system integration tests ran smoothly and revealed only a few design anomalies.

The last layer of testing before the NASS was allowed to be installed at the RCC was called Interaction testing. This was carried out at the offices of another HA contractor, Peek Traffic, and involved running NASS on a rig which included NMCS2 equipment in exactly the same configuration as the live NMCS2 system. The intention here was to ensure that NASS could interact correctly with the other live systems at the RCC.

Lastly, Site Acceptance tests were held at the RCC to demonstrate that the live NASS was in fact operating correctly and safely with the rest of the NMCS2 system. See Table 3 for a summary of testing levels within the NASS development project.

8 Conclusions from Project

This paper illustrates that a properly run 61508 project, even at a relatively low SIL, can be demanding on test time. It is intended to reinforce the point that testing is, on one level, about providing reassurance to developers that they can move with reasonable confidence from one stage of the project to another. At a different level it can provide confidence to other stakeholders (e.g. the customer) that the system will work safely and reliably when installed on site.

Table 3. Complete hierarchy of testing on NASS project, at third phase of the project

Name of tests	Testing	Tool	Comments
Class/Unit tests	C++ classes	Cantata++	283 in total. 100% Entry-point, statement and condition coverage. Test plan is in the class specification.
Component tests	Components (individual executables or DLLs)	Cantata++	23 of these in total. 100% Entry-Point coverage. Test plan is in the component specification.
Regression tests	Re-runs of Unit and Component tests	Cantata++ and IPL-developed framework	Run nightly
Integration testing	Aspects of ADS and SSDS	IPL-developed simulators	
System Test	Entire System	IPL-developed simulators	Dry-run of Factory Acceptance Tests, witnessed by IPL QA staff.
Factory Acceptance Test	Entire system	IPL-developed simulators plus HA 'Portable Standard'.	Formal run of System Tests at IPL offices, witnessed by HA.
Interaction tests	Entire system	Test Rig at Peek Traffic	Formal run of tests at Peek, witnessed by HA.
Site Acceptance Test	Entire system	Live at RCC	Formal run of tests at RCC, witnessed by HA.

A good project will work from a test strategy (i.e. determine in advance at what stages and levels in the lifecycle testing should be carried out), and will demand that test plans exist for each entity to be tested. Testing needs to generate results as evidence of test completion (i.e. be self-documenting). Furthermore, testing needs to be conducted in a repeatable fashion because the one certainty is that tests will need to be run and re-run at all levels many times.

Some thoughts arising from experiences gained over the 5 year duration of the project include:

- The software class test plans were arguably too detailed. In some cases they extended to many times the length of the basic class specification. The result was that they took longer to write than the tests themselves took to prepare and run. This was felt to be rather unproductive effort, and it might have been better to concentrate test planning on core 'black box' functionality, leaving the rest to be covered by the developers as they aim to achieve the full structural coverage level established in the project's standards.

- While the standard did not explicitly state the test coverage analysis level appropriate for the adopted SIL (see Section 9.2, below) the project's decision to aim for 100% of statement, decision and condition coverage was felt to be a good one. The project team was comfortable working to that degree of detail, and it does give high confidence for a relatively low level of extra effort. A useful by-product will be that if the System is ever re-classified to SIL 2, then there should be no trouble in justifying a claim that the class testing is already conformant.

- Testing C++ classes needs to be a combination of black-box and white-box testing. There was possibly too much focus on testing individual methods within classes, and not enough on testing the class as a whole object. The only work package where full 'end-to-end' functional testing on classes was carried out was the database interface package. This principle could have been extended to the other work packages.

- The integration testing was very useful and fully justified its inclusion in the project's Quality Plan. It enabled the timely detection of errors in low-level class specifications i.e. classes which successfully verified (by test) that they conformed to their specifications, but where the specification itself had not implemented the higher-level design intention.

9 Reflections on IEC 61508 and Testing Requirements

The IEC 61508 standard was first published in 1998, which makes it now about 10 years old. It is reasonable to suppose that the thinking and guidance that went into it dates from the 10 years or so preceding that. So potentially the practices mandated and recommended in the standard are 20 years old. This raises two related questions in the authors' minds:

- Are the recommendations still recognised as valid and useful by current standards?

- Are there any current practices not present in the standard which might usefully be considered candidates for any revision?

The rest of this section is devoted to a brief attempt to answer these questions.

9.1 Are the recommendations still recognised as valid and useful by current standards?

Starting from the standard's sections 7.4.7 [Requirements for Software Module Testing] and 7.4.8 [Requirements for Software Integration Testing], this leads to Tables A.5., B.2, B.3 and B.6. Making reference as needed to Part 7 of the published standard ('Overview of techniques and measures'), and taking these tables and their contents in turn we have a number of observations.

Even the term 'software integration' in Table A.5 is somewhat vague. As has been seen from the above case study the term integration can be applied at several discrete levels, so what is appropriate at one level of integration testing may not be so at another. The choice of appropriate integration testing levels becomes a matter of engineering judgment based partly on balancing cost with SIL constraints. It is not objectively definable.

Table 4. Comments on IEC 61508 Table A.5 'Software Module Testing and Integration'

Technique	Comment
1. Probabilistic testing (HR at SIL 4)	The authors are not convinced this is a useful activity for module/integration testing activities as software is usually deterministic at these levels. It is probably more suitable for use in higher levels of testing, though potentially difficult/expensive to set up.
2. Dynamic analysis and testing (HR at SILs 2-4)	See Table 5, below.
3. Data recording and analysis (HR at all SILs)	It seems a little unnecessary to include this 'technique' in this table. It does not particularly relate to the detail of software testing but may be considered as part of overall project development documentation. What 'analysis' is intended at the testing stage is not specified other than to suggest it may 'establish a wide variety of information'. On the NASS project the Cantata++ tool was able to generate all the evidence deemed necessary.
4. Functional and Black-box testing (HR at all SILs). See also Table 6, below	This corresponds most closely to what software developers would recognise as verification by testing at these levels. The former would allow for simulation of external calls, whereas the latter would expect all modules to be present in the test build. To be successful written functional specifications must exist for all items under test.
5. Performance testing (HR at SILs 3-4) See also Table 7, below	The authors contend that applying performance testing at these levels is questionable as performance requirements are very rarely specified. It is much more usual to define performance requirements at system test level, so this technique is arguably best omitted from here.
6. Interface testing (HR at SILs 3-4)	The detail of interface testing as documented in Part 7 would seem to impose an unjustifiable burden on developers. A more proportionate approach would be to verify that each interface variable (typically subprogram parameters) is checked for the correct (i.e. expected) value on each call but not to be demanding that the full range of possible values be explored. This requirement is probably better left to the tests of the individual sub-programs using boundary-value analysis.

Table 5. Comments on IEC 61508 Table B.2 'Dynamic Analysis and Testing'

Technique	Comment
1. Test case execution from boundary value analysis (HR for SILs 2-4)	This is a valid activity (in the authors' opinion) when combined with equivalence class testing, as a means of boosting confidence in software beyond that already achieved with basic functional/structure-based testing.
2. Test case execution from error guessing (R at all SILs)	Based on the description of the technique given in Part 7 this seems a somewhat random (though based on 'experience and intuition') approach to test case generation. As such it would not seem to have much to recommend its continued inclusion.
3. Test case execution from error seeding (R at SILs 2-4)	This is not really testing but a way of attempting to gauge the effectiveness of existing tests. It is highly arbitrary (i.e. who decides what error to seed?) and has, in the authors' opinion, very little to recommend its use.
4. Performance modelling (HR at SIL 4)	It is unclear why this is included in this table. Modelling is not testing. If it has a role it is probably at a higher level, under the heading validation.
5. Equivalence classes and input partition testing (HR at SIL 4)	See comment for 1 above.
6. Structure-based testing (HR at SILs 3-4).	This relates to the widely used and accepted technique of measuring test coverage to gauge test effectiveness and thus assign a (subjective) confidence to the value of testing achieved by other means. The big flaw in its inclusion in this standard is that it provides no specific recommendations as to types and levels of coverage that should be achieved. See next section (9.2).

In addition to the use of functional/black-box testing in module/integration testing, Table B.6 of the standard also recommends these testing types at system level. The comments in Table 6 are related to the latter.

Table 6. Comments on IEC 61508 Table B.3 'Functional and Black-box Testing'

Technique	Comment
1. Test case execution from cause consequence diagrams (R at SILs 3-4)	Applicability depends on the prior production of cause-consequence diagrams. It is not evident that this is a recognised technique in modern terms, though an equivalent might be sought in current UML terminology.
2. Prototyping/animation (R at SILs 3-4)	These techniques appear to be far more related to a validation activity than anything that can reasonably be termed testing.
3. Boundary value analysis (HR at SILs 2-4)	It is questionable whether this approach to generating test inputs is a practical proposition at system test level. The combinatorial effect of generating all possible boundary values for an entire system is likely to lead to the collapse of the enterprise under sheer weight of numbers. If a 'selective' approach is adopted how does this improve on simple functional testing? This type of testing is best left to the module/integration testing stages.
4. Equivalence class and input partition testing (HR at SILs 2-3)	Same as above.
5. Process simulation (R at all SILs)	Similar comments as 2 above. Simulation is not a testing technique. It should not be included in this table.

Comments in Table 7 all relate to use of techniques at the system test level.

Table 7. Comments on IEC 61508 Table B.6 'Performance testing'

Technique	Comment
1. Avalanche/stress testing (HR at SILs 3-4)	Stress testing is a valid and useful technique provided that some performance indicators are laid down in advance.
2. Response timings and memory constraints (HR at all SILs)	These are valid and useful techniques but why have they been combined as one entry? They should arguably be treated as separate requirements, though it is noted that memory limitations can lead to performance degradation.
3. Performance requirements (HR at all SILs)	This is a valid and necessary part of system testing, but as with stress testing it does require that performance indicators be defined in advance.

9.2 Are there any current practices not present in the standard which might usefully be considered candidates for any revision?

The aim in this section is to highlight a deficiency (in the authors' opinion) in the current standard as it relates to software testing, namely the omission of defining any testing coverage standards. This is in marked contrast to the DO-178B standard for Civil Avionics (RTCA, 1992) which lays down both the types and percentage coverage to be achieved in software testing. The nearest current standard approach is to recommend (HR) the use of structural-based testing (Table B.2 item 6) for SILs 3-4.

There are many ways to define code structures (statements, decisions, conditions etc) and the current 61508 standard does nothing to specify what should be used. The 'Overview' (Part 7) of the standard does list the various types and gives brief notes on them, but limits any recommendation to saying they should be achieved 'depending on the level of rigour required'. In the authors' opinion this is far too subjective considering what an important role that structure-based testing usually plays in code verification.

Based on the DO-178B standard it should be fairly easy to include a table of recommended types and levels such as that shown in Table 8.

Table 8. Recommended coverage types and levels

Coverage Type	SIL 1	SIL 2	SIL 3	SIL 4
100% Entry points	HR	HR	HR	HR
100% Statements	R	HR	HR	HR
100% Decisions	R	R	HR	HR
100% MC/DC[1]	R	R	R	HR

The value of MC/DC coverage can be debated but within the civil avionics software community it appears to have stood the test of time. A revision of the DO-178 standard (DO-178C) is in the process of being prepared, and it will be interesting to see what emerges from this. If and when IEC 61508 goes back for revision the authors would contend that there are several important elements which could be improved.

Acknowledgment This paper is an extended version of an article that first appeared in Safety Systems, the Safety-Critical Systems Club Newsletter.

References

Chilenski J, Miller S (1994) Applicability of modified condition/decision coverage to software testing. Journal of Software Engineering 9:193-200
IEC 61508 (1998) Functional Safety of Electrical/Electronic/Programmable Electronic Safety-related Systems Part 3. International Electrotechnical Commission, Geneva
RTCA (1992) DO-178B Software Considerations in Airborne Systems and Equipment Certification. Radio Technical Commission of America, Washington DC

---

[1] MC/DC = Modified Condition/Decision Coverage (Chilenski and Miller, 1994)

Defence Standard 00-56 Issue 4: Towards Evidence-Based Safety Standards

Catherine Menon, Richard Hawkins and John McDermid

Software Systems Engineering Initiative, Department of Computer Science, University of York

Heslington, York YO10 5DD

Abstract Defence Standard 00-56 Issue 4 is goal-based, and requires system developers to demonstrate how they have achieved safety. To this end, evidence is used to support claims relating to software safety. One of the most subtle questions when constructing a safety argument is the determination of whether the evidence presented is sufficient to assure the safety of the system to the level required. This paper presents a framework for assessing the assurance of evidence and claims. We also present a vocabulary for discussing factors which influence assurance. This framework and vocabulary together enable us to construct and discuss safety arguments for software. Using this framework and vocabulary, we present some sample discussions which demonstrate how the factors influencing assurance can interact.

1 Introduction

DS 00-56 Issue 4 (Ministry of Defence 2007) is goal-based – it sets out requirements relating to safety management, but does not prescribe how those requirements will be met. In general, before a system can be deployed, it is necessary to produce a safety case setting out an argument and supporting evidence that the system is acceptably safe.

The UK Ministry of Defence has adopted a principle that standards should be 'as civil as possible, and only as military as necessary'. DS 00-56 Issue 4 deliberately moved away from prescription to allow, for example, the software elements of a system to be developed to appropriate civil standards, e.g. DO178B (RTCA and EUROCAE 1992) for aircraft software. However, it would also be equally valid to use a standard such as EN 50128 (British Standards 2001) for software in a railway signalling system, or a bespoke approach for military-unique systems. In all these cases there is an issue of what amounts to an acceptable argument and

C. Dale, T. Anderson (eds.), *Safety-Critical Systems: Problems, Process and Practice*,
DOI 10.1007/978-1-84882-349-5_15, © Springer-Verlag London Limited 2009

what constitutes sufficient evidence – which we can perhaps best summarise as sufficient assurance of evidence and argument.

The MOD has funded the Software Systems Engineering Initiative (SSEI) as a centre of excellence for defence software systems. One of the initial tasks to be undertaken by the SSEI is to provide guidance on software safety, in the context of DS 00-56 Issue 4. One of the key issues to be addressed by this work is to provide a sound basis for assessing, or measuring, assurance in evidence. This paper focuses on the core technical issues in assessing assurance, and the conclusions outline how the model set out here will fit into the guidance to be produced by the SSEI.

One of the most subtle aspects of the evidential approach is assessing whether the safety requirements have been satisfied by the arguments and evidence presented. The assurance of a system is the measure of how much confidence we have in the safety argument and supporting evidence. That is, the assurance of a system is the extent to which we are confident that the safety requirements have been met. The assurance requirements on a system vary with the risk of the system hazards, and any failure to meet these requirements must be justified. We recommend that the justification take the form of an argument based on the ALARP principle, and will refer to this as ACARP (As Confident As Reasonably Practical).

We present here a framework for assessing the assurance of a safety argument. This framework identifies the major factors which influence the assurance of a claim, and therefore influence the confidence we have in the safety of a system. The framework also provides a means of calculating assurance from these factors. One of the primary advantages of such a framework is that it provides a generalised foundation for calculating assurance in any system, and furthermore for verifying the accuracy of any assurance claimed to have been achieved by a safety argument and the associated evidence. In addition, this framework establishes a vocabulary to discuss safety arguments. Thus, it is possible to communicate to the people responsible for providing evidence – such as testing evidence or formal analysis of the system – precisely what evidence would be needed to achieve the required assurance.

Section 2 establishes a framework for addressing assurance in arguments, and section 3 extends this to evidence presented in support of an argument. Section 3 also identifies questions which should be asked when determining the quality of the evidence presented. Assurance is a multi-faceted concept, and there is a risk of 'double-accounting' when assessing assurance; section 4 discusses this issue and considers how to combine assurance. Section 4 also considers the issue of propagating assurance through argument structures, and section 5 draws conclusions.

2 Claims and Arguments

Throughout this paper we will be referring to the constituent parts of a safety argument. Our terminology for discussing arguments is based on GSN (Kelly 1999), although there are other acceptable methods of presenting safety arguments (Adelard 1998). We define the key concepts we will use below.

Definition 1. Within a system safety case, a *claim* is a statement made about the system which may or may not be true.

For example 'All omission failures are detected and handled acceptably' is a claim about a system.

Definition 2. An *argument* is a connected sequence of statements intended to establish a claim.

For example, 'All omission failures are detected and handled acceptably, because Components A and B are present in the system, and tests show that they detect and handle all possible omission failures' is an argument.

Definition 3. A *higher-level claim* is a claim which is supported by other claims.

For example, the claim 'Software safety requirements mitigate all system hazards' is supported by the three claims 'Software requirements are adequate and address all hazards', 'Software requirements are met' and 'Software requirements are traceable'.

Definition 4. A *leaf claim* is a claim which is supported directly by evidence.

For example, a leaf claim might be 'Function X has no side effects', being supported by static analysis.

In the course of refining an argument, it is possible for a claim which was originally presented as a leaf claim to become a higher-level claim. It is also possible for claims to be simultaneously higher-level claims and leaf claims, depending on whether they are supported exclusively by other claims, by evidence, or by a mixture of both.

The assurance of a higher-level claim is dependent upon the assurance of its supporting claims. However, the assurance of the higher-level claim may not be dependent upon every supporting claim to an equal extent. In the following section, we identify some factors which influence the degree to which a higher-level claim may be dependent upon a specific supporting claim. We also identify some more general influences which can increase or decrease the assurance of a claim. In this way we will present a means of analysing an argument to identify where assurance deficits (discrepancies between the assurance required and the assurance achieved) may have been introduced.

2.1 Assurance Factors

Throughout this discussion our model argument will consist of a higher-level claim HC supported by two supporting claims SC_1 and SC_2. That is, the purpose of the safety argument will be to justify the inference $SC_1 \wedge SC_2 \rightarrow HC$ (where the symbol $\wedge$ is to be interpreted as conjunction). The assurance of HC is a combination of the assurance of SC_1 and SC_2 and the strength of the inference $SC_1 \wedge SC_2 \rightarrow HC$. The strength of the inference is subject to the following factors.

2.1.1 Scope of Supporting Claims

Definition 5. *Scope* is defined as the degree to which the supporting claims entail the entirety of the higher-level claim.

Scope is most easily understood where it refers to the extent of the claim HC which is addressed by either SC_1 or SC_2. For example, consider the argument $SC_1 \wedge SC_2 \rightarrow HC$, where the claims are instantiated as follows:

HC: 'Function X is fault-free in all 10 operational modes'
SC_1: 'Function X is fault-free in operational modes 1, 2, 3, 4, 5'
SC_2: 'Function X is fault-free in operational modes 6, 7'

In this case, we deduce that the *scope* of $SC_1 \wedge SC_2$ is most, but not the entirety, of HC (in practice, we would also be interested in other variables such as the time spent in each operational mode during typical use). We can also deduce that the scope of SC_1 is larger than the scope of SC_2. Consequently, the assurance of HC is dependent upon the assurance of SC_1 to a greater extent than it is upon the assurance of SC_2. A more complex example of scope can be observed in the following example, where HC is supported by claims SC_1, SC_2 and SC_3.

HC: 'Software safety requirements mitigate all system hazards'
SC_1: 'Software requirements are adequate and address all hazards'
SC_2: 'Software requirements are met'
SC_3: 'Software requirements are traceable'

Here, several supporting claims each address a different facet of the higher level claim. In the absence of any argument to justify why one supporting claim is more important than another, we assume each of these to have equal scope.

To avoid confusion, we will use the expression *equal scope* to describe the situation where multiple supporting claims influence the higher-level claim to the same extent. That is, equal scope implies that each supporting claim addresses different aspects from the others, but all these aspects are equally important to the higher-level claim. We will use the expression *identical scope* to describe the situation where multiple claims address the same aspect of the higher-level claim. This has also been referred to as convergent support (Govier 1988), and is described more fully in Section 2.1.4.

The advantage of identifying scope as a factor in assurance is twofold. Firstly, it formalises the idea that a higher level claim can be dependent upon one supporting claim to a greater extent than the others. That is, in the absence of all other factors (see below) we can state that the assurance of the higher level claim is most strongly influenced by the assurance of the supporting claim with the greater scope. Secondly, scope helps us to understand why assurance deficits may have been allowed within a safety argument. Where the combined scope of supporting claims does not address the entirety of the higher level claim, this is an indication that the argument structure is flawed or limited. In other words, this indicates that an essential premise of the safety argument is missing, meaning that some aspects of the higher level claim are not supported in any way. The visible consequence of this is that the assurance of that aspect of the higher level claim is zero, and the assurance of the entire higher level claim is therefore diminished. In general, such assurance deficits would need to be justified along ACARP principles if they remained in a final safety case.

2.1.2 Independence of Supporting Claims

Definition 6. *Independence* is defined as the diversity between the sets of evidence used to support the claims SC_1, ..., SC_n in the inference $SC_1 \wedge ... \wedge SC_n \rightarrow HC$.

More specifically, independence is the measure of how qualitatively 'different' the evidence supporting SC_1 is from the evidence supporting SC_2 (note that if SC_1 and SC_2 are not leaf claims, then evidence can only support them via other supporting claims). If the evidence that supports SC_1 shares some significant characteristics with the evidence which supports SC_2, then SC_1 and SC_2 are said to demonstrate low independence from each other, and the assurance of the higher-level claim HC will consequently be diminished.

Independence may be *conceptual* or *mechanistic*. Items of conceptually different independence are based on different underlying theories, while items of mechanistically independent evidence are obtained by implementing the same underlying theory in different ways (Weaver et al. 2003). For example, formal methods and testing will produce conceptually independent evidence, while conducting testing alone using a variety of techniques will produce mechanistically independent evidence.

One illustration of the consequences of a lack of independence is the effect that common-cause failures can have on the assurance of a claim. If the evidence for SC_1 is generated using a particular tool, then any undetected failure in that tool will result in flaws in the evidence and consequently an incorrect (often unjustifiably high) confidence in the truth of SC_1. Because the assurance of higher level claims depends upon the assurance of the supporting claims, the assurance of HC will also be affected by this tool failure. If the same tool is then used to generate evidence for SC_2, the effect of the tool error on the assurance of HC will be compounded. In other words, a high degree of conceptual and mechanistic independence between the evidence supporting SC_1 and SC_2 will reduce the impact of any common-cause failure when generating these groups of evidence. Section 3.7 contains further discussion on how to estimate the independence of items of evidence.

2.1.3 User-defined Importance

Definition 7. *User-defined importance* is the additional weighting placed upon one or more supporting claims due to legislative or other precedents.

Legislation and standards often identify certain safety principles as carrying more weight than others in an argument. This can lead to a supporting claim SC_1 being considered more 'important' than another, say SC_2, even though SC_1 and SC_2 may have equal scope. Consequently, the assurance of HC is then affected by the assurance of SC_1 more than the assurance of SC_2.

The safety of children or the general public as compared to the safety of adults or defence force personnel is a common example of this (Health and Safety Executive 2001). For example, consider the argument $SC_1 \wedge SC_2 \rightarrow HC$, where the claims are instantiated as follows:

HC: 'Personnel in all 4 rooms of the nuclear plant are acceptably protected against failures'
$SC1$: 'Safety systems are in place for rooms 1 and 2 (approx. 10 people)'
$SC2$: 'Safety systems are in place for rooms 3 and 4 (approx. 10 people)'

The scope of SC_1 is equal to the scope of SC_2, because they both address equal extents of the claim HC. However, if rooms 3 and 4 are the nuclear plant childcare centre (assuming there is one), then guidance for decision-making issued by the Health and Safety Executive (Health and Safety Executive 2001) would consider the claim SC_2 to be more important.

User-defined importance therefore allows us to consider many of the unstated or 'intuitive' considerations which can affect the quality of a safety argument. While theoretically it is certainly the case that the safety of the power plant in the example above is dependent equally upon the assurance with which we can state both sets of rooms are safe, a doubt as to the safety of the childcare centre is far less palatable than a doubt as to the safety of the other rooms. That is, this example demonstrates a situation where a doubt about one supporting claim SC_1 is more easily justified than a doubt about another supporting claim SC_2, even though both these doubts would logically have the same impact on the assurance of the higher-level claim HC. In other words, due to user-defined importance SC_2 has a potentially much greater impact on the assurance of HC than SC_1, so the consequences of failing to meet assurance requirements on SC_2 will be correspondingly greater.

Previous attempts to define assurance (Weaver 2004) have not formally codified this factor. In general, however, arguments are always written with an intended reader in mind, and are written to be compelling from the point of view of that reader. Consequently, all arguments consider user-defined importance to a certain extent. By formalising this, we make it possible to assess, for example, the impact of public feeling upon the required assurance for safety-critical systems.

User-defined importance is usually expressed in general terms, meaning that certain principles (such as the safety of children) are defined to be of greater importance than others (such as the safety of defence force personnel) when constructing a safety case. In some cases this has been codified in legislation, standards or guidance (Health and Safety Executive 2001). An example of the latter case is the prioritisation of certain types of evidence expressed in DS 00-56 Issue 4 (Ministry of Defence 2007). Section 3.6 discusses this in further detail.

2.1.4 Reinforcement

Definition 8. *Reinforcement* is defined as the extent to which multiple supporting claims address the same aspects of a higher-level claim.

Arguments where reinforcement is relevant are those where two (or more) supporting claims SC_1 and SC_2 have *identical* scope. That is, where SC_1 and SC_2 address the same aspects of the higher-level claim HC. A high degree of reinforcement within the supporting claims means that the assurance of HC will be increased.

When assessing the effects of reinforcing a supporting claim SC_1, it is important to consider the assurance of the other claims which will be used to reinforce SC_1. While it is certainly true that the assurance of the higher level claim HC can be increased by introducing a claim SC_3 which reinforces SC_1, the extent of this increase can vary. If both SC_3 and SC_1 are strongly assured themselves, the reinforcement will have a significant positive effect on the assurance of HC. Equally, reinforcing a supporting claim SC_1 which has low assurance with a claim SC_3 with high assurance will greatly increase the assurance of HC. However, where two supporting claims are only weakly assured themselves, a high degree of reinforcement between these claims will only marginally increase the assurance of HC. The interaction of independence and other factors will influence the effect of reinforcement, as we discuss in Section 4.1.4. Nevertheless, the value of reinforcement within each individual safety argument must be assessed on its own merits.

Reinforcement can also be used to express the effect of *counter-evidence*, a quantity recommended for consideration by DS 00-56 Issue 4. This is discussed in more detail in Section 3.8.

2.2 Applying Assurance Factors

We can use the factors introduced in Section 2.1 to provide a means of calculating the assurance of a higher level claim. The assurance of any claim HC is dependent upon:

- The assurance of each supporting claim, allowing for:
    - The scope of this supporting claim relative to HC
    - The user-defined importance of this supporting claim

- The independence of all supporting claims
- The degree to which any supporting claims are reinforced

That is, the assurance of the claim HC is dependent solely upon the assurance of the supporting claims SC_1 and SC_2, the independence of these supporting claims, and the extent of reinforcement between these claims. The degree to which each the assurance of an individual supporting claim SC_1 affects the assurance of HC is determined by the scope of SC_1 and any additional importance placed upon principles which affect SC_1.

The two primary advantages of decomposing assurance as described above are an ease in communication, and a more standardised approach to safety arguments. This framework makes explicit a number of different ways to improve the assurance of a claim, as well as providing a means to assess the impact of each individual claim on the assurance of the entire argument. Because safety arguments depend ultimately on the assurance of leaf claims, we devote the next section to a discussion of how to ensure maximum assurance at this level.

3 Leaf Claims

As described above, assurance within a safety argument 'cascades upwards', with the assurance of higher-level claims being determined from the assurance of supporting claims. This means that the assurance of the leaf claims is of vital importance, supporting as they do the entire safety argument. Unfortunately, when generating evidence it is common for there to be limited visibility of the proposed safety argument structure. Consequently, it is often difficult to determine the value of an item of evidence to the safety argument. Furthermore, the people generating the evidence may not be system safety experts and may not have the resources to interpret abstract principles for increasing assurance, and apply them to evidence. To negate this problem, we have provided sample checklists of questions which will help determine the quality of an item of evidence. These checklists facilitate discussion between safety experts and system developers, by providing an accessible language to discuss those properties which are required for the evidence to support a compelling safety argument.

3.1 Assessing the Assurance of a Leaf Claim

The assurance of a leaf claim depends upon the quality, or rigour, of the evidence provided. We have identified seven factors which must be considered in determining the assurance of a leaf claim from evidence. Four of these, *scope, user-defined importance, independence* and *reinforcement* have been discussed previously in Section 2.1. There are also three factors which apply solely when assessing the assurance for a leaf claim: *replicability, trustworthiness* and *coverage*. These factors are as follows:

- Replicability: the ease with which the evidence could be replicated.
- Trustworthiness: the likelihood that the evidence is free from errors.
- Scope: the extent of the claim which this type of evidence could be reasonably expected to address.
- Coverage: the extent of the claim which is actually addressed by the evidence, relative to the scope.
- User-defined importance: the additional weighting placed upon certain types of evidence by legislation, standards or client preference.
- Independence: the diversity of the evidence, as well as the different tools and methods used to obtain evidence.
- Reinforcement: the extent to which multiple items of evidence support the same aspects of a leaf claim.

The following sections discuss how each factor is to be interpreted with respect to evidence. We also present sample checklists of questions which can be used to assess the quality of evidence. These checklists require neither visibility of the overall safety argument, nor a background in software safety management. Section 3.9 then describes how to estimate the assurance of a leaf claim from these factors.

3.2 Replicability

The replicability of evidence is the extent to which this evidence can be reproduced. Evidence may not be replicable for two reasons:

- The circumstances under which the evidence was obtained no longer hold.
- The evidence is by nature subjective.

The first situation commonly arises for evidence which is the result of discussion or analysis during an early part of the development. HAZOP analysis is a good example of this, in that it cannot be reproduced at a later date. Firstly, the system may have changed so that hazards which were present have now been removed entirely, or new hazards introduced. Secondly, even if this is not the case, the discussion and thought-processes of the participants will not be exactly the same as before. Consequently, it is impossible to reproduce the analysis and gain the same results. Another common example of evidence which lacks replicability is in-service or historical evidence.

The second reason for a lack of replicability is a lack of objectivity in the evidence, a situation which commonly arises with review evidence. Although the competence of multiple reviewers may be judged to be equal, there is no guarantee that they will produce identical reviews. Similarly, any evidence which relies on interpretation is said to lack replicability.

Supporting a leaf claim with replicable evidence will increase the assurance of that claim to a greater degree than supporting it with evidence which is not replicable. This is a commonly accepted principle, to the extent where replicable evidence is often officially preferred within standards and contract conditions. For example, DS 00-56 Issue 4 (Ministry of Defence 2007) expresses a preference for analytical evidence, whereas in DS 00-55 Issue 2 (Ministry of Defence 1997) the emphasis is on formal techniques.

3.3 Trustworthiness

The trustworthiness of evidence is the faith which we place in the integrity of the evidence. Untrustworthy evidence is often characterised as evidence which is 'buggy' (Weaver et al. 2005) and can greatly reduce the assurance of claims it supports. Questions to consider when determining the trustworthiness of evidence include:

- Was the evidence gathered in accordance with any documented standard (for example, a COTS product developed to DO-178B will have some evidence in its safety case, gathered according to the principles of this standard)?
- Are the evidence-gathering personnel competent? Are they certified to an appropriate standard? Have they performed the tests before?
- How valid are the assumptions and simplifications that were made?
- Is there a culture of safety in the environment where the evidence was gathered?
- For COTS products especially, has the evidence been obtained from disinterested sources?
- Is there any counter-evidence (see Section 3.8.1)?

Supporting a leaf claim with trustworthy evidence will increase the assurance of that claim to a greater degree than supporting it with evidence which is not trustworthy. It is important to note that evidence which is deemed trustworthy may still contain flaws. For example, while there may be every indication that a tool is trustworthy, it is still possible that the results produced by applying this tool contain false negatives. Consequently, independence (Section 3.7) is still an important factor in guarding against common cause failures no matter how apparently trustworthy the evidence. Section 4.1.6 explains more about how trustworthiness can interact with the other factors which influence assurance.

3.4 Scope

Scope has been introduced in Section 2.1.1 and, for evidence, is to be interpreted as the extent to which a particular type of evidence can imply the truth of a leaf claim. Questions to consider to help determine the scope of a particular item of evidence include:

- Does this type of evidence typically produce results which would support all parts of the leaf claim? For example, evidence produced from formal analysis is unlikely to support a claim about a lack of timing failures in the system.
- If the evidence is to be obtained from testing, how much of the relevant functionality referred to in the leaf claim will be tested?
- If the leaf claim refers to multiple components, do you envisage testing all these components and their interactions?
- Will all applicable operational modes be examined when generating this evidence?

In keeping with the earlier notation, if E represents an item of evidence, and LC a leaf claim, the scope of E helps determine the strength of the inference $E \rightarrow LC$. The higher the combined scope of all evidence supporting LC, the higher the assurance of LC will be. If two items of evidence are provided to support a claim, the evidence with the greater scope will have the greater effect on the assurance of the claim.

3.4.1 Scope and Evidence

If the evidence does not cover the full scope of the leaf claim, this will result in diminished assurance for the leaf claim. While this does not necessarily imply that the assurance of the system will not meet the requirements, it does signal the need for an ACARP argument to justify this decrease in assurance. Such an argument would provide reasons as to why it is not necessary to generate further evidence to address the missing scope. The scope of evidence is determined mainly by the type of the evidence, and the extent to which it is possible for such evidence to fully address the leaf claim. This could also be referred to as the intent of the evidence.

The scope of evidence can be determined before the evidence has been generated. Scope is affected by considerations such as the fidelity of any models used in formal analysis, the planned coverage of tests, the number of operational modes for which historical data can be sought and so on. There is a closely related concept to scope, which determines how well the evidence gathering processes have been implemented, or the intent has been achieved: *coverage.*

3.5 Coverage

The coverage of an item of evidence supporting a claim is the extent of the claim addressed by this evidence, relative to that which could reasonably have been expected from evidence of this type (that is, relative to the scope of this evidence). Questions to consider when determining coverage are:

- How much of the relevant software functionality was examined, compared with what could have been examined?
- To what degree was consistency of configuration maintained?
- In how many different valid operational modes or environments did the evidence-gathering take place? Was there a reason why not all operational modes were examined?
- For historical evidence, were all major sources considered?
- To what extent did the evidence gathering processes match the usage profile of the system?
- How thorough was any review evidence? Were all relevant documents made available to the reviewers, and was the system adequately completed at the time of review?

Supporting a leaf claim with evidence demonstrating high coverage will increase the assurance of that claim to a greater degree than supporting it with evidence demonstrating low coverage. An evidence-gathering process which is implemented and executed exactly as planned will theoretically generate evidence with maximum coverage. If a leaf claim is supported solely by evidence which does not provide maximum coverage, an argument using ACARP principles will be required to justify why this evidence is thought to provide sufficient assurance.

3.5.1 Coverage and Scope

Scope and coverage illustrate different reasons why the assurance of a leaf claim (and consequently of any higher-level claim it supports) may be lower than desired. If low scope is the cause of the low assurance, this indicates that the evidence-gathering processes were not appropriate to the task. For example, modelling a system using formal methods is not an appropriate technique to gather evidence about a lack of timing failures. Similarly, normal-range testing will address only a small part of a claim that a system is robust to erroneous input. In both these situations, therefore, the proposed item of evidence will have low scope and will not strongly support the claim.

By contrast, if low coverage is the cause of the low assurance, this indicates that the evidence-gathering processes, while appropriate, were not implemented as well as expected. For example, review evidence may be used to support a claim that the system was developed in accordance with good practice. The scope of this evidence may be quite high. However, if the review is undertaken midway through the development lifecycle the coverage will be low because many life-cycle activities would not yet have been completed.

3.5.2 Rigour: Coverage, Trustworthiness and Replicability

Coverage, trustworthiness and replicability together make up what is termed the *rigour*, or quality, of the evidence. Presenting evidence which is highly rigorous will increase the assurance of a leaf claim more than presenting evidence which is less so. That is, to achieve a given assurance, the quantity of evidence required will vary inversely with its rigour. Similarly, *counter-evidence* (Section 3.8.1) of greater rigour will decrease the assurance of a claim more than counter-evidence of little rigour.

3.6 User-defined Importance

The user-defined importance of a type of evidence is the additional weighting which is to be placed on that evidence by historical or legislative precedence, or by client preference. For example, DS 00-56 Issue 4 presents five evidence categories in order of importance. The assurance of a higher level claim is to an extent dependent upon the presence of evidence which is defined as important in this way. That is, providing a type of evidence which is defined to be more 'important' will increase the assurance of a leaf claim to a greater extent than providing a type of evidence which is not deemed so. Questions to consider when determining if there is any explicit user-defined importance on certain evidence types are:

- Has conformity to a particular standard been requested? If so, does that standard place a weighting on evidence types?
- Does the contract for the work state that particular types of evidence are preferred?
- Has the client specifically stated a preference for certain evidence-gathering processes (perhaps based on the track record of the supplier)?

An item of evidence which is deemed to be of greater importance than the others provided will have a greater effect on the assurance of the leaf claim.

It is important to remember that there may be no *explicit* description of the types of evidence which are deemed to be most compelling. In this case, user-defined importance is taken to be neutral. That is, any *implicit* user-defined importance cannot be considered as binding when determining assurance of claims.

3.7 Independence

Providing multiple items of independent evidence will increase confidence in the claim they support. Conceptual independence is preferred to mechanistic independence, and providing both will maximise the increase in confidence. Questions to consider when determining the degree of independence which has been obtained are:

- Have multiple items of conceptually diverse evidence (e.g. testing, formal analysis, review evidence) been presented?
- Has evidence been gathered in a number of mechanistically different ways? For example, if testing is performed using an automated tool, have a number of different tools been used?
- Have reviews been endorsed or approved by a number of different people?
- For COTS products, does evidence originate from a number of different sources?

Increasing the independence of the evidence provided to support a claim will increase the assurance of that claim. By contrast, if only one type of evidence is provided to support a claim, an argument using ACARP principles will be required to justify why this evidence is thought to provide sufficient assurance to the claim.

3.8 Reinforcement

Reinforcement is the extent to which multiple items of evidence support identical scope of a leaf claim. The assurance of a claim will be increased if the evidence supporting it is adequately reinforced. Note, however, that if evidence does not address the full scope of a leaf claim, then reinforcing this evidence will not increase the scope. That is, the assurance of the claim will still be negatively affected due to inadequate evidence scope.

One of the important aspects when considering how to reinforce evidence is to ensure that the items of evidence in question are independent. We discuss this in more detail in Section 4.1.4. When assessing whether one item of evidence is reinforced by another, the following questions should be considered:

- Do the two types of evidence have identical scope?
- If the two types of evidence do not have identical scope, can the results from one be extrapolated to provide reinforcement for the other?
- Is there another item of evidence which ought to be reinforcing, but in fact contradicts the claim? If so, this is *counter-evidence* and will greatly diminish the assurance of the leaf claim.

In general, the assurance of a leaf claim will be increased if multiple items of evidence can be presented which reinforce each other. However, when determining the extent of this effect, it is necessary to consider the rigour (Section 3.5.2) of the evidence in question. That is, two items of evidence which reinforce each other and both have a high degree of rigour will have a greater positive impact on the assurance of the leaf claim than two reinforcing items of evidence which do not demonstrate this high rigour.

3.8.1 Counter-evidence

Counter-evidence refers to the provision of an item of evidence which has the potential to undermine a claim. Some standards, such as DS 00-56 Issue 4, mandate the search for counter-evidence. If found, counter-evidence will greatly reduce the assurance of a claim. The degree to which the assurance of the claim is reduced will be directly dependent upon the rigour (Section 3.5.2) of the counter-evidence. However, even counter-evidence with a relatively low degree of rigour will have a negative impact upon the assurance of a leaf claim – and consequently on the assurance of any claim supported by this leaf claim.

Furthermore, the provision of counter-evidence may have an effect on the assurance of other claims which are not themselves refuted by the counter-evidence. This is because the presence of counter-evidence which refutes a claim may lower the trustworthiness of any evidence E_2 which supports this claim. If E_2 is also used to support a second claim, then the assurance of this second claim may be lowered due to the lowered trustworthiness of E_2. Section 4.1.5 discusses this in more detail.

3.9 Leaf Claim Assurance

When determining the assurance of a leaf claim, it is necessary to take into account all factors discussed above, for all supporting items of evidence presented. With that in mind, the assurance of a leaf claim is dependent upon:

- The rigour (replicability, trustworthiness and coverage) of each item of evidence, allowing for:
  - The scope of this evidence
  - The user-defined importance of this evidence

- The independence of all evidence supporting this claim
- The degree to which all items of evidence are reinforced

By noting the parallels between this definition and that given in Section 2.2 we can deduce that, for evidence, assurance is interpreted as being rigour. This observation, combined with the decomposition of rigour as described in Section 3.5.2, provides us with a vocabulary for assessing whether evidence is 'good enough', or 'sufficient' to support a particular argument.

4 Separating and Combining Assurance Factors

In the previous section we discussed how the assurance of a leaf claim is dependent upon the rigour of the evidence presented, and we described factors which influence this dependence. Unfortunately, in the process of determining the assurance of a claim it is inevitable that information is lost. To see this, note that an item of evidence may be judged to lack rigour for three reasons: a lack of trustworthiness, replicability or coverage. All these situations will have the same end result – a decrease in rigour and therefore a decrease in the assurance of the leaf claim supported by this evidence. Consequently, given the situation $SC_1 \wedge SC_2 \rightarrow HC$, if HC has a lower assurance than is required, it is difficult to immediately see how this could be rectified without 'propagating up' specific knowledge about how the assurance of SC_1 and SC_2 were determined.

To obviate this problem, we recommend propagating the elements of rigour (replicability, trustworthiness and coverage) up to higher-level claims. This allows us to retain as much information as possible, and to structure the argument in a way which best compensates for any deficiency. Consequently, we will speak of the trustworthiness factor of a leaf claim as being obtained from the trustworthiness of all supporting items of evidence. The trustworthiness factor of a higher-level claim HC is a combination of the trustworthiness factors of SC_1 and SC_2, in a degree which is proportional to the scope and user-defined importance of each. Similarly, the replicability and coverage factors of HC are a combination of the replicability and coverage factors of supporting claims SC_1 and SC_2 in a degree proportional to the scope and user-defined importance of each. Finally, we will also refer to the independence factor of HC; this is the degree of independence between the evidence gathered for supporting claims SC_1 and SC_2 (see Section 2.1.2 for more details).

4.1 Interaction of Assurance factors

While it is impossible to prescribe a single optimal strategy for constructing every argument, there are some general observations which can be made about the interaction of those factors which influence assurance. In the sections below, we discuss how to extrapolate from particular combinations of assurance factors to conclusions about how a safety argument should be structured. Similarly, we provide some examples of where particular combinations of assurance factors can appear to have a more pronounced effect on the assurance of a higher-level claim than would actually be the case. These are anticipated to form the basis of anti-patterns (Weaver 2004), which are used to analyse common fallacious arguments. It should be emphasised that this section is not intended to be an exhaustive list of all possible interactions, but rather to demonstrate some of the 'flavour' of what is required in terms of propagating assurance upwards.

4.1.1 Trustworthiness and Independence

If a claim *HC* has a low trustworthiness factor (that is, the evidence which eventually supports this claim is not particularly trustworthy), then the assurance of *HC* will be decreased significantly if *HC* also has a low independence factor. That is, a combination of low trustworthiness and low independence factors will result in a significantly lowered assurance, perhaps to a greater degree than another combination of low assurance factors. The reason for this is that a low trustworthiness factor signals that the evidence has been gathered in a manner which would be likely to introduce errors. Furthermore, a low independence factor signals that all the evidence shares some common characteristics. That is, errors which affect one item of evidence are highly likely to affect the others. Consequently, combined low trustworthiness and independence factors signal that errors are likely to be present, and they are likely to affect all of the evidence presented. As a result, the assurance of *HC* will be lowered to a greater degree than would generally be the case.

4.1.2 Coverage and Trustworthiness

A low coverage factor for a claim means that there are parts of this claim that have not been addressed by any evidence, even though they are theoretically within the scope of the types of evidence which have been generated. This indicates that we might expect to see a correspondingly low trustworthiness factor for this claim. The reason for this conclusion is that the implementation of the evidence-gathering process was obviously not as thorough as expected (hence low coverage). This fact indicates that the evidence may have been generated in a careless manner (hence low trustworthiness). In other words, a low coverage factor combined with a high trustworthiness factor signals a possible deficiency in the assessment of the evidence.

4.1.3 User-defined Importance and Replicability

One of the most common examples of user-defined importance is the statement of a preference for a particular type of evidence (Ministry of Defence 2007). In many cases this preference can reasonably be judged to be due to this evidence being highly replicable (for example, formal methods and static analysis have a high degree of replicability). In this situation, when considering the extent to which the assurance of a leaf claim depends upon the rigour of an item of evidence, the user-defined importance should not also be taken into consideration. If it were, then evidence with a high replicability factor would have a disproportionate effect on the assurance of a leaf claim. To understand this, note that firstly high replicability would – in the absence of all other factors – cause this evidence to be judged highly rigorous, thereby increasing the assurance of any leaf claim it supports. Furthermore the leaf claim would be dependent upon this evidence to a greater degree, due to its high user-defined importance. Correspondingly, the assurance of the leaf claim will be "increased twice" solely because the evidence is highly replicable. This type of 'double-accounting' can result in imbalanced arguments which disproportionately favour some claims or types of evidence.

4.1.4 Reinforcement and Independence

The assurance of a claim HC is dependent upon the degree to which items of evidence reinforce each other (otherwise known as convergent support). However, reinforcement by independent items of evidence will increase the assurance of a claim to a greater degree than reinforcement by evidence which lacks independence. To see this, consider an item of evidence supporting some claim and resulting from execution of a test suite. It is possible to run this test suite again to obtain a second item of evidence with which to reinforce the first – however, most people would judge that this would not noticeably increase their confidence in the claim! However, reinforcing these test results with evidence obtained from formal analysis (i.e. evidence which is conceptually independent) is likely to increase confidence in the claim. Thus, a high degree of reinforcement coupled with a high degree of independence will increase the assurance of a claim to a greater degree than would generally be the case.

4.1.5 Counter-evidence and Trustworthiness

If counter-evidence is found which has the potential to undermine a claim, then this finding may cast doubt on the trustworthiness of evidence which supports that claim, requiring a reappraisal of the trustworthiness of this evidence. This situation arises when the counter-evidence and the supporting evidence have identical scope – that is, they address the same aspects of the claim and would otherwise be assessed as reinforcing items of evidence.

For example, let E_1 be the results from a test suite, showing that no omission failures in the system have been detected from the tests. If E_2 is an item of counter-evidence showing that there are omission failures in the system that should have been detected by these tests (that is, E_2 and E_1 have identical scope) then this finding will lower the trustworthiness of E_1. Furthermore, the trustworthiness of any evidence sharing certain characteristics with E_1 will be lowered by this finding. Using the example above, the trustworthiness of that test suite is called into question by the existence of counter-evidence. Consequently, all evidence resulting from iterations of that test suite will now be judged to lack trustworthiness. There are multiple types of counter-evidence, all of which undermine a claim in different ways (Toulmin et al. 1979). Thus, the effect of counter-evidence on each individual safety argument must be explicitly assessed.

4.1.6 Trustworthiness

Trustworthy evidence is evidence which is judged to be free of 'bugs' and which has been gathered in a manner which is unlikely to introduce errors. By contrast, the provision of untrustworthy evidence implies that evidence-gathering processes and assessments were not carried out with the necessary care. If one item of evidence is judged to have a low trustworthiness factor, it is reasonable to suppose that this should be the case for all other items of evidence with which it shares certain characteristics, such as a common origin. If this is not the case, then this signals a potential discrepancy in the assessment of evidence. In this way, low trustworthiness functions in a similar manner to counter-evidence (Section 4.1.5).

5 Conclusions

In this paper we have presented a framework for assessing and communicating the assurance of a safety argument. We have identified several factors which determine the confidence we have in the truth of a claim. We have also provided a vocabulary with which to discuss these factors. By making use of the concepts of scope, independence, user-defined importance and reinforcement, we can determine the extent to which any claim depends on those which support it. These concepts also aid us in constructing a safety argument, as they can be used to determine exactly where assurance deficits have been introduced.

Furthermore, we have provided guidance for assessing the quality of any evidence supporting a safety argument. This guidance is written in a way that clearly expresses why one item of evidence may be judged to provide less assurance than another. We have also defined rigour, and shown how the assurance of a claim is dependent upon the rigour of supporting evidence. By using the concepts of coverage, replicability and trustworthiness we have established criteria by which evidence of different types maybe compared. Finally, we have provided some examples of how assurance factors can interact, and discussed the effect these interactions have on the assurance of claims. The principles underlying these discussions may then be used to construct a justifiable and compelling safety argument.

5.1 Context and Further Work

The guidance on software in the context of DS 00-56 Issue 4, to be produced by the SSEI, has two primary audiences: MOD Integrated Project Teams (IPTs) and the industry supply chain, including Independent Safety Auditors (ISAs). The intention is to produce guidance for the supply side, which enables prime contractors to specify evidence requirements, to assess the evidence which is supplied, e.g. coverage versus scope, and to identify any assurance deficit. The guidance will also address arguments about the acceptability of any assurance deficit, probably as a form of ACARP argument and will build on the notion of assurance set out here, and will include questions to help elicit measures of assurance. The guidance will be supported with case studies illustrating the approach and, if practicable, argument patterns showing how the principles can be applied in practice. These patterns will be 'grounded' in evidence types, e.g. review results, test evidence.

The IPT guidance will dovetail with the supply side guidance, but will be presented in a way which does not require expert knowledge. The aim is to identify means of articulating assurance requirements, to help understand the assurance achieved at each milestone in the project, and to provide the ability to challenge what is being done to address any assurance deficit. This should enable IPT staff to engage effectively in assurance decisions, with the relevant experts.

There are many benefits of moving to goal-based, or evidence-based, standards not the least of which are avoiding situations where 'perfectly good' systems have to be re-engineered at high cost, but with minimal added value, because they do not meet some prescriptive standards. The downside is that it is difficult to articulate 'how much is enough' when it comes to evidence – and arguments, for that matter. This paper has outlined an approach to assurance which we plan to use to underpin guidance for software in the context of DS 00-56 Issue 4. We hope that this will help the MoD to realise the benefit of the standard, whilst reducing the uncertainty that can arise in using goal-based, or evidence-based, standards.

Acknowledgements   The authors would like to thank the UK Ministry of Defence for their support and funding.

References

Adelard (1998) ASCAD - The Adelard Safety Case Development Manual. ISBN 0 9533771 0 5
British Standards (2001) EN 50128:2001, Railway Applications – Communications, Signalling and Processing Systems – Software for Railway Control and Protection Systems
Govier T (1988) A Practical Study of Argument. Wadsworth
Health and Safety Executive (2001) Reducing Risks, Protecting People. http://www.hse.gov.uk/risk/theory/r2p2.pdf. Accessed 15 September 2008
Kelly T (1999) Arguing Safety – A Systematic Approach to Safety Case Management. DPhil Thesis. Department of Computer Science Green Report YCST99/05
Ministry of Defence (1997): Defence Standard 00-55 Issue 2: Requirements for Safety Related Software in Defence Equipment

Ministry of Defence (2007) Defence Standard 00-56 Issue 4: Safety Management Requirements for Defence Systems

RTCA, EUROCAE (1992) Software Considerations in Airborne Systems and Equipment Certification. Radio Technical Commission for Aeronautics RTCA DO178B/EUROCAE ED-12B

Toulmin S, Rieke R, Janik A (1979) An Introduction to Reasoning. Macmillan Publishing Co., New York

Weaver R (2004) The Safety of Software – Constructing And Assuring Arguments. PhD Thesis. University of York

Weaver R, Fenn J, Kelly T (2003) A Pragmatic Approach to Reasoning about the Assurance of Safety Arguments. In: Proceedings of the 8th Australian Workshop on Safety Critical Systems and Software. Australian Computer Society, Darlinghurst

Weaver R, Despotou G, Kelly T et al (2005) Combining Software Evidence – Arguments and Assurance. In: Proceedings of ICSE-2005: Workshop on Realising Evidence Based Software Engineering